W9-AYQ-282

A BLACK NIGHT
FOR THE BLUEGRASS BELLE

Collector's Edition # ___ of 500

Ian Punnett, Author

A BLACK NIGHT FOR THE BLUEGRASS BELLE

A BLACK NIGHT FOR THE BLUEGRASS BELLE

THE MURDER OF
VERNA GARR TAYLOR

AND THE
KENTUCKY HONOR CODE KILLING
THAT GAVE HER JUSTICE

IAN PUNNETT

Acclaim Press
MORLEY, MISSOURI

Acclaim Press
—— Your Next Great Book ——

P.O. Box 238
Morley, MO 63767
(573) 472-9800
www.acclaimpress.com

Book Design: Rodney Atchley
Cover Design: M. Frene Melton

Copyright © 2016, Ian Punnett
All Rights Reserved.

No part of this book shall be reproduced or transmitted in any form or by any
means, electronic or mechanical, including photocopying, recording or by an
information or retrieval system, except in the case of brief quotations embodied
in articles and reviews, without the prior written consent of the publisher. The
scanning, uploading, and distribution of this book via the Internet or via any other
means without permission of the publisher is illegal and punishable by law.

ISBN: 978-1-942613-47-3 / 1-942613-47-4
Library of Congress Control Number: 2016910945

First Printing 2016
Printed in the United States of America
10 9 8 7 6 5 4 3 2 1

This publication was produced using available information.
The publisher regrets it cannot assume responsibility for errors or omissions.

CONTENTS

ACKNOWLEDGMENTS

Verna Garr Taylor's story was so central to my upbringing that I cannot remember a time when I did not know about her. I thank my mother, Ann Garr Hill Punnett Artze Brown, for her role as family archivist and for showing us how stories like this need to be told correctly. This would never have been a book if my mother had not done so much preliminary research with the hope of publishing it herself. I also thank my brother, Spencer, for his initiative in tracking down the lyrics to "The Garr Ballad," learning to sing and play it, and letting me sing along when I was a kid.

A Black Night for the Bluegrass Belle was improved every day through the editorial skills of my wife, Margery, and our patient sons that carry treasured names from each of us: My older son, Garr, and my younger son, Campbell. I am grateful that not only did Margery accept my marriage proposal, she accepted my proposition that one of our kids would have to be named Garr in order to carry on my mother's family name. Margery felt the same way about the name Campbell from her mother's side, so we agreed that if we were to get married, Garr and Campbell would be the names of our children. It was our second date. I love you.

It's impossible to prioritize the impact of so many others. Ann Rule helped me understand true crime better, but it was her daughter Leslie, and Leslie's husband, Glenn, that set up our first meeting, and they have been friends ever since. Each of the professors at Walter Cronkite School of Journalism and Mass Communication contributed in some way, but I will single out Craig Allen for all the good advice, the members of my dissertation committee, Dennis Russell, Joe Russomanno, Kristy Holtfretter and Dr. Bill (you only need to say his first name; it's like Cher—if she were a PhD). The enthusiasm of Leslie-Jean Thornton, the human hug, was often just the juice I needed.

Tim McGuire read the damn thing at crucial stages and gave me the benefit of his insightful, editorial perspective; Candice Hadley McGuire was the perfect cheerleader and conversation partner over dinner. I never would have gotten this far without my PhD cohorts, Cee-Cee, Shuo-Shuo, and Waffles. We have been with each other since the beginning, and they will be with me wherever I go until the end.

At the Filson Historical Society, James M. Prichard, Aaron Rosenblum, Jana Meyer, Heather Potter, and Johna Picco were not just informed, helpful professionals, their contributions fundamentally improved my work. Thank you, Jim, also, for hooking me up wth Doug Sikes and Randy Baumgardner at Acclaim Press, just when I needed folks like that the most. Nancy Theiss and her staff at the Oldham County Historical Society pointed me in several key directions.

Big props must be given to my mother-in-law who made so many valuable observations and corrections to the original text. Thank you, Mary, for your experienced, eagle eye.

Just as my Kentucky grandmother was forever connected to her Kentucky cousin regardless of distance, Verna, so I have been connected with my Kentucky cousin, Brian Curella, and now his family, Heather, Emeri and Hali (and Toni!). In particular, it was the conscientious attention of Heather Curella to a small, local story about the discovery of the Denhardt trial transcript that changed the trajectory of this book. After her email, I was on the first flight to Louisville and Filson Historical Society. Thank you, Heather. I hope you enjoy reading the fruit of your labor.

A shout out to all my radio and social media friends, and to my colleagues at Ohio Northern University. Go Polar Bears.

And then there is my dog, Jack. He did nothing but snore and chase after things in his sleep. Not much of a literary contribution, I'll grant you, but sometimes just the diversion I needed to keep going.

I dedicate this book to Verna Garr.
I wrote everyday looking at your picture.
You were my muse. I hope I did not fail you.

AUTHOR'S NOTES

Nonfiction murder narratives—described by author Jean Murley as stories of "real events, shaped by the teller and imbued with his or her values and beliefs about such events"— are as old as Creation. In the Holy Bible, the first human born on Earth also became the first murderer: "Now Cain said to his brother Abel, 'Let's go out to the field.' While they were in the field, Cain attacked his brother Abel and killed him" (Genesis 4:8, New International Version).

For Bible literalists, Cain's killing of his brother is arguably the first, complete murder narrative: A motive was established, the murder was committed, a cover-up was attempted, the crime was solved, and the perpetrator was brought to justice. With the question to Cain, "Where is Abel, your brother?" (Genesis 4:9), God became the first homicide detective, and when God wondered, "What have you done? The voice of your brother's blood cries out to me from the ground!" (Genesis 4:10), God was also the first crime scene investigator. Regardless of whether the reader chooses to view Genesis 4 as merely an apocryphal life lesson or not, the biblical model of communicating "morality through murder stories" has been a part of Judeo-Christian culture ever since.

Like all nonfiction murder narratives, the story of Verna Garr Taylor is shaped by me and imbued with my values and beliefs about two killings and two trials from two generations ago, a murder-trial-murder-trial saga that only for the first time can be told in full. The material in this book comes directly from various familial, journalistic, historic and legal sources.

Due to events that will be made clear, however, the Verna Garr Taylor murder remains officially unsolved, and this has allowed the accused, Brigadier General Henry H. Denhardt's few supporters, then and now, to create the impression that he was innocent, gunned down for a crime he did not commit. This book will resolve the issue of Denhardt's guilt once and for all and prove that not only did he kill Verna, but he also *may* have been a serial killer.

Recently discovered correspondence, memoranda, news articles, and court transcripts reveal the herculean effort undertaken by Denhardt's lawyers to cover for their client. These dusty files from his own defense team expose the real Henry Denhardt as a hotheaded, violent drunk prone to impulse rage. In order to improve the image of their client to a jury, the defense team attacked the character of the popular victim, her friends, and her family in the ugliest of ways. Sadly, fictions about Verna created by the Denhardt defense team are still quoted online as though they were fact. These lies are merely the antique smoke of a scorched earth defense strategy lingering from 1937.

Old fashioned as it may sound, a sense of ancestral chivalry calls me to set the record straight on this murder. Verna was my grandmother's first cousin and friend, and I have been hearing about her and her brothers, "the Garr Boys," my whole life. Because of the discovery of these revealing documents, though, for the first time, we can do more than hear *about* Verna; finally, we almost can hear *from* her. #HistoricalJusticeMatters.

Preface

The murder narrative of Verna Garr Taylor is a story as dark and twisty as an old Kentucky backroad on a moonless night. I could not have written it if my path had not been lit by the late Ann Rule.

Ann Rule was the most prolific true crime magazine writer and the author of more than forty-five true crime books. At last count, her seminal *The Stranger Beside Me* (1980) ranked third in all-time true crime sales, right behind Truman Capote's *In Cold Blood* and Vincent Bugliosi's *Helter Skelter*. A complete list of the Top 20 true crime books, however, is dominated by Rule's many other works. There may be many claimants to the title of "king," but Ann Rule reigned as the indisputable Queen of True Crime right up to her death in July 2015. I had the privilege of visiting with her several times in Seattle and once on the phone before her passing. What she taught me greatly influenced the structure of this book.

The research for my dissertation is primarily the form and function of true crime magazines that began to be popular in the late 1920s, became a sensation the 1930s, thrived for decades, and then were subsumed by other forms of murder media. Rule and I discussed her studies of the human psyche, especially the mindsets of evil men who brutalize women. Rule was a lifelong student and teacher of criminology, psychology, and forensic science, an interest that started when she was little girl reading the true crime magazines that were collected in the office of the local county sheriff, her grandfather. "True crime magazines seemed like fairytales to me—rude fairytales," Rule told me. True crime magazines of the period wrote about Verna often, but not always accurately.

When we met, I told Rule about Denhardt, Verna, and her dedicated brothers. By coincidence, her daughter Leslie had written about an aspect of that story once, too, which will be revealed later. I asked Rule, "What is the most important thing to remember about great true crime writing?" Her answer inspired me to push on telling Verna's story.

"Give the victims a voice. That's the one thing I wanted to do since I was a little girl, give the victims a voice."

There were other takeaways from my audiences with the Queen of True Crime, but giving Verna Garr Taylor her voice back, regardless of the age of her case, resonated with me the most. Unfortunately, because Verna's killer survived the night and she did not, it is Denhardt's version of the events eighty years ago that has filtered Verna's story. In Denhardt's testimony, one hears only a hand puppet of Verna that Denhardt created, saying the things he wished Verna had said or the things he needed her to say in order for a jury to believe his defense that he did not shoot Verna, that Verna committed suicide with his gun.

To better understand how to hear Verna's voice through Denhardt's distortions, I turned to another prolific source, Dr. Les Carter, a psychologist and nationally recognized expert on infidelity, anger, and narcissism who has authored many books, including *Enough About You, Let's Talk About Me: How to Recognize and Manage the Narcissists in Your Life*. Dr. Carter took a look at a fact file on Denhardt and sketched out his opinion.

"Unquestionably, (Denhardt) was a narcissist/sociopath," Dr. Carter said. For the narcissist/sociopath, "morality is defined by the whims or desires of the moment. Classic narcissist/sociopath traits when it comes to character means that truth is expedient, loyalties are fluid, morality is relative."

It goes without saying, therefore, because Denhardt lacked a moral conscience and said anything to protect his own fragile self-image, Denhardt's version of Verna's final hours cannot be trusted. For a second opinion, I asked Dr. Katherine Ramsland, a professor of forensic psychology and the author of about fifty books on crime, forensic science, and the minds of predators to take a look at this case, too. She offered to work up a "suicidology" on Verna—a kind of psychological autopsy of the decedent. As it was with Dr. Carter, Dr. Ramsland's assessment was blunt and concise. She told me a suicidology was impossible.

"The case is so obviously not a suicide, just based on the physical evidence... There is no evidence for suicidal ideation, aside from (Denhardt's) absurd, self-serving story, and plenty of behavioral evidence against it." In order to hear Verna's voice for the first time, then, Denhardt's hand had to be pried from Verna's throat. This meant that some of the dialogue between Verna and Denhardt on the day she died had to be either reconstructed from other sources or created to bridge known segments in her narrative. In many instances, I believe that Denhardt was hiding Verna's story in plain site by repeating actual things Verna would have said but framing them in a different context to make her quotes sound as if she was talking about suicide. Some of Verna's dialogue from the day she was killed is exactly what Denhardt claimed she said, but freed from his "absurd, self-serving" spin.

By introducing previously unknown evidence, reevaluating the existing facts, seeking new expertise, and creatively filling in those missing puzzle pieces on my own, the result is that Verna's story can now be seen more clearly from a fresh, credible, and challenging perspective. Because of that conceit, however, this book should not be seen as an attempt to be the definitive historical record of the case, rather a historical true crime book that seeks the truth. Even those few speculative exchanges between Verna and Denhardt that I included are supported by the evidence that Denhardt was an unrepentant abuser and the impulsive killer of one—and *perhaps* even two—women.

Some people have said that only Verna and Denhardt will ever truly know what happened on November 6, 1936. With Ann Rule's passing, I cannot help but smile every time I think that she is finally on the case. That's the nonfiction narrative of Verna's murder I would love to read. Until Ann Rule's book drops from heaven, I humbly submit that mine might have to do.

A BLACK NIGHT FOR THE BLUEGRASS BELLE

THE MURDER OF
VERNA GARR TAYLOR

AND THE
KENTUCKY HONOR CODE KILLING
THAT GAVE HER JUSTICE

CHAPTER ONE

Of the many famous ghost sightings of The Lady in Blue at the Seelbach Hotel in Louisville, most seem to happen in summer. On a hot July Sunday in 1987, according to *The Seelbach Hotel* by Larry Johnson, chef James Scott saw The Lady in Blue float through closed elevator doors on the hotel's mezzanine level while he was making brunch omelettes in front of the AAA Five Diamond-rated Oakroom Restaurant. A few minutes later, an 8th floor maid witnessed a similar spectral performance. It was also summertime in 1992 when Seelbach housekeeper Missi Nussbaum caught a glimpse of a ghostly head in a hotel room mirror—twice.

In the summer of 2015, a couple taking wedding photos in the Seelbach's famed Rathskeller banquet room appeared to be photobombed by The Lady in Blue. If there is any logic to the supernatural, then that all makes a kind of sense. It was July 15, 1936, when a twenty-four-year-old woman fell to her death down the Seelbach's service elevator—wearing a blue dress.

Her name was Patricia Wilson, and decorum aside, it was likely not a blue dress she was wearing the night of her death, more like a silk slip and sheer stockings. Mrs. Wilson and her husband had moved to Louisville from Oklahoma a few years earlier but had separated shortly thereafter. Her estranged husband had been killed in a freak auto accident a few weeks prior to Mrs. Wilson's death. During their legal separation, Mrs. Wilson was living independently, fully supporting herself in a house on 847 South First Street. The assistant manager of the Seelbach Hotel that night identified Mrs. Wilson and told reporters and police, "She often 'visited' here." On the evening of July 14, Mrs. Wilson had been attending "a drinking party" in a Seelbach Hotel room. The party had been going on up to the time she went down the elevator shaft.

According to the press, the coroner did not rush to judgment, and a complete investigation took place. The police determined that Mrs. Wilson was a "party girl," a euphemism for a type of escort/prostitute (think Holly Golightly in *Breakfast at Tiffany's*). According to Louisville police, Mrs. Wilson lived to party; according to the coroner, she partied herself to death. It was ruled that Mrs. Wilson had been killed "through her own carelessness." After that verdict, the Seelbach was exonerated of any blame. Interest in the tragic death of a beautiful, shapely, dark-haired young woman faded like a ghost in the mist. The day after her fall, "the party girl" was buried in an unmarked pauper's grave at Evergreen Cemetery.

And perhaps it was that simple. It is possible that Mrs. Wilson was so drunk she foolishly forced herself through "a seeming defect in the service (elevator) door on the eighth floor." Upon police inspection, the metal service elevator's collapsible gate—there was no solid door to the elevator back then—was found to be partially pried open, but anybody familiar with those old elevator gates knows that getting through a closed one would have taken some doing, even for a sober woman.

So, despite the decision to list cause of death (COD) as "accidental," the indelicate whispers would not go away. Was Mrs. Wilson suicidally despondent over the death of her unreconciled husband? Was she sleepwalking? Could it have been murder?

As reported in *True Detective* magazine as late as 1955, there continued to be testimony that contraindicated any facile conclusion that Mrs. Wilson's death resulted from her drunken negligence or depression. Similar to the occasional reappearance of The Lady in Blue, the alternative narratives of the predawn hours of July 15, 1936 haunted the official inquiry. This is one of those stories.

On the night Mrs. Wilson died, the Seelbach's ornate, French Renaissance-style, Italian marble lobby had been empty and quiet. Although there had been some loud parties earlier, the hotel patrons appeared down for the night when the switchboard phones rang cacophonously. Looking at the rush of blinking lights, the overnight desk clerk, Charlie Evans, bent over the shoulder of the phone operator and asked, "What's up?"

The operator broke off for a minute. "On the eighth floor—some kind of commotion. And on the second, rooms 206 and 210 heard a terrible crash. The guest in room 817 says she distinctly heard a woman pleading, heard her scream."

Rushing up the main staircase to the second floor, the overnight clerk and the phone operator encountered the guest from room 206, "a startled-looking little man in a bathrobe," as he was described in the true crime magazines. He had heard the crash for sure, and he thought he had heard a moan. Evans and the bellman went first to the passenger elevator shaft and then around to the service elevator shaft. Drops of blood were seeping through the exit hatch in the service elevator ceiling.

After the police and ambulance drivers arrived, Mrs. Wilson was found to have a faint pulse, barely breathing. The men carefully removed her broken body from the roof of the service elevator, using a hotel blanket as a makeshift stretcher. Sadly, Patricia Wilson never regained consciousness, and she neither gave a statement nor made it to the operating table before she died. Perhaps only The Lady in Blue's body ever truly left the Seelbach Hotel at all.

Concerned and curious hotel guests had gathered in the lobby to watch the police and ambulance drivers desperately try to save the young woman's life. The small, "startled-looking" man from room 206, still in his bathrobe, spotted and worked his way over to a fully clothed, tall, barrel-chested gentleman that he thought he recognized in the murmuring crowd.

"General Denhardt? I dare say you don't remember me, sir, but—" the man from room 206 began deferentially.

"No! And you don't remember me, either," the big man shot back. He continued imperiously, "My name is not General anything. As a stranger to Louisville, I'd had this dump recommended as a quiet place to spend the night."

The man from 206 gulped out an apology, but it was ignored, and the gentleman with the ramrod military bearing stalked out of the lobby.

In the weeks that followed, Louisville police interviewed every witness to the event that night, including the man from room 206. Despite his certainty that he had recognized Brigadier General Henry H. Denhardt, the then-current adjutant general of the Kentucky National Guard, the former lieutenant governor of Kentucky, former judge, and thought-to-be wealthy lawyer, publisher, and politically connected local businessman, the startled-looking man stayed quiet about his lobby encounter when questioned by the Louisville police.

A few months later, when another beautiful widow died suspiciously in the company of Denhardt, the man from room 206 felt he had to say something and contacted the authorities. The second widow's name was Verna Garr Taylor, and she lived in the quiet, nearby town of La Grange, Kentucky, about forty-five minutes northeast of Louisville. Verna was forty-years-old, an independent, successful, shapely, dark-haired mother of two who *Time* magazine reported was "the prettiest woman in two counties."

The night of Verna's suspicious suicide, however, Denhardt's where-abouts were well established. He was mere yards from where Verna lay, shot through her heart with Denhardt's gun, on State Road 22, a very cold, lonely place to die.

CHAPTER TWO

The last of rural Kentucky's fall colors were gone by early November 1936. What few leaves clung against the typical autumn winds had been challenged by an early snow. For the most part that snow, too, had melted by the first week of November. Save for some soggy roadside ditches, all that remained from the first wave of winter was colder air and stiffer breezes. The bluegrass for which this area is named was already dormant for the winter under what historians call the "dark and bloody ground" of Kentucky. Not that travelers driving down State Road 22 (SR 22) through Oldham County toward New Castle, the Henry County seat, would be watching the scenery at night, anyway. Without street lights or a full moon, SR 22 was a black void.

The porch lights on the modest farmhouses set back from the road could tell you where you weren't, but they did not burn bright enough to tell you where you were going. The night of November 6, 1936, SR 22 was even more treacherous for a woman to be stuck in a disabled car with a man intent on murder. If anybody deserved better than that, it was Verna Garr Taylor.

When people referred to Verna in the press as "the prettiest woman in in two counties," it was not just a reference to her classic, gentle facial features and youthful 135 pound, 5'7" appearance, it was for Verna's inner beauty, as well. From the very first news reports of her death in *The Louisville Courier-Journal* on November 7, Verna's popularity might have been inflated a touch, but nobody would deny she was admired by both men and women for being a hard worker and a "fashion plate" who shopped at the finest stores in Louisville. Her happy marriage with her high school sweetheart ended too soon and left her with two young daughters, Mary Pryor and Frances.

Instead of selling her husband's laundry and dry cleaning business when he died in 1931, Verna took it over and made it even more successful through an exclusive contract with a nearby boarding school, the Kentucky Military Institute (KMI). She was a respected lady in the community, but she did not condescend to her employees; she was a popular, pious churchgoer who still liked to have fun. More importantly, Verna's life revolved around family, the foundation of Kentucky culture. In fact, Garr is considered a "blueblood" Bluegrass Country family name because there were Garrs in the New World *before* there was even a Commonwealth of Kentucky.

Spelled "Gaar" or "Gar" by the first German immigrants, the earliest Garr settlers sailed from Rotterdam, South Holland, on the British ship *Loyal Judith* in 1732. With his wife, Eva, and an unspecified number of young children, patriarch Andreas Gar, a Lutheran lay leader in search of religious freedom in the colonies, was bringing his family to an area called Germanna, Virginia, which had been populated by two previous waves of German immigration. This third wave was blown off course, however, and all the passengers disembarked in Philadelphia on September 25, 1732. It would be five years before Andreas and Eva had saved enough money to finally catch up with the others in Germanna. Once there, Andreas played a key role in the fundraising and building of the Hebron Lutheran Church, the oldest continuously operating Lutheran church in the United States, still holding services on Blankenbaker Road in what is now called Madison, Virginia.

Eventually, Andreas and Eva would have thirteen children. Sadly, there were many more funerals than weddings. Not long after landing in Germanna, however, Elizabeth Barbara Garr, the third oldest child, was married to Michael Blankenbaker, and a pattern was established that still repeats almost three hundred years later: the intermarriage of Garrs and Blankenbakers. Not exclusively, mind you, and not incestuously—the reader should be cautious not to think in unfounded Southern stereotypes—but the name Garr and Blankenbaker reoccurs *often* in *both* family trees, along with the name Tyler. The Tylers were descendants of the brother of the tenth President of the United States, John Tyler. (Later, genealogists argue, the Tyler family would produce one more presidential descendant in Harry S Truman).

Another frequent family name is Pryor, and historical speculation links Pryors to Meriwether Lewis and other members of the Lewis and

Clark Expedition. Garrs and Blankenbakers, too, appeared to have shared that pioneering spirit. Many members of each family followed Squire Boone, Daniel Boone's brother, from Virginia into the territory that would become Shelby County, Kentucky, to homestead near each other. Later, "Squire Boone's Station," one early name by which the settlement was known, would be defended by General George Rogers Clark, the older brother of William Clark, the other half of the Lewis and Clark Expedition. Naturally, Garrs and Blankenbakers depended on each other for survival on the frontier. Apparently, they also were huddling together for warmth.

In the tradition of this inosculation of the family trees, Labon William Blankenbaker (1850) also married a Garr, Ann Eliza Garr, known as "Annie" (1855), in 1875. Labon and Annie had twelve children, all born in the late 1800s, one of whom was my grandmother, Ethelle (pronounced "Ethel Lee") Blankenbaker (1892). All of their children were both Blankenbakers and Garrs. Ed Garr, Labon's half brother, married Mary Herndon Pryor (1866). Ed and Mary Pryor Garr had six children in all: Mary Lillian Garr (1886?), Edward Staunton Garr, known only as "E.S." or "Doc" (1888), Roy Pryor Garr (1891), Florence Juanita Garr (1893), Verna Elizabeth Garr (1896), Sarah Catherine Garr (1898), and Davis Tyler Garr, known as "Jack" (1899). Sarah Catherine did not survive to adulthood.

Rowan Barclay Taylor, known as "Barc," was a man of similar pedigree. So similar, in fact, like his future wife Verna Elizabeth Garr, Barclay's mother was also named Mary Pryor! Barclay Taylor's great-great-great-great-grandfather was James Taylor III, son of James Taylor II, or "the Younger," whose father arrived to Virginia in the 1600s "in an unknown year on an unknown ship." James Taylor III's younger brother Zachary, born in 1703, was the great-grandfather of the 12th President of the United States, Zachary Taylor. James Taylor III's sister, Francis Taylor, married Ambrose Madison in 1721 and was the grandmother of the 4th President of the United States, James Madison.

Whatever Barc and Verna might have lacked in monetary riches at the beginning of their young marriage, they had in family heritage equity, which, in the Old South, was its own kind of currency. Yet, true to form, no matter how financially successful Barc and Verna became, family was still everything to the Taylors. Verna, her father, Ed, her mother, Mary Pryor Garr (who, it is said in the family, was a lousy cook), and her brothers, Doc, Roy, and Jack, grew up making the drive almost every Sunday to Elliott Avenue in Louisville to have supper with Labon and Annie Blankenbaker. The three brothers and Verna had been considered inseparable growing up in their respected, historic La Grange family, and it was a bond that did not weaken after marriage.

In short, to the Garr-Blankenbakers, family was everything. Only a fool would try to come between them.

Even while Henry Denhardt (1876) was still in short pants in Bowling Green, Kentucky, he seemed to thrive in conflict. Denhardt's neighbors knew him "as a bully who tyrannized boys smaller than himself and ran from those he feared." Later as a prosecutor, "Bowling Green saw a man hard of mouth and cold of eye." In politics, many of his fellow legislators condemned his "Prussian tactics." According to *The New York Times* coverage, Brigadier General Ellerbe Carter of Louisville, a former political rival who nonetheless served with Denhardt in the National Guard, described him under oath once as "one of the most violent, domineering, and unscrupulous men I ever knew." His former aide, Lt. Lew Ulrich of Louisville, testified that Denhardt was "power drunk" and "officious" while another former comrade summed up Denhardt as "cruel and inhuman—a veritable Jekyll and Hyde." *Time* magazine reported the same anomalies when it assessed Denhardt in November 23, 1936:

> In the 60 years since he was born in Bowling Green, Ky., 6 ft.-2 in., 220-lb. Brigadier General Henry H. Denhardt has made his mark in law, journalism, war, and politics. He served ten years as Bowling Green prosecuting attorney, two terms as Warren County judge. With his brother, he has long published the *Bowling Green Times-Journal*. He organized a company in the Spanish-American War, served as major in the 3rd Kentucky Infantry on the Mexican border in 1916, went to France with it in 1918. In the St. Mihiel offensive he was cited for valor, promoted to Lieutenant Colonel. As the head of a troop of Kentucky National Guardsmen in 1921, he put down a riot in strike-torn Newport, was promoted to Brigadier General of the National Guard. Grateful Newporters presented him with a saddle horse... But as the years

passed, hard-bitten General Denhardt won the dislike of many a Kentuckian for his use of troops in labor troubles. As Lieutenant-Governor of Kentucky from 1923 to 1927, he was praised as one of the best presiding officers in the history of the State Senate. In 1931 his good friend Governor Ruby Laffoon made him his Adjutant General. Last year, defying a court order, he marched his Guardsmen into bloody Harlan County to supervise the Democratic primary, charging that the forces of Albert B. ("Happy") Chandler were planning to steal votes from the Laffoon-backed candidate. Cited for criminal contempt of court, he hid for days, issued (defiance) to Harlan County authorities, was pardoned by Governor Laffoon before going to trial.

Further fleshing out the *Time* reference to Denhardt's strong arm tactics in using seven hundred fully equipped guardsmen to swing Harlan County to his political friends, Denhardt was formally "indicted for violation of election laws, intimidating voters, sending troops within illegal distances of polling places, keeping voters from approaching polls and illegal arrest." But charging Denhardt was one thing, arresting him was another. "Sheriff Middletown, of Harlan County, immediately sent out fliers offering a reward for General Denhardt's arrest. The size of the reward—98 cents—made the 'Iron General' the laughing stock of the state." But before anybody could arrest Dehnardt and claim the ninety-eight cent bounty, he was pardoned by his friend, the outgoing governor. When this "favorite son" of Bowling Green returned home after losing his bid for re-election as lieutenant governor, however, there was no marching band and no parade to meet him.

Somewhere between his 1905 marriage to Elizabeth Glaze and his many rapid promotions, Denhardt had developed the reputation as an arrogant and belligerent martinet. Rigid, cold, and brutal in his punishments, when Denhardt was given the nickname "Iron General" by his men, it wasn't a compliment. "His former friends in Bowling Green frankly diagnosed his 'ailment' as a 'swell head,'" wrote a reporter for *True Detective* in 1937. This was a folksy way of identifying the empowerment of Denhardt's narcissism and the growing flagrancy of his sociopathy.

Denhardt once reportedly said, "I only tell the truth when it is to my advantage." Whether that quote is apocryphal or not, it appears to describe his willingness to play both ends to the middle and to use coercion to get what he wanted.

In November of 1931, the family of Republican Charles A. Smith, a fellow citizen of Bowling Green who was running for State Senate, experienced Denhardt's callousness in a particularly cruel way. Denhardt considered himself at war with all Republicans, and they happily hated him in return. Making no attempt to hide his identity, Denhardt called Smith's home to threaten him. When Smith's young daughter answered the phone, however, Denhardt was undeterred. Denhardt told the little girl to pass this message to her daddy: "If he continued to run for office, he would be killed." Sobbing, the girl ran and told her father immediately. The story flew around Bowling Green. Smith's nephew, Willie Dent, "polished up the family revolver and went looking" for Denhardt. Dent found him walking along Bowling Green's main thoroughfare. As soon as Denhardt saw Dent, the general started running. Dent got off five shots, but only one hit Denhardt in the shoulder. In keeping with small-town Southern tradition, Dent turned himself in to the police, handed over his guns, and threw himself on the mercy of the court.

Despite the fact that Denhardt was a former prosecutor in Bowling Green, a former judge in Warren County, a former lieutenant governor in Kentucky, and an active high-ranking official in the National Guard and Reserve, Dent was fined just $250 for shooting Denhardt—and "That fine," said one court official famously, "was for being such a rotten shot."

In January of 1933, Denhardt's wife sued him for divorce on the grounds of cruelty. Did he regret the other women that his wife found out about? For all that he had done for God and country, for all of his public service, Denhardt felt he had earned his pleasures. He was a robust, youthful sixty-one, and as he saw it, he had more to offer the right woman. In *Front Page Detective*, Elsie Frank Mayer wrote, "Having lost all personal discipline at that dangerous period in a man's life when late resurgence of sexual power and desire flares up like Indian summer, the General stepped up his tempo to the rapidity of heedless youth."

She added, "But an older man is seldom as successful in evading trouble as is youth. Perhaps it is because others look with less sympathy on wild oats sown at harvest time." After his divorce and his ill-conceived death threat against a campaign rival, Denhardt retired from politics to an eight hundred-acre tenant farm in Oldham County in January 1936. There, he lived with his unmarried older sister, Miss Bertha, and drew an income as the landlord.

If a two-word motto could sum up the Garr-Blakenbaker clan, it might be "family first." Miss Bertha aside, in the case of Denhardt, his family philosophy seemed to be "me first." A study in contrasts does not end there. Whereas forty-year-old Verna Garr was respected, adored, beautiful, and considered a model of motherhood and self-sufficiency, sixty-one-year-old Denhardt was amoral, pugnacious one moment and obsequious the next, a public figure "cloaked in respectability," but considered by many to be "the most hated man in Kentucky."

Denhardt credited his success to his win-at-all-cost approach to life. Politics was a game of influence, and although Denhardt had won more than he had lost, a few times he had had to "take one for the team." For example, in 1921, on Christmas Day, when Governor Edwin P. Morrow called on then-Colonel Denhardt to restore order to Newport, much of Campbell County turned against Denhardt personally. The same could be said of the infamous labor wars of Harlan County when Denhardt's Kentucky National Guard troops became the *de facto* goon squad of the coal company owners in 1931 and again in 1935. After the indictments for intimidating voters the second time around, Denhardt was wise to stay out of "Bloody Harlan," even after things cooled down.

Balancing out the counties where Denhardt was *persona non grata* were other counties such as Henry and Shelby, where a relatively small handful of families owned the farm land. New Castle, the Henry County seat with a population of just five hundred, was quaint with a few rows of shops, no tourism or industry to speak of. Denhardt launched his successful campaign for lieutenant governor on the steps of the Henry County Courthouse. Farmers in the Bluegrass counties had very little sympathy for the left-leaning coal mine strikers in Eastern Kentucky, so they appreciated Denhardt's reputation for keeping them in line.

In fact, according to *The Kentucky Miner's Struggle: The Record of a Year of Lawless Violence*, published by the American Civil Liberties Union in May of 1932, it was common practice for hardline anti-labor judges to move trials of protesters from pro-union Kentucky counties to Bluegrass counties like Oldham, Henry, and Shelby because the juries were made up of tobacco farmers who were likely to be much harder on the defendants. In Kentucky, being in a friendly jurisdiction might be all one needed to get out of trouble.

In a way, Denhardt's career in Kentucky was a testament to how a public figure's popularity could go up or down, depending only on what county he was in, but that's not how he chose to look at it. To Denhardt, his troubles were linked to an "invisible government" that conspired to ruin his political ambitions. He retired only because there were no offices left for him to run for, but he was not ready for the rocking chair yet. Louisville could be a city where the party did not have to stop for a guy with enough money and the right addresses. A gentleman's farm in La Grange would keep him near the all-night action.

Verna was introduced to Denhardt through her eldest brother, Doc, after plans for a real estate transaction fell through in early summer 1936. Doc had served in the Great War with Denhardt, but although Doc knew who Denhardt was, Denhardt knew nothing of Doc. Denhardt was thinking about renting some property that the Garrs owned. When he gave the family a courtesy call to turn down the offer to rent a house, he and Verna made small talk.

"How are you?" Verna asked Denhardt over the phone.

"All right, except that I am lonely."

Verna laughed and said, "I am pretty lonesome, too."

"We lonesome people ought to get together." After that, she invited him over to sit on the porch. In the weeks ahead, they visited in modest, appropriate settings once or twice a week. She found him fascinating, apparently. Denhardt was educated and had been everywhere Verna hoped to go someday. Except for his bad first marriage, as he told it, his life had been pretty much perfect, and he knew just about every important person in the state. He would have been governor, but powerful people in Frankfort made sure he did not get a break, as Denhardt described it. In a good way, Denhardt's big personality and the way he talked with his hands reminded Verna of her dad, and he had this boyishness about him that was kind of endearing at first. For all of her grace and position, Verna enjoyed being the center of a man's world. Denhardt's attention was flattering.

With one daughter engaged to be married, it was only natural for a still-young widow to think about companionship. When Denhardt went on his annual war maneuvers with the National Guard at Fort Knox, the cordial courtship continued, and they exchanged frequent letters. Verna and Denhardt went to clubs for dinner and even brought Frances and two of her girlfriends along for a football game at the nearby Kentucky Military Institute. Despite the Depression, Denhardt spent big on a $1500 engagement ring, one whole carat surrounded by twenty-six little diamonds set in white gold, worth around $20,000 today. Verna had not yet agreed to marry Denhardt, but she had agreed to think about it.

The general told a different story, though. He said they were openly engaged and boasted that they would be married any day now. Eyewitnesses contradicted that claim. Her friends had the feeling that Verna was in love with the ring, not the man who gave it to her. Only the night before Verna was killed did she finally show Denhardt's ring to some of the laundry ladies, but only then because they asked to see it. She didn't wear the ring at work; she mostly kept it wrapped in a handkerchief in her bra. She never told anyone whether it was an engagement ring or a friendship ring, just that the general had asked her to marry him. One of the laundresses teased Verna about moving onto Denhardt's farm, but Verna did not respond. Verna never told her workers that she was returning the ring to the general.

Mary Pryor and Frances had never been sure if their mother actually considered herself engaged or just friends, but they did suspect that Friday, November 6, was going to be the day their mother was going to give the ring back. Verna had been putting it off too long, and the longer she waited, the more the older man appeared to be getting the wrong impression. Mostly, Verna's procrastination was due to a character flaw.

"The prettiest woman in two counties" had a tendency to be a "people pleaser," but a few things had happened in her last few weeks that showed her there was no pleasing "the most hated man in Kentucky." Denhardt had a bad reputation for a good reason, Verna was learning. She was still willing to be a part of his life as an encouraging friend in his efforts to stay sober, but she decided her missional work as a devout Methodist did not have to include marriage.

For his part, Denhardt loved Verna so much. In fact, he came to understand he loved her *too much*. How much is too much? As Denhardt repeated in his defense overlooking the wet ditch that ran alongside SR 22 where Verna's body was found, "I loved her too much to kill her."

CHAPTER THREE

Verna Garr Taylor was just as comfortable exploring the rapidly changing 1930s fashion trends as she was learning the finer points of commercial laundry maintenance. She might have preferred to discuss a butterfly collar over a butterfly valve, but in order to get timely repairs and capital improvements on her business, The Community Laundry, Verna also had to be technically fluent enough to negotiate with Roy Stewart, the L&N Railroad boiler specialist. On the night before her death, Verna had roughed out the plans for a new brick smokestack and three new flues with Stewart in just under thirty minutes. On any given week, the employment of up to fifteen people depended on Verna's business running smoothly. Verna was not intimidated by machines, and she was not afraid to spend money to make money. She knew her way around a farm, and she was just as good a driver as any of her brothers, and probably better than Doc.

Driving eastbound on SR 22 on the evening of November 6, 1936, crossing over into Oldham County, however, Verna might have been driving a little recklessly. She so much wanted to get home in time to see Frances and her girlfriends off to the dance at the Mary D. Shop, a soda fountain and sweet shop at the center of town. If she could only be there, Verna would be so grateful that she wouldn't even fuss at Frances if somebody at the Mary D. Shop snuck the teenager a beer. And those boys who smuggled in hard liquor from the place down the street? That was the least of Verna's worries right now. Approaching La Grange, the man next to her held all the cards. And, well, he held the gun.

The ladies in the laundry had seen something like this coming, but nobody thought it would ever be this bad. Mrs. Coleman and Mrs. Powell noticed how Verna had been acting differently. She seemed worried, distracted, sometimes afraid. She wasn't depressed, Verna was still smiling and encouraging, but her resting face was recently one of concern. Mrs. Powell also thought that the usually particular Verna was not as "tidy" in her appearance as she typically had been. Verna tried to hide her worries from all her girls. The ladies wondered whether it might have something to do with the rumors that Denhardt had given Verna a ring.

It was amusing, at first, how Denhardt like to show Verna off by bringing people past the laundry to meet her. Increasingly, though, there were the times when the general would come and Verna would pretend not to be there. In late October, Verna had been in the back when Denhardt asked for Verna at the counter. Verna said in front of all the laundresses, "I will not see him." This was unusual for Verna. She seemed resolute in this decision at first, then faltered, changed her mind, and told one of the girls, "Well, I will see him because I don't want any scene here in the laundry—or anywhere."

The general smothered her, some felt. What had started off as fun attention was turning into an annoyance. He would drop by for what felt like surprise inspections, as if he were trying to catch her doing something nefarious. One time, Denhardt caught her avoiding him. As Verna had instucted them, the ladies in the front had told the general that their boss had been there, but she was gone. Only a few seconds earlier, Verna had left by the back door. Suspecting that he was being ditched, Denhardt pushed past the women in front, but by the time he got to the screen, Verna was running halfway up the road. She yelled, "I didn't want you to see me with my hair such a fright, and I have to run home to catch my chauffeur to Cincinnati." The ladies in the laundry could only smile. That just didn't make any sense. If Verna were late, why not have the general drive her home instead of running on such a hot day? And what was all this about a chauffeur to Cincinnati? "Okay" was all the general could say in front of others.

Mrs. Powell said, "Mrs. Taylor was a proud woman. I believe she was fearing for her life, but she did not want people to know that they were having troubles." As it was, Verna worried that she was the subject of enough gossip, so discretion was as much for Denhardt's benefit as for hers. Despite being somebody that wanted to be friends with everybody, Verna even discharged Mrs. Roberts—the one whose daughter worked at the post office—when it was learned that Mrs. Roberts was spreading rumors about Verna and Chester Woolfolk, Verna's twenty-six-year-old righthand man at the laundry, just because he would drive Verna home at night in the delivery truck or bring by the day's receipts if Verna was already home. "Ches" also gave Frances saxophone lessons for a while. That was the limit of their public interaction, of course, Ches just doing his job, but people in small towns like Mrs. Roberts would always talk.

Verna and Denhardt's relationship soured further when Verna's sister, Juanita, came to town. Juanita was known in the family as warm-hearted, articulate, and intelligent, with a good sense of humor. Juanita had a beautiful marriage to Major Holmes, dean of the School of Ceramics at Alfred University in Alfred, New York. Major and Juanita adored each other but never had children. The students were like her children, and Juanita was celebrated for her grace as a Southern hostess at the university.

The general egotistically took Juanita's charming hospitality as flirting when she came to visit her sister. Verna was embarrassed by Denhardt's behavior. Although Denhardt seemed to enjoy implying that he and Juanita were becoming "close," there was absolutely nothing between Juanita and Denhardt as far as Juanita was concerned. That did not stop the general from sitting between the sisters and portraying himself as somebody they were fighting over. When Verna drew the line on his conduct in the car on the ride home after a movie, Denhardt acted like Verna was being a silly, jealous woman. What Denhardt took as "pouting" was really disgust. This was no way for a would-be husband of Verna's to act; Barc never would have done that.

And there other little things. Verna expected a certain, modest level of romantic affection, but that was often an afterthought with Denhardt. Instead, he was often quick to criticize. Once, Mary Pryor was in the next room and overheard Denhardt "storming about using bad language." It was probably about Chester Woolfolk again, a recurring subject for Denhardt, and how the general felt that Woolfolk needed to be fired because it did not look right for Verna to be getting rides home at night in the laundry truck from a younger man. Denhardt also had insisted that if they were to get married, Verna would have to sell the laundry. Mary Pryor was trying not to eavesdrop, but there was no mistaking Denhardt's tone and his vulgar words. Maybe the whole neighborhood heard it when Verna raised her voice to the general and said, "You can leave now." He did.

But Verna put the ring on one last time on the morning of November 6 before Denhardt picked her up for their weekly trip into Louisville for business and lunch. Perhaps she wanted to show how grateful she had been, focus on the good times, and not make it seem that the ring had not been generous enough, or that Denhardt had done anything wrong that he was capable of correcting. Verna wanted to remain friends in the neighborly Southern way. She had not made a big deal about the proposal going in—there had been no public announcement in the paper or the church bulletin—and she did not want to make a big deal of it going out.

When Verna felt stress, she tended not to feel well, and the anticipation of knowing that she was going to disappoint Denhardt was giving her a bit of a tension headache. She was not morose or melancholy about what she knew she had to do, but Verna looked forward to the end of the day when it would all be over. She really did enjoy her routine drives into the city with Denhardt because the luncheons, the card games, and the shopping sure made the business errands more tolerable. She and Denhardt could still do that together as friends.

Perhaps Verna sensed that being around people after Denhardt got his ring back would be good thing. Verna was not sure exactly how or when she would tell Denhardt, but she had prayed about it. The general seemed to take awhile to process his emotions. Perhaps Denhardt would be distracted enough by their busy social schedule that he'd have a chance to feel less angry by the time they went home later in the afternoon.

Frances, in her typical, sullen, teenage mood, was off to school by 8 a.m., but Mary Pryor was still around when Verna made a breakfast of bacon, eggs, tea, oatmeal, and toast with preserves. Verna was looking forward to bridge with Mrs. Bessie Lee, another cousin and one of her best friends, in honor of Bessie's guest, Mrs. Robert Lucas. Verna had some banking to do, too, and that new flue for the boiler to arrange, so she dressed up a little for the luncheon and light business. Crepe fabric, which had traditionally been something people wore only in mourning, had become very "in," so Verna wore a stylish black crepe dress under a black cloth coat, black leather gloves, black low-heeled "opera slippers," a black toque hat, and a black pocketbook. Verna added a karakul fur wrap around her shoulders to protect her from the November chill.

When Denhardt pulled up in his Chevrolet Master Sedan around 9:30 a.m., Verna was not quite ready, so Mary Pryor came to the door. Denhardt followed her back to the kitchen where the young woman had been working. Standing there, they chatted until Verna came down. While collecting her things in the front room, Verna started to say her goodbyes. She told her older daughter to expect her home for supper and that she was planning to chaperone Frances' dance that night. Despite the light tension headache, Verna was in fine spirits when she left, Mary Pryor thought, showing no signs of worry or stress. Mary Pryor had no idea that that was the last time she would ever see her mother alive.

All seemed well when Verna stopped by the home of Mrs. Mildred Connell, a young friend in La Grange who had a package that Verna had agreed to return for her in Louisville to Stewart Dry Goods Company. Mrs. Connell noted that Verna was her usual convivial self, assuring Mrs. Connell that this little favor was nothing at all. From there, it was over to the Community Laundry so that Verna could make a couple of quick long distance calls and line up the next day with Norman Rankin, the carpenter and bricklayer who had started laying the groundwork for the new flues. Verna asked Mr. Rankin if he could meet her back at the laundry on Saturday to help install the flues Mr. Abbott was delivering. There were some parts that still needed ordering, and Verna wanted to make sure she had all the pieces in place for next week's workload. That was about 10 a.m. As promised, the calls did not take long, and Denhardt was happy to be her companion as they started the forty-one mile drive west to Louisville down State Road 22.

"How are you this morning?" the general asked cheerily as they drove.

"I'm a little tired. I did not sleep well last night, Henry. I've got a little bit of a headache, but it will pass. The drive will do me good. How about you?"

"I've had a touch of cold since Wednesday."

As was their Friday custom, Denhardt stopped at KMI. They had done this together many times because of the general's connection to the institution and so that Verna could call on one of her larger accounts. Before Denhardt, Verna would have made the drive by herself, but he preferred that she spend time in his company, so he always made himself available for this particular Friday errand. This time, the general stayed by the car because Verna thought it would not take long to check the "shortages" from last week's delivery and to collect the balance due for laundry services with A.S. Rueve, KMI's business agent. When Verna did not return as quickly as he expected, the general got a little exercise strolling the grounds. Inside, Verna looked out the window at the cadets practicing a parade march. "My, don't the boys look splendid out there today," she remarked to Mr. Rueve. Getting back in the car, Verna said there had been a discrepancy in the order, and she apologized for keeping the general waiting. The whole errand had taken about fifteen minutes.

After they were back on the road to Louisville, though, Verna took the opportunity to say, "There was another reason why I was late, Henry. While I was in there, I stood by the window and looked out, and I saw you walking around. Did you see me looking at you through the window?"

"I did not."

"Well, I have been making up my mind in regard to a very serious matter that concerns you. As I mentioned, I did not get much sleep last night because I did not know how I was going to say this. You have been so kind. That ring you gave me was the nicest thing I ever got, but I don't think we ought to get married, so I must turn down your proposal. It does not mean that my feelings for you have changed. I just do not love you in that way, I've come to realize. I hope that we can always be friends, but I need to give you back your ring. I do want so much to be friends."

At first, Denhardt was speechless. He tried to imagine how a Southern gentleman might respond, but the words did not come quickly. Denhardt finally said, "Do you love me as you said you always do?"

"Yes, Henry, you've been very sweet to me."

"If you do, then keep this ring. Just when you look at it, be reminded that I love you," Denhardt said.

"Oh, Henry, I could not accept such a beautiful ring as a gift."

"Keep the ring," Denhard said. This time, it sounded a little more emphatic. Verna had heard that tone shift before and likely knew where it could lead. If it meant not rocking the boat, she decided, she would agree to keep the ring—for now. Relieved, thinking the worst of it was over, Verna flung her arms around Denhardt's neck and kissed him on the cheek. "Henry, you're one of the finest men God ever put on this

Earth." Why had she been so nervous? That had not been so bad. She had tossed and turned all night for no reason.

After a brief pause, however, the storm clouds started to form. "Can I ask 'why'?" Denhardt said with forced composure. This is why a woman gets nervous around a man of Denhardt's temperament.

"Well, lots of reasons, I suppose," Verna said calmly. "My daughters are against me getting married at this time, and they're being a handful these days. I need to set a good example for Mary Pryor, who would run off tomorrow and marry Allen if I weren't slowing her down. They're both so young, I think. A wedding will be fine in time, someday, but right now I need to focus on them. My brothers are also not so keen on the idea, and you know how important family is to me."

"We could go get married today, and then they wouldn't have a say in it," the general said over-brightly. "We could get married at your cousin's after lunch. Bessie could be your maid of honor."

After what she had just said, Verna wasn't quite sure at first if Denhardt was joking or just not listening, so Verna answered with a smile, "Now, wouldn't that look silly for a couple people our age running off and finding a preacher like a couple of kids that *had* to get married! It just wouldn't look right. Besides, I was going to have my sister, Mary Lillian, as my maid-of-honor, remember? No, I think it's just best if we call the whole thing off and stay really good friends. You know how important you are to me, though, right?"

"If you won't marry me today, then you never really loved me. It was all a lie."

"Now, Henry, please don't make this any harder than it has to be. I am sorry if your feelings are hurt, I am, but I just have to say 'no.' Do you forgive me?"

Verna knew that Denhardt's temper got the better of him sometimes even when he was not drinking, but he, usually, eventually, made amends. She did not want a scene, and she had faith that Denhardt would start to accept it. As they motored toward Louisville, it got harder to read Denhardt's mood, but at least he was not storming, so that was a plus. It would have been unladylike to keep the ring, of course, but for now it kept the peace as they drove in relative silence. They were still on time for Bessie's luncheon for Mrs. Lucas, and even with a couple of errands, they would be back in La Grange in time for supper and chaperoning.

Sometime after 11 a.m., though, things changed. It might have been the flat tire. Denhardt's moods were tested often by small stuff. Close to where State Road 22 and Route 60 intersected near St. Matthews, a first-ring city that bordered Louisville, they had a puncture of the left hind tire. Denhardt pulled his Chevrolet Master over to the side of the road and inspected it, then walked back down the road to a garage they had passed to pay a man to come exchange the tire.

When Denhardt got back into the car, his demeanor had spoiled. Was it the frustration of a flat tire right after Verna broke things off with him? Was it going to a luncheon with Verna's friends? Denhardt likely sensed that Verna would have a great time while he was miserable.

After the tire was changed, Denhardt did not start up the sedan.

"Henry, Bessie will be waiting for me. I'm the fourth for bridge. She's been so looking forward to this."

"I don't want to go. I think we have a lot of things to talk about. I don't understand what has changed. We were just about to be married."

"But, Henry, that's just not true. We were never 'just about' to be married. I don't know where you got that idea. When you proposed, you told me that I did not have to give you an answer right away. You told me that you knew it was sudden, but that you wanted me to think about it, so I did. I have thought about it for several weeks now, and we have had lots of dreamy conversations and talked some things out, but I thought you deserved an answer. You have been so good to me and that ring is the nicest thing that anybody has ever given me, and I love you for that. You stopped drinking so much because I asked you, and I know that wasn't easy. I really enjoyed sitting next to you in church, too, Henry, and I was proud to be seen with you. I just don't want to get married right now. It's sometimes hard to run a business and raise two girls, but we were moving too fast. You can understand that, can't you?"

"It's Chester Woolfolk, isn't it? You're in love with him and not me."

"Henry, I am so tired of telling you that there is nothing between me and Ches. He is a loyal employee, he's a hard worker, he's been so good to the girls, and he's like a member of the family, but I'm not having a love affair with a twenty-six-year-old boy. First of all, it would not be decent. Secondly, I do not love him."

"But you admit that he loves you. He worships the ground you walk on. He follows you around like a puppy. He's jealous every time I come in to the shop. I can see it. Admit that much. You drive around with him in that truck every night and talk about me."

"Now, you're being silly. Ches gives all the ladies a ride home at night to be safe. Ches might have been crushing on me at one time or another, but I have never reciprocated his attention in that way. He gave me a note once telling me how much he liked me; it was very sweet. I dismissed the subject, of course—I felt like his school teacher—and we parted in our usual manner that night, and that was the end of that. It has never come up again. There is nothing to that rumor that Mrs. Roberts started because the delivery truck was parked in front of my house. I like Ches, he's been good to me, but I do not love him, Henry. Every time you bring up Ches, it sounds so crazy."

"Isn't that why Doc and his wife got divorced? Because she also knew about you two?"

"Doc and Theresa had lots of problems. Since the war, Doc has trouble sleeping and he kept her up all night talking sometimes. We all know about Doc's nerves, and Theresa could not take it anymore. Nobody blames her. I think she said some mean things about me to get back at Doc because he loves me dearly, as I love him. He's my brother."

Nothing Verna said did anything to mollify Denhardt's growing anger. He felt like he was in a terrible dream. Not only was his fiancée breaking off their engagement, but now she was denying the obvious– it was because of her affair with another man. On her account, Denhardt thought, he had acted better than he ever had in his whole life. The more Denhardt thought about how hard he had strived to avoid even the appearance of evil in their relationship, all the while he was certain she was intimate constantly with a twenty-six-year-old boy in the delivery truck, the madder he got. Ches was allowed to come by the house every night, but here he was, her fiancé, and he was only there two or three times a week.

"You're lying," Denhardt said derisively. Verna had been the idealized woman, venerated in an important part of his psyche where she was lavished with gifts in hopes that she would stay where she had been installed. But now she had dislodged herself, and where Verna had been a near holy object, she now had become like a wrecking ball swinging freely at Denhardt's fragile, internal structure of self-worth.

"Henry, I don't have any other relationships with any other men. I just don't want to get married. When you asked me to marry you, you told me that you wanted me to think about it. Now I have. Take that back, take me to Bessie's, or take me home."

Wordlessly, Denhardt started up the car and pulled back on to the road heading toward Louisville. "I don't want to go to Bessie's for lunch. I'm not hungry. You can go. I'll sit in the car."

"Oh, Henry, that would look ridiculous. I don't want you to make a scene. Let's go, have a bite, nobody has to know anything about this."

"I'm not hungry, and I don't feel like socializing. You go, and I'll wait for you in the car."

"Henry, why would you do that when Bessie is honoring a guest? It would be so embarrassing. Bessie is counting on me to be fourth for bridge, and I do not want to ruin her luncheon. You like Bessie. She's always been nice to you."

"Then you should call her and tell her you have a terrible headache and you don't want to come over."

"I will do no such thing. First off, that would be a lie, plus I have been looking forward to this lunch all week. If you don't want to go, then you'll have to be the one to make our excuses. You call her. You tell her that we have had car trouble if you want, but do it in time for her to find somebody else for bridge. Then we'll do our errands and then we'll head home, okay?"

Within a few minutes, Denhardt was pulling into the Aetna Parking Lot beside the Pendennis Club, one of Louisville's oldest and most prestigious social clubs. The Aetna was a full-service parking facility that would wash your car, change your oil, and/or change a tire while you shopped. While Verna stayed in the car, Denhardt found the house phone and called Bessie at 12:25 p.m., just five minutes before the lunch was about to start.

"Mrs. Lee? This is General Denhardt. Mrs. Taylor has asked me to call you to say that she will be unable to keep her engagement with you because she has one of her terrible headaches."

"I'm so sorry to hear that. I'm so disappointed," Mrs. Lee said. "Might I speak to Mrs. Taylor?"

"No, no, she's in the car outside. She cannot come to the phone," explained Denhardt. "I'm sick, too, I'm afraid, so I can't come over, either," Denhardt said. Denhardt highlighted his sickness by repeating it twice, as Mrs. Lee remembered it. She thought it odd that he kept bringing it up.

Denhardt returned to the parking lot where Verna was waiting in the passenger seat.

"What did she say?" Verna asked.

"She understood. She told me to tell you that she hopes you'll feel better."

"Henry, did you tell her that I had a headache?"

"C'mon, let's get some lunch. I'm starving."

"I thought you told me that you weren't hungry, and that's why you did not want to go to Bessie's?"

"I wasn't hungry then. I'm hungry now. Let's go get something to eat."

"I'm not hungry. I just want to do my errands and go home."

"I'll take you home, but first, really, I need to eat something. You should, too. Let's go inside at the Pendennis Club and have some lunch. I insist."

"How would it look if Bessie hears that I'm sitting having lunch in Louisville after calling and canceling her luncheon? Too many people know me in that club."

"Fine, we'll go someplace where no one will see you."

"And then we'll do our errands and go back to La Grange?"

"Just like that, I assure you."

Verna grabbed her pocketbook and got out of the car and followed Denhardt the few blocks to the Walgreens lunch counter right off the lobby of the Seelbach Hotel. They were seated at a booth in the back. Denhardt ordered a sandwich, but Verna ordered only tea.

"You really ought to eat something," Denhardt insisted.

"No, thank you, my headache is getting worse. I am not hungry. I just want to go."

They sat in dignified silence. Verna drank her tea. When Denhardt finished his sandwich, Verna grabbed her purse and started to slide out of the booth.

"I'm going to order another sandwich," Denhardt said.

"You said we could leave after lunch."

"We can, but I'm not done with lunch."

So, Denhardt ordered another sandwich, and Verna slid back into the booth and went back to her tea.

"Did you hear about the woman who was killed falling down the shaft at the Seelbach back in July?"

"I saw it in the paper."

"I was in this hotel that night," Denhardt whispered.

"Did you know her?"

"A lot of people knew her. I knew her last."

Denhardt did not explain any further, and Verna did not want to encourage his menacing tone. He was obviously still mad about the engagement, and when he was mad, it had been Verna's experience, Denhardt was bound to say anything to irritate. Verna felt responsible for his anger. She thought she had played fairly with him, but now she doubted herself. She probably waited too long to give him an answer. She did not feel that she had led him on, but she was sensitive to his disappointment. The last thing Verna wanted was for Denhardt to start yelling or using ugly words in anger in Walgreens. Verna could just imagine Denhardt shouting about her and Chester Woolfolk at the top of his lungs. If she were patient, she could cheer him up, and the day could go by without creating more gossip for the ladies back in La Grange.

Finally, by 1:00 p.m., the storm seemed to pass. Denhardt finished his second sandwich, he paid for his lunch and her tea, and they left. They first stoppped at Stewart's Dry Goods where Verna bought some stamps, mailed some letters, and dropped off Mrs. Connell's package. At 1:10 p.m., Denhardt followed Verna into the Citizen's Union National Bank as she tugged at her gloves and smiled to everyone as she entered. Pausing for a moment to fill out her deposit slip, she approached the man in charge of the savings department, Harry Gorman, and had him deposit the seven hundred dollars that she had with her from the week's receipts. They chatted about whether there would be any other type of savings account that would bring her more compounded interest, and Mr. Gorman said there was and that he would be happy to set one up. Today was too busy, Verna said, but she expressed a desire to take care of that next time she was in. The general said nothing during this visit, except "good day" to Mr. Gorman, and they were gone.

When Verna and Denhardt parted at the corner at 1:30 p.m., they agreed to meet back at Denhardt's car in the Aetna Parking Lot at 4:30 p.m. It would be an easy drive home from there. She and the general could part as friends when he dropped her off back at her house, in plenty of time for supper and chaperoning the dance at the Mary D. Shop. This was going to work out just fine after all, if she just kept the general on the right track.

The general went to get a shave at the Tyler Hotel, then he "loafed around" the Pendennis Club, got a room at the Kentucky Hotel for about an hour, then headed back over to the Seelbach Hotel where he "loafed around" some more with his old cronies. Even though he was in the "men's only" billiard and bar area on the Seelbach's mezzanine floor, Denhardt abstained from the cold beer. So he said.

For Verna, the next few hours were spent in a mix of business and pleasure, and her worried mind lightened with both. As was her inclination, Verna still was concerned about whether the flue parts would be delivered on time to fabricate the new chimney that Mr. Rankin was building. The business could only afford to miss a few days without the old boiler. The obvious truth was, however, that the entire physical plant for the laundry was due for an overhaul, an expense that Verna was preparing to meet. With the right advice and a new interest bearing account, that could happen in the next couple years if Verna planned ahead. In the meantime, there were fabrics to look at and some clothes to try on. Maybe it was not the time to buy anything new until she had a better handle on the capital improvements she needed to make. Verna shopped, but she left without any brightly colored parcels to bring home this time.

By 4:00 p.m., Verna was making her way cheerily back to the Aetna lot. Approaching 3rd and Walnut in downtown Louisville, Verna was excited to see a familiar face. Walking up the street next to a younger gentleman was J. Ballard Clarke, a lawyer and family friend who Verna had known her whole life. Clarke and the young man were standing at the intersection waiting for the light to turn green when Verna caught up and hooked Clarke by the arm.

"Hello, how are you?" Verna said happily.

"Well, this is a nice surprise! How are you?" Clarke replied warmly.

"I have bad headache today, but I won't get into it. I'll be rid of it soon."

"Mrs. Verna Taylor, this is Mr. Clare Smith," said Clark.

The light turned green as Verna hooked her arm through Clarke's young friend's arm, too, and all three walked across the street.

"Hello, Mr. Smith. Nice to meet you."

"My pleasure, Mrs. Taylor."

"Where you headed?" Clarke asked as they strolled up the sidewalk near the Pendennis Club.

"Just up a ways." Clarke noticed that she seemed to avoid being specific on purpose.

"This is where we'll leave you then, but it was so good to see you!" Clarke said with a friendly hug.

A half a block was not near long enough for old friends, but Verna was eager to get back to Denhardt's car and home for supper. She was sitting in the passenger seat for a few minutes when Denhardt showed up—with a tire inner tube in his hand.

"What's this?" Verna asked suspiciously.

"Oh, we have to put the spare back and fix the punctured tire with the tube before we start driving home," Denhardt said with a smile. Denhardt started the car and rolled it to the little house in the back of the parking lot where an old man washed cars and did basic maintenance.

"Why couldn't you have done this already? We were supposed to be driving home now."

"Well, I just bought the inner tube. It'll only take a few minutes."

"What were you doing for the last three hours that this had to wait until now?" Vera demanded.

"Nothing," Denhardt said airily. "Just loafing."

While he was saying that, Denhardt unlocked the glove compartment and pulled out the biggest handgun that Verna had ever seen, a .45 caliber Smith & Wesson United States Army Model 1917 service revolver, and placed it into his righthand overcoat pocket. "Now, I have to get this tire taken care of, but don't even think about leaving. We still have a lot to talk about tonight."

Verna said calmly, "Henry, you don't have to do that. I'm not going to do anything."

Denhardt replied with a grin, "Of course you're not. I hadn't even thought about it."

Verna slumped over to the passenger side window and stared out the window while Denhardt negotiated the replacement of the ruptured inner tube. Now it did not look like they would be in La Grange in time for supper. Denhardt did this on purpose. When he returned to the driver's seat, he seemed almost giddy.

"Turns out, there's one more car in front of us he has to tend to, and then he'll get to us right away, he promised."

"Henry, how long is this going to take?" Verna pleaded.

"Not long, probably less than than an hour."

Even as she said, "But, Henry, I'll miss supper," Verna realized that this was just what Denhardt wanted. He was goading her. She could get out and make a scene, but she thought better of it. Denhardt had not actually threatened her with that gun, but it appeared he was going to make breaking up as slow and painful as possible. All she had to do was be patient and play along until they got home.

"We can eat supper after we get married," Denhardt said calmly.

Verna shook her head in dismay and decided to try a different tact, "I cannot get married in this, Henry. I'm wearing black. My sister is coming in a few days. We can get married then. Let's get me home now, and we can discuss it all later. It's only a few days off, and in the meantime, we could make some bit of preparation for the wedding, and it would look better that way," Verna said calmly in return.

Denhardt said, "If you don't marry me now, you never intended to marry me. You were just leading me on. You were playing me even while you were carrying on with Chester Woolfolk."

"Henry," Verna said breaking down slightly, "I will marry you, if you want, but I am not having an affair with Ches. Look, I'm still wearing your ring," Verna said showing her hand. "Now, let's just get home tonight and chaperone the children together as we planned. Wouldn't that be nice?"

During this time, the parking lot attendant who had been working on replacing the tube put the repaired tire on the car and started getting the spare loaded back into the trunk. Before he started jacking the car up, Denhardt left and said, "I'll be right back." He went into the Pendennis Club for a few minutes and came out. The car was almost finished.

"Country Club for dinner then?" Denhardt asked.

"I can't go, you know that. Remember when you said you would take me home tonight for supper with my girls and then help me chaperone? Being around the children will be bright and cheerful, and you will feel much better if you go."

"We could just grab something at the Pendennis Club, then we could be on our way."

"Henry, I don't know how much clearer I can be. I want to go home. I do not want to go out for dinner, not at the Country Club or the Pendennis or any place. I promised Frances that we would be home in time for supper and that you and I would chaperone the children tonight. Can't we still just do that? Won't that be fun?"

When the attendant was done, he came to the driver's side window, and Denhardt paid him for the repairs. Denhardt then pulled out into traffic and began to make his way back to SR 22 and home. They were heading into St. Matthews again when Denhardt pulled off the road and started driving in the direction of the Sada San Restaurant.

"We need to eat something. You haven't had anything to eat all day, so you need to get something to eat."

"Henry, you know that Frances is expecting me home for supper tonight. I'll eat at my house when I get there, I promise."

"She's not expecting you. You have time for dinner. I called Frances when I went inside the Pendennis Club and told her that you would not be home for supper, but you would be home in time to chaperone the dance," Denhardt said. "Don't get hysterical, Verna," said Denhardt flatly. "Really, with the history of imbalanced people in your family, you ought to be more careful. Besides, we're not married yet. You cannot tell me what to do. You need something to eat. You'll feel better when you eat something."

"I'm sorry," Verna said calmly. "I just want to get home."

"I forgive you," said Denhardt. Although Denhardt had not said anything about the gun in his pocket, he had not put it back in the glove compartment yet, either. It was bulging in his overcoat. Denhardt caught her eyeing the gun as he pulled the car over to park. "Would you feel better if I put this away? I can just lock it up while we're getting something to eat."

As they got out of the car, they started walking over toward Sada San Restaurant when Denhardt stopped on the sidewalk.

"You know, this day has been very trying for me," Denhardt reflected, and Verna agreed. "I still feel a little sick from a cold earlier this week, and the news you've given me has left me depressed. I know how you feel about me drinking, but I think I am entitled to have a drink in order to get over the shock of you breaking off our engagement. I have not been drinking on your account, and I won't do it if you don't consent, but I could really use a drink."

"It's all right, Henry. I think you're entitled to one drink, and it might do you some good."

"So, it's okay with you?" Denhardt said sarcastically.

"I want you to have it," Verna said.

"Problem is, I'll have to write a check," Denhardt said getting flustered. "Today has been very expensive for me to drive you around and see your friends and be your chauffeur. I had to pay the man to fix the tire, I bought you lunch, then I had to fix the inner tube and replace the tire. I haven't any cash left with me."

Calming him, Verna said, "Don't do that. It's not necessary. I have a dollar here, a silver dollar I have been keeping to give to you anyhow, you know, for your collection."

"You were going to give this to me, anyway? Because I never want to take your money."

"I had been saving it to give it to you for your collection. It's yours to do whatever you want. I can get another silver dollar for you. They come in at the laundry all the time. I only ask that I get to drive on the way home. You go get your drink, we'll have supper, and then I'll drive home. If that's all right with you."

"I'll be right back!" Silver dollar in hand, Denhardt went across the street to Bauer's, a bar and packaged liquor store, where he bought a pint of whiskey for fifty cents. After purchasing the flask-shaped bottle, Denhardt asked the bartender for a glass. Filling the glass with two fingers of whiskey, Denhardt chugged the shot and then, taking some water from the bar, filled the bottle back up again and put the cap on. As Denhardt crossed back over the street to the waiting Verna, Denhardt waved the seemingly unopened whiskey bottle at her before taking a long, slow drink as he walked. Slipping the bottle into his overcoat pocket, the general and Verna went in and found a table.

Verna did not enjoy being around Denhardt when he was drinking. He was a known combative drunk, but originally Verna did not think that was his true nature sober. She believed in his redemption. At first, he had been a gentleman when he was not drinking, very charming and sweet to her friends, although they did not care for him much. There was a part of her that saw it as a kind of Christian mission to show him how kindness could usurp his need for whiskey and beer. When she gave him an ultimatum that she had no interest in considering marriage to a habitual drinker, Denhardt appeared to give up alcohol and started coming with Verna to church. That was even before his proposal. His sincerity impressed her. It fueled her willingness to take her time in answering his proposal. But that night, was whiskey her ally? Verna paid for Denhardt's booze.

Dinner at the Sada San Restaurant was twenty-five cents for a plate with a meat and two vegetables and a cup of coffee, no pie. When the waitress came up, Denhardt pulled out the two quarters change left-over from the silver dollar Verna had given him for the whiskey and said, "Dinner is my treat." He asked for a glass from the waitress and poured another two fingers into the glass.

"I think we should cancel the dance plans tonight, don't you? I don't want to chaperone tonight, and I think you would not want to either considering your headache," Denhardt proposed.

The plate dinners were served with the coffee. R.H. Kirchdorpher, the Sada San's owner and manager, came by to greet the two diners who had been in many times before.

"Good evening, General Denhardt, Mrs. Taylor. It's so wonderful to have you back tonight," Kirchdorpher said.

They both thanked him for his hospitality and commented on how delicious dinner looked, but Verna was not her usual self. She was not smiling, and her voice carried no joy in it. When Kirchdorpher withdrew to a remote part of the room, he continued to watch the couple. Neither of them were eating their food. They both had forks in their hand, but Verna picked at her plate while the general sat grim-faced, staring at Verna. Kirchdorpher was concerned that the food served to them was unsatisfactory. He could not hear what they were saying, but whatever it was, it was not pleasant.

Although Denhardt's Smith & Wesson was safely in his car's glove-box, something was keeping Verna in line and preventing her from leaving.

"With the number of people out there conspiring against me, I never go anywhere unarmed, Verna," Denhardt said, speaking of the brownish-green metal pen sticking up from his vest pocket. "That's a pistol pen gun. It was given to me as a gift by Major Topmiller, a fine man from Bowling Green who knows me very well and respects me so much. He was an executive on my staff. I have had it for five years. You can never be too careful these days. It fires little tear gas canisters, but I keep it loaded with a .22 caliber cartridge. Just the other day, a big Negro was leaning up against my car, and when I told him to get off, the boy gave me lip about it. He wasn't laughing when I told him it was a pen pistol, and I had no problem shooting him on the spot in self-defense. And I would have, too, if a cop hadn't shown up."

Baxter Taylor, cousin to her late husband, happened to be in the Sada San that night, too. He had been watching the stiff conversation between Verna and the general from his table and was concerned about how Verna appeared. Taylor thought a friendly face would shift the mood of the quiet but public argument, so he dabbed his mouth with his napkin and greeted Verna with a big smile.

The general turned on him quickly through clenched teeth. "Sir, are you not mannered enough to know that you never interrupt a lady when she's having dinner with her gentleman?"

"Henry, this is Mr. Baxter Taylor. He was not speaking out of turn. Mr. Taylor is one of my late husband's favorite cousins. He and Barc were very friendly."

"General Denhardt," Mr. Taylor said without raising his voice, "you, sir, are a very rude man. I have every right to speak to Verna. She is family."

"Well, that may be," Denhardt said. "But Mrs. Taylor does not have the right to speak to anyone tonight."

Verna interceded. With apologies to Baxter, Verna suggested that tonight was a bad night to catch up, but she would be in touch soon.

This was the kind of public ugliness that Verna found mortifying. Verna was fighting her natural tendencies by standing up to Denhardt as much as she was. She enjoyed being the center of attention when it was positive about her girls, her business, or the dress she was wearing, but she was susceptible to people talking behind her back or spreading rumors about her. She would do just about anything to avoid not being liked.

The two had begun to garner stares from nearby tables, so Verna tried to eat as if nothing were wrong. Sitting straight up, she took some bites of her dinner and drank her coffee. Denhardt, too, shoveled in some food. When he thought no one was looking, he discreetly poured a splash of whiskey into his coffee. At 6'2", 240 pounds, it took a lot of liquor to get Denhardt drunk, but his shoulders were sagging a bit and his head was tilting a little to one side. Denhardt had had two big chugs and one sip of bourbon, but nobody could know about the shot he had downed in Bauer's or if he had had any beers in his clubs. All total, the general could have had as many as five drinks. For a big man who could hold his booze, this might not make him fall-down drunk, but it would make him sleepy. If Denhardt really did have the remnants of a head cold from earlier in the week as he claimed, it might not take long for a sixty-one-year-old man with a full belly of food and whiskey to nod off in the car.

"I want to go on a drive like a proper romantic couple should," Denhardt said without slurring or any outward sign of drunkenness.

"I agree, that sounds lovely," Verna said with a phony happiness. "I'll call Frances right now and tell her to find another chaperone because we're too sick. Eat everything up. We won't be stopping." Verna then made sure to drink all of her coffee for energy. She could not afford to get drowsy now.

Three phones were on the wall behind where they were sitting. Verna reversed the charges and called home. Having a home phone in 1936 was a luxury, but Verna's house was actually on a party line with the Community Laundry, a convenience she needed to manage the business and raise two daughters. It came in handy on nights like this. Without trying to worry Frances or sound like she was in trouble, Verna explained to her daughter that she had a terrible headache and that Frances needed to find another chaperone for the dance. Verna also begged her daughter not to leave until she made it back to the house. If there was a tone of desperation in her voice, this time it was picked up by Kirchdorpher, who overheard Verna stressing how important it was that Frances stay put. "Do not leave until I get home to see you!"

Shortly after that, Verna and the general were gone, this time, per their agreement, with Verna behind the wheel. There was no stumble in Denhardt's walk, no physical signs that he had been drinking, but the increased coarseness of his language and the shortness of his tone were telltale signs that the alcohol was having an impact. Denhardt might have been slowing down, but Verna was a long way from the safety of home.

On the open road, Denhardt's breathing became more labored, and the light of passing cars would have revealed that his eyelids were getting droopy. They had driven SR 22 from Louisville back to La Grange many times at night, and even without alcohol in his system, the sixty-one-year-old man could doze off at the end of the day. Tonight, she needed a little luck or divine intervention. She would have taken either.

As Verna approached a certain part of the road that had a very wide shoulder, though, Denhardt perked up and told her to pull into one of their usual spots. Maybe his "droopy eyes" had been wishful thinking.

It had been their custom on several late night drives back from Louis-ville to park and cuddle and talk about their possible future in the long driveway of a farm that had white milk cans lining the front. It was possible to pull a car slightly into the driveway and be obscured from the road and passing cars.

For a while, it had been a place for dreaming. If they were to get married, Denhardt's stately, but tattered, farm house would have to be remodeled and updated. Eventually, the Community Laundry and her home would have to be sold, Denhardt insisted on that, but he had been willing to discuss deeding her a part of his farm to do with as she pleased in return. The high point of their intimacy had been there, along that road well west of La Grange, obscured from passing cars, where they canoodled innocently and shared the possibilities of what a marriage might mean.

"Henry, I don't want to do this tonight. Please, can't we just go home?"

In the headlights of an oncoming car, Verna perhaps saw Denhardt had quietly removed his .45 caliber service revolver from the glove compartment and was cradling it in his lap. Taking another swig from his bottle, Denhardt had other plans.

Verna complied. A bolder woman might have kept on driving and dared a man to shoot the operator of a moving vehicle, but another fifteen miles or so and they would be pulling into La Grange. Verna glided the big Chevrolet off the road into their usual spot and turned off the car and the lights after they came to a stop.

"Leave the radio on," said Denhardt.

"Aren't you afraid you'll kill your battery?"

"The battery is fine," Denhardt said as he slid a little closer to Verna across the big bench front seats of his Master Sedan.

"Henry." Verna sighed. "It has been such a long day. You're sick. I have a headache. I have a big day tomorrow with the new steam flues going in. You've been better to me than anybody ever was. I think we owe it to ourselves to just call it a night."

But Denhardt had another idea of what was owed to whom. Accord-ing to two sets of doctors who examined her body later, a large, deep bruise on Verna's inner, upper right thigh was consistent with sexual assault, perhaps the heel of Denhardt's hand or a knee trying to force her legs apart. It is too gruesome to contemplate exactly how Denhardt tried to satisfy himself against Verna's body, and the autopsy revealed no sign of intercourse, no sign of bodily fluids, only that six-inch diameter, fresh, intimate inner thigh bruise, the lining of her coat had been ripped, and there was a tear in her slip.

How was a half-in-the-bag Denhardt repelled by the much smaller Verna? Did she talk him out of rape by reminding him that "marriage" would be just weeks away and that that would be the decent way? Was she able to get the physical upper hand somehow? People who saw him later saw no scratches on his face, no bruising, no sign of a struggle on his body.

Perhaps she threatened the general with the only reliable weapon always at her disposal: her protective brothers, Doc, Roy and Jack. Denhardt was an experienced bully who knew not to pick on a kid with much bigger brothers. Denhardt had 100 pounds on Verna and he had a gun, but if the autopsy was correct in suggesting that a fresh upper, inner thigh bruise was indicative of sexual assault, something made Denhardt reconsider in the front seat of the Chevrolet Master. Later at his trial, lawyers for Denhardt would argue that the Commonwealth of Kentucky failed to to establish a motive for why the general would murder Verna. One possibility was the sobering awareness that if Verna had made it back to her house alive, she would have told her brothers that Denhardt had attempted to rape her, and then there would have been hell to pay. If the brothers for some reason doubted her, she would have had the bruise to prove it.

Forensics can only fill in this blank so much, but this much is known: for the rest of the night, Denhardt would be fixated on the wrath of the Garr Boys. Coincidence?

Even after an undetermined amount of time on the side of the road with the engine off but the radio on, Verna was able to get the car started and continued driving eastbound on SR 22. Leaning on the passenger side window, consistent with other drives home from Louisville at night, Denhardt appeared to be falling deeper into drowsiness. The Chevrolet Master Sedan had a bench front seat as cozy as a living room sofa, and those springy, super-soft tube tires bumped across the La Grange city limits like a baby buggy. Up ahead, Verna could almost make out the upcoming intersection at First Avenue. One left turn and Verna would be almost home in time to see Frances, her friends, and all those pretty dresses. Braking slightly, Verna would have prepared to make the left turn into La Grange. Instead, something happened at that crossroads that sent her farther and farther away from her happy ending.

At the laundry once, Denhardt was overheard saying to Verna crossly, "If you don't marry me, no one will marry you," a comment that could have been construed as either an insult or a threat. Perhaps if Verna had been allowed to turn left, "no one will marry you" would have been merely an insult. By being forced to keep driving straight into moonless uncertainty, Verna must have realized that "no one will marry you" had been more of a threat all along.

Chapter Four

Looking at the night's events in the rearview mirror, perhaps Verna erred by being too eager to get back to La Grange. If she had not driven so fast, perhaps, Denhardt might have been rocked more gently to sleep—and stayed there.

"If anything happened to me, Henry, you'd be committing suicide, Henry. You know my brothers will hunt you down like a dog. You'd be dead fifteen minutes after you got home, you know that."

After four or five more miles in silence, Denhardt's eyelids were closed, and his head was bobbing. He looked sound asleep. Verna drove for another couple of miles east on SR 22 toward New Castle to be sure and then looked for a place to turn around. There were some lights at the Sligo Road intersection (pronounced "Sly-go"). It was referred to as "the Sligo Road" because it was *the* road that went to Sligo, Kentucky. Verna was concerned that sudden brightness might wake up the general. About a hundred yards before the Sligo Road, there was a driveway for the old state-owned Pendleton Schoolhouse that dated back to the days before Henry County had its own school system. The building was now being used by the county for small events, such as coroner's inquests and other official business.

The grassy parking area in front was dark, but Verna could pull in and turn around easily enough and get back to La Grange before Denhardt woke up. The general could sleep it off outside her house, they could talk it over in the morning over a cup of coffee and part as friends. Nobody would have to know anything about how he attacked her earlier, God forbid, or how awfully Denhardt had behaved. The general would keep his distance in exchange for Verna keeping her silence, and everybody would live happily ever after. Verna had been away from home for almost eleven hours. At this point, turning around in the old Pendleton Schoolhouse parking lot would literally turn around her night.

A car coming from the east would have helped illuminate the driveway, but the roads were quiet, so Verna tapped the brakes, shifted into neutral, and did her best to roll onto the gravel driveway entrance from the paved road. She was off to one side a bit on her approach. Verna was trying to go slowly so as to not wake the general, but the unevenness of the road surface caused her to slow down more than she wanted. Verna had to shift back into first, but as sometimes happens with big heavy cars, the Chevrolet lurched and then stalled. Verna put on the brakes and tried to start it again. It turned over, but would not catch. She tried to start it again. And again.

How long had they been parked at that farm with the engine off but the running lights on? With the key in the ignition, the Chevrolet's headlights dimmed a bit more every time Verna tried to start the car until, finally, she heard nothing. Other than the light coming from Browning's Filling Station at the Sligo Road intersection, Verna and Denhardt were sitting in darkness, and the car was dead.

"Looks like we're here for the night," Denhardt said with a sly smile, rolling over to rest his head on the window.

"There's a filling station right over there. I'm going for help."

Putting the gun in his pocket, Denhardt said, "You stay here. I'll handle this."

"Henry, why don't I go? You're... um, sick... and I think these people might know me, so it'll be easier for me to get help."

Rolling over back to the window, Denhardt said, "Okay, well, then, leave me out of it."

Pulling her karakul fur wrap tighter around her shoulders, Verna assessed the car's situation and then worked her way up to the paved road. The tail end of the large black Chevrolet was a few feet off the roadway. The front end was pointed down slightly toward the school. Without any lights on, the black car was quickly fading into the black, almost moonless night as Verna walked east up SR 22 toward the Sligo Road intersection and Browning's Filling Station.

Farmers George and Nettie Baker were neighbors of Barney Browning and his wife. The Bakers lived just off SR 22 a little further west from where Denhardt's car was parked—Verna had passed the white, one-story farmhouse as she was driving away from town but probably wouldn't even have noticed it because it was set off the road by about seventy-five feet.

Browning's Filling Station (just gas, oil, and water—no car repair) was similarly modest. Business in front, living quarters in the back, with a sweet sitting porch on the side of the house part of the building. Browning's had two big Standard Oil gas pumps on an island and a bench in front, where some of the locals would gather to drink a sodapop and catch up. That night, Baker had an errand to run. He dropped his wife off at Browning's at around 6:45 p.m. so that she and Mrs. Browning could visit a spell. After a quick trip to another neighbor's house, Baker went back to Browning's, where the two men and their wives socialized for several hours in the sitting room in the back. Except for the odd customer here or there, it had been a lively night of dessert and conversation between the friendly couples.

The Bakers were fixing to leave at about 8:45 p.m. when they heard the knock on the front screen of the gas station door. Browning stepped into the gas station from the adjoining door, but Baker and the wives remained in the back rooms. Verna appeared to him as a fashionably dressed woman who opened the front door of the gas station but did not enter. She seemed in a hurry and a little nervous as she pleaded, "Please help me! I'm having car trouble. It has no lights. I can't get the car to start."

Despite the chatty sounds coming from the setting room, Browning said, "I'm alone here tonight. I don't think I can leave. Besides, I don't know that much about automobiles." Disappointed, Verna said, "Oh, thank you, anyway," and closed the screen door behind her.

Browning went up the door and took one more look at the woman as she walked away and thought better of it. He decided that, if the car were not too far away, he would agree to help. She was about thirty steps in front of him when Browning threw on his coat and followed her. From the ambient light of his gas station, almost right away Browning could make out the faint silhouette of a large sedan parked in the old schoolhouse driveway. Baker also followed a few steps, saying, "I might try to help some way." Baker stopped and went back for his car, as he said to nobody in particular, "I'll get my machine and swing it around for some light."

When Verna saw Browning walking behind her a few yards, she stopped for him to catch up a bit and then introduced herself.

"I don't believe you know me," Verna said.

"I don't," confirmed Browning.

"I am Mrs. Taylor from La Grange. I operate the Community Laundry there."

Still walking in front, Verna got to the car first and took the seat behind the wheel. Browning looked over the car and asked, "What do you think? Should we try and tow or push the car a bit? If you drop it in gear while it's rolling, we can see if we can start it that way."

"I'd like to try either, thank you."

It was then that Browning was startled to see that a man sitting in the passenger seat. He made no motions, and he did not speak. Verna did not introduce him, and Browning did not ask who it was. Browning went around to the front of the car to try to push it back onto the highway. Verna put the gear in neutral, got out, came around to the front bumper, and tried to help push.

Looking in the direction of Denhardt, Browning asked, "What's wrong with this fellow that he can't help push the car off the driveway?"

"He's kinda... sick," stated Verna flatly. Verna said "sick," but Browning understood that as "drunk."

Denhardt did not try to disguise his presence or appear to be engaged in anything. He just sat there.

About that time, Baker arrived in his car to help push. The men had been giving the Chevrolet the shoulder for a few minutes when Baker stepped around to see how much farther they had to push. That was the first time Baker noticed Denhardt sitting in the passenger seat.

"Uh, Mr. Browning," Baker said. "What is that gentleman doing in the car?"

"She said he was kinda... sick," Browning reported. Thinking that meant "drunk," too, Baker just shrugged it off, got in his car, and with Verna steering, Baker and Browning were able to push the Chevrolet back up on the road. Verna had turned Denhardt's car so that it coasted backward, closer to Browning's gas station, but facing toward La Grange.

During this time, Verna, her window down, exchanged suggestions and encouragement with the two men while Denhardt sat stone faced, staring ahead, aloof, as though nothing was going on around him. After Verna safely came to a stop, Baker swung his car around on the road to go back to the Browning's porch to pick up his wife. Nettie Baker said her goodbyes and got in. Just then, the Bakers and the Brownings saw headlights racing westward down SR 22—and Verna standing out in the middle of the road waving, trying to flag down a maroon '34 Chevrolet Coupe. It was brave, Browning thought, because if that driver did not notice her, one of them was going to get killed. Browning thought he was going to witness this lovely woman get run over, but the driver suddenly stopped in time.

J.B. Hundley, a local barber, was driving home to La Grange from his sister's place in Pleasureville when he saw a frantic Verna waving for assistance. Unlike the other gentlemen, Hundley recognized her as "Mrs. Taylor," the operator of the Community Laundry, where he had been a customer for three years. Still hoping for a push into La Grange that night, Verna was talking to Hundley as Baker and his wife pulled back up again in their car. Feeling that Verna was in the hands of much more competent men now, Browning begged out of the group to shut down the filling station for the night. The last thought Browning had of the whole affair was that Mrs. Taylor and her anonymous sick friend would be all right. Even though Browning's Filling Station was just a mile up the road from the Baker farm, he would know nothing of her death until the next morning when he opened the filling station for business.

Verna asked if it were possible for her to be pushed into town. Pushing a car without any lights over a long distance in the dark brought up some serious, potentially fatal, safety considerations. Because she asked so nicely, though, Hundley tried to use his car to push Denhardt's Chevrolet up the road even a little bit but the two cars locked bumpers right away and had to be separated. While Hundley and Baker worked on the interlocked vehicles, Denhardt just sat in the car.

The gathered men were in consensus. There were no phones nearby, Baker said. The nearest phone was at Baker's son's house in Pendleton, quite a ways up the Sligo Road. None of them had a tow rope to take the Chevrolet back into town, and all agreed it would be unwise to push the general's car very far on SR 22 at night because the car would be rolling without lights, so the driver of the stalled car could not know for sure where they were steering. Furthermore, the driver's view in the car that was pushing would be obstructed by the stalled vehicle. SR 22 had some sharp turns, and the ditches on either side were too steep to try to push a car with no lights all the way back to La Grange. Verna was visibly disappointed, but this ad-hoc roadside committee knew how easy it would be to die on this highway.

As Denhardt got out of the car to give Hundley access to the battery under the seat, Hundley confirmed that everything appeared fine except for the battery. "The battery were dead," Hundley observed. "Has it been starting the car alright tonight?"

"Yes, it had," Verna said, but not being her car, she looked toward Denhardt for confirmation.

"Yes!" the general said with annoyed emphasis, not really facing the others. A small introduction was made at some point as to who he was. "Yes!" was the first word that any of these men had heard Denhardt utter all night. After that, Denhardt just leaned on the car's quarter panel and looked out into the night, bored, answering questions occasionally. Everybody smelled the liquor on Denhardt's breath.

After some debate about who might be open at this hour, Hundley volunteered to take Verna and Denhardt with him back to La Grange to get a battery from Cuba E. Shaver at Ellis's, a full-service gas station. This would have left Denhardt's car on the side of the road. Denhardt rejected that plan: "We don't want to leave the car setting on the road with no light and nobody around it."

It was Baker's plan that Hundley drive in front of Denhardt's car with his headlights on while this time Baker pushed with his car from behind. That way, at least, the bumpers would not lock and Denhardt's car would be safe at the Baker farm until more help arrived. Verna thanked the men effusively and then moved around to the driver's side door. Denhardt sat on the passenger side and resumed silence.

"I believe this is yours," said Hundley, as he handed Verna a woman's leather glove that had fallen on the running board. "Make sure you have the other one."

"Yes, thank you," Verna said as she looked in the dark car. "There it is!" Too cold a night to be going without gloves.

"Okay," said the barber to the farmer. "I will drive slow in front, and you can see how to push the car."

With Hundley lighting the way, Verna steering and leaning out the driver's window, Baker and his wife used his bumper to nudge the Chevrolet westward up SR 22. With her head and left arm fully exposed to the night air out the driver's side window, Verna very subtly let her left glove drop onto the road in front of the Baker house just as she turned left to the flat, grassy area along the Baker's farmhouse driveway. Denhardt remained emotionless.

Once the Chevrolet had been pushed in straight but just off to the side, Baker rolled in carefully past the Chevrolet to get his "machine" drained for the night in the barn. These were the old days before antifreeze in cars, and whenever temperatures at night were expected to go below freezing, wise and cautious men drained the water from their radiators, a process that could take up to twenty minutes. While Baker drained the water from his car in the garage, Mrs. Baker went into the house and started a fire to warm up.

Just after Baker had gone past, Hundley hollered back to Verna and Denhardt, "Y'all want to go to town, too?" He wasn't sure if he could tell who said it, but somebody said, "We'll wait right here," and Hundley left to find Shaver and a new battery. The Bakers did not hear any of that, though. They'd just assumed that Verna and Denhardt had gone with Hundley to town to stay warm, arrange for the battery, or to drop off Verna. It only made sense. What kind of gentleman would insist that the woman he loves stay in a car until the battery was replaced when she could be home, safe and sound? The only living soul in the Baker house who knew the couple was still out there was Trixie, their dog. If the Bakers had known that Verna and Denhardt were outside in the car, they would have begged them to come in.

Inside the Chevrolet, the only thing that had changed was Denhardt's appearance. Since the car had stalled, Denhardt's eyes had gone empty.

"We're not getting out of this car," Denhardt declared. "We're never getting out of this car."

"Henry, that's just crazy talk. You don't mean that." Verna always tried to give people the benefit of the doubt, to forgive their trespasses, as it were.

"I don't have to tell my brothers anything. You can just let me go, I promise. I'll sign anything. You're a lawyer, just draw up a contract, and I'll sign it. When I get home tonight, I'll write a letter to you swearing that I will never divulge what happened in this car tonight. You will be blameless, Henry. We don't ever have to speak of this, and my brothers would never have to know. You stopped tonight, Henry, before things went too far, and that's to your credit. It can just be our secret.

"So, let's just get the car fixed and go to the Mary D. Shop and chaperone the kids like we talked about, you and me," Verna said trying to placate him. "I just need to get out of this car and start heading home. I've been in and out of this car for twelve hours now, and I have a head-ache, and I'm going a little crazy."

Inside the farmhouse, Trixie was growling out the window at the anger coming from the Chevrolet. Denhardt's whole face seemed to change as if a mask had loosened and revealed a demon that had been hiding behind human flesh. Verna had attributed his temper flares to alcohol, but this time, for the first time, Verna understood that this evil went much deeper than whiskey and beer.

In the distance, Verna could hear Trixie's agitated barking.

"Clearly, Henry, you are under a lot of stress, and that is not your fault, but you are too great a man to be trapped in this little car, either. You've got too much to offer the world yet. You could still be governor someday; you're young. Better yet, with your war record, you could be a senator. Senator Denhardt would not be out of the question."

"There are too many people against me now," Denhardt said defeat-edly. "There are invisible powers that decide who gets what."

"They just don't know you like I know you, Henry. This state still needs you. Don't let anything get in the way of that."

Verna spoke softly as she searched around her coat and front seat. "Where is my other glove? Do you see it here?" It was hard to see any-thing inside that car. "So, are we done with all this crazy talk? This ring you gave me was the nicest thing I have ever received in my life." With that, Verna kissed her ring. "But I still don't think I deserve to keep it."

"No, no," Denhardt mumbled. "I want you to have it."

"Well, then I have a present for you." From her pocketbook, Verna withdrew some tattered pages of a small, yellowed, tape-covered book of sayings. "I have a little tract here that has given me more help than anything. I have read this over and over, and I want to give this to you and I want you to read it."

Denhardt took the small bundle of papers and tried to look at them in the dim light, but he couldn't tell what it was. He smiled and put it in his coat pocket. Once more, Verna reached over and hugged Denhardt's neck and said, "You've been better to me than any man ever was."

After Verna and Denhardt had sat in the car in the Baker driveway for some minutes, Denhardt seemed calm and more like his usual self.

"Henry," Verna asked, "Do you think you could ask the Bakers for a phone so you could check on what is taking the garageman so long?"

Inside the farmhouse, the Bakers had settled in front of the fire of the middle room, the dining room. After all the excitement of trying to help stranded motorists had passed, they hoped for some quiet time. Trixie never stopped barking, though, as she went from window to window, agitated at something outside. No verbal commands would quiet her for long, so Baker got up and went over to the front door window to see if he could see what she was barking at. Suddenly, Trixie was barking again, watching Denhardt moving quickly down Baker's driveway in the direction of the side porch where the lightbulb was on. Where did he come from? Baker was frightened because, to his knowledge, the tall, silent man was in La Grange seeing to his battery. In fact, Denhardt walked in a straight line so "fastly" that for the first time that night, Baker wondered whether the general was not as drunk as he thought he was. Either that or he sure sobered up fast.

Out by the road, quietly, the second that Denhardt disappeared up the Bakers' driveway, Verna quietly had unlatched the driver's side door, picked her glove up from the roadway, and started walking quickly westward. Every step she took toward La Grange was one more foot toward home and her girls, she thought.

When Baker opened up the side porch door off the kitchen, Denhardt said quickly, "Have you a telephone?"

"No, I hadn't," said Baker, who thought Denhardt had heard him say there were no phones around those parts.

"It seems like the garageman is taking so long I wanted to call them."

"Well, then, won't you folks come in to the fire until the garageman comes?"

"No," Denhardt said, "I guess not," and then he turned and started slowly back toward his car.

Right about that exact moment, bright lights from a fast moving car coming from La Grange toward New Castle poked through Baker's trees and seemed to be slowing down as they neared the driveway. Baker closed the porch door and went to the front room window, fully expecting that it was Hundley with the mechanic and the battery pulling up to the farm. But even though the car slowed down to about 35 m.p.h. after the bend west of Baker's place, the fast-moving car then sped up, flying down SR 22 at about a mile a minute. Curious now about what else was going on outside, Baker shut the middle room door and moved around to the front room window to peer out in the darkness. Around the Denhardt car, he couldn't see anything, just blackness, and certainly no signs of the woman or her silent friend.

Baker would not have been able to get a good look at it, but the fast moving car was a 1934 sedan belonging to Bernard Shephard and his wife, Lottie. The Shephards had been visiting with Mr. Shephard's mother in her home on SR 22 about a mile east of La Grange. Being that he was driving a V-8, the night was clear, and there were no other motorists around, Shephard tapped the gas a bit and let the engine unwind for a few miles toward New Castle. He figured he was doing around 55 m.p.h as he came up to the bend in the road just before the Baker farm.

Hugging the side of the road, Verna held tight to the glove she had dropped earlier, as it was her excuse for having left the car. Verna moved swiftly in her low-heeled opera shoes toward the trees on the south side of SR 22. She wanted to go to the Bakers' house, but Denhardt was there, and, frankly, she was not sure if Denhardt would just start shooting. Verna almost heard the '34 V-8 sedan as soon as she saw it. The loud engine, the bright lights were coming fast. Verna was only a few yards west of the driveway, but she faced a moment of truth. Were these headlights from Hundley's car with the mechanic? Should she chance stepping out in the road in case it was? If the car did not stop, Denhardt would see her for sure. She stayed against the tree, hidden, and let the car go past.

Slowing down as the Shephards came up to the Baker farm, they saw a black Chevrolet sedan parked off to the side of the driveway. For just a second, his headlights shone on a large man in a dark overcoat standing next to the open passenger door of the sedan. The big man did not wave or smile; he just stood there as the Shephards blew past. There was nobody visible inside the car. Safely by, Shephard accelerated again down the long, straight stretch of SR 22 until he turned left at Browning's Filling Station and went north up the Sligo Rd. The Shephards saw no other person on the road that night, before or after the Bakers' driveway.

When Denhardt had left the Baker's porch just a half minute before the Shephards drove by, he could tell almost immediately that Verna had left the car while he was gone. Running up to the car, he looked in the driver's side window and then into the darkness eastward toward New Castle. First, he ran a few yards up the road but knew right away that was pointless, so he ran back to his car to grab his keys and flashlight. Denhardt had just opened the passenger side door when he saw headlights coming fast from the west. The big man just froze. If that oncoming car was Hundley with the garageman, Denhardt was as good as dead. That would mean that Verna had escaped, and she would tell the Garr Boys what he had being doing all night to their sister, and they would kill him, plain and simple. In that moment, Denhardt felt like he was having a heart attack. His breath went shallow. He had never been so afraid in his life. The faster the car came, the faster his heart beat.

But the car flew on. It had slowed down a little, but obviously it was not Hundley. The car with the garageman might be coming at any minute, though, so if Denhardt could find Verna, he still had one chance to control the situation. Inside the Baker house, a worried Trixie was still barking at a monster not visible to Baker, patrolling in front of the farm. Baker walked back toward the kitchen window near the back porch to see if he could get a better look at the Chevrolet up by his driveway.

Denhardt opened up his glove compartment and found his flashlight and took the keys. The flashlight was fading, but the batteries still had some juice. He walked a few steps up SR 22 toward the Sligo Road until it occurred to him that if Verna had been going that way, he would have seen her in the headlights of that speeding car. Inadvertently, the Shephards had helped Denhardt narrow the scope of his search. Instead, he turned to go west. She was trying to get back to La Grange. She was trying to get home.

"Verna! Verna!" Denhardt screamed into the night, but all anybody heard was Trixie barking.

Perhaps in the long history of women who have struggled to get away from narcissist/sociopaths, Verna got farther than most. About thirty yards up from the Bakers' driveway, Verna was walking briskly along the side of SR 22, hoping for any sign of Hundley's car. Unfortunately, Ellis's had been closed for the night, and Cuba Shaver had gone home. Concerned for the woman he knew from the laundry and the drunk guy with her, Hundley went to Shaver's residence and talked him into helping. Hundley drove Shaver back to the garage to get a battery and some tools.

Running at full speed along the same path, it took Denhardt a few seconds to catch up with Verna. Even with an overcoat on, Denhardt was showing no signs of perspiration in the cold night air. As Verna spun around, her hands up to block the fading light from Denhardt's flashlight, Verna would have made her last defense.

There was no clear, apparent motive for Verna's murder, but there rarely is with rage-killing. Denhardt may have been experiencing a build up of fear in connection with Verna's brothers finding out about his controlling and boorish behavior that night. As a narcissist/socio-path, Denhardt would have been hypersensitive to his world becoming disordered after being exposed. In the buildup, people who rage are prone to hate most those that are a threat to their sense of well-being; the combination of fear and hate was enough to lead to Denhardt's explosion. According to Dr. Duncan Cartwright in his article *The Narcissistic Exoskelton: the Defensive Organization of the Rage-Type Murderer*, "the act is not premeditated in any way, some degree of disassociation appears to take place, and the act is typically provoked by a relatively innocuous external event." Like a woman getting out of a car without permission, for instance. A rage-kill culminates after "a build up of affect or psychic energy that has a cathartic or relieving effect after a rupture in the ego has occurred," according Dr. Cartwright's research.

The Iron General was dangerously close to the Bluegrass Belle. Perhaps he gave her the impression that she had nothing to be worried about. Maybe he felt true pity for what he knew was about to happen: "You were the finest woman I ever knew..."

Facing Verna, the gun held low by the right-handed man, perhaps just above the righthand-side overcoat pocket, Denhardt's .45 pointed upward toward Verna's heart. Unless he closed his eyes when he fired, Denhardt would have watched the life drain quickly from Verna's pretty face after the single bullet passed through her. As the shot echoed and Verna fell backward, likely, Denhardt's momentary sadness over what needed to be done was washed away by the relief of knowing the existential threat to his self-image had been eliminated.

Chapter Five

M r. Baker was standing by his kitchen window near the side porch, peering out when he heard the first gun shot. Not a small caliber weapon, mind you, not a kid's first hunting rifle or a woman's gun, but the booming, echoing explosion of a military grade weapon, a bullet that was designed to kill, not just to wound. Baker didn't see a muzzle flash or any movement in the dark. The gunshot could have come from anywhere, but it still seemed to be echoing when Baker went back to the middle room where Mrs. Baker was sitting, frightened.

"What was that?" Nettie Baker said.

"It was a gun shot, and I'm afraid something serious just happened. It was so close," said George Baker. They talked for a minute or two—the Bakers were never quite clear how long—about the characteristics of the shot, whether it was a large pistol or a shotgun, before Baker moved halfway back toward the kitchen window, stopped, turned around, and then walked on. He was about to step out to the side porch when Mrs. Baker called him back from kitchen.

"George, can you shut the middle door? It's kind of cold." When he had secured his wife, Baker stepped tentatively out on to the side porch, but he could neither hear nor see much past his own driveway. Except for Trixie barking at shadows, the night was still again.

After Denhardt pulled the trigger, Verna fell back to the road surface like a marionette that just had her strings cut with one bullet. Verna's coat was open when Denhardt fired, so the bullet cut through her dress just below her left breast. There were no final words, no dramatic gestures. Verna was alive one second and dead the next—and that's about as much thought as Denhardt gave it. In order for him to avoid the wrath of the Garr Boys, however, Denhardt knew Verna's death had to look like something else—and fast. She had talked about suicide that night, hadn't she? Of course, she meant it as HE would be committing suicide if he did anything to her, but close enough. Or maybe it was robbers on the road; could be random highway robbers. Anyway, it had to look like it was not his fault. The minds of narcissist/sociopaths are wired for situations like this. Denhardt's ability to reason was not constrained by empathy or guilt.

Picking up Verna's hat from the road and stuffing it in his pocket, Denhardt closed her coat over her entrance wound so that he did not get any blood on his own coat, turned her 135 pound body onto its stomach and carried her across his arms with the exit wound facing up to the night sky. He had gone a ways past the car down SR 22 when he stopped to rest for a moment and pull out his flashlight. In the process of trying to juggle Verna's body and use the flashlight to find the perfect spot to stage the body drop, Denhardt fumbled the contents of his coat pocket—flashlight and keys—somewhere on the road.

About a tenth of a mile east from the farmhouse, on the farm side of the road, was far enough. Denhardt carried Verna to the edge of the roadway surface before it sloped down to the drainage ditch. First, he put her hat back on, and then with his hands under her arms, Denhardt could have easily bear-hugged Verna and walked her back like a mannequin as far as possible on the road without falling off himself. Denhardt then gently tossed her body onto its back in the bluegrass as though she had shot herself and fallen backward. He then tossed the gun to land close to her right hand, but he missed and it ended up by her head. Looking down, Denhardt saw a glove and Verna's left shoe. He realized that they had fallen as he was manipulating her body. He tried to get the shoe near her left foot but overshot that, too. He made quick work of the glove and then he started to hustle back to the car. There was just one more thing Denhardt had to do—and he had to be fast.

Denhardt's service revolver had no safety feature, so like anybody who knows their way around a six-shooter, Denhardt always kept a spent cartridge in the first chamber. That way, if the hammer got caught on something, the revolver would not discharge a live bullet; instead, it would hit a dead shell. That simple trick kept a lot of old cowboys from blowing a hole right through their best boots.

To account for the two spent casings in the revolver and also to give the illusion that somebody else was doing the firing, Denhardt needed a decoy shot. Denhardt did not have a second .45 in his possession, but he did have his pen pistol that fired a .22 caliber bullet. It would have to do. He'd have one chance, and he'd have to time it just right. He had to be close enough for somebody to hear the pen pistol but not close enough for somebody to see him shoot it.

Meanwhile, Baker was gathering the courage to brave the cold darkness. Fear was the only reason for not going out faster to determine what was happening so near his farm. Fifteen to twenty minutes had passed since Denhardt had startled Baker by appearing at his side porch when the farmer thought the general was in La Grange; ten to fifteen minutes had passed since the loud gunshot that had made Baker concerned something more serious had happened. Baker told his wife where he was going, and then he walked out into the black night.

Over on the neighboring Parker farm, Preston and George Carpenter were doing some night hunting. George had just bought a new hunting breed pup, and he was testing the small dog in the post-harvest fields about a mile from the Baker house. They hadn't yet fired a shot when they heard a loud report in the distance.

"Did you hear that?" one brother said to the other. "It sounded something like a shotgun or a large revolver." Somebody else shooting at something in the darkness was a good enough reason for the Carpenter boys to head back to their place on the Parker farm. In the twenty minutes it took them to get home, that was the only shot they heard.

By the time Denhardt was almost back to the Baker house, he had the pen pistol ready. Just as the name suggests, these were little, single-shot guns disguised to look like pens. They were not working pens that fired a pellet, it is important to point out, but a spring-loaded, percussion-fired, single chamber gun that one could clip into a breast pocket. As a novelty, they were sold through mail-order ads in the back of comic books and other magazines. In the 1930s, there were only a couple manufacturers of these personal protection devices, but the best-known pen pistol was the Faultless Pen Gun from Federal Laboratories in Pittsburgh, Pennsylvania, now owned by Mace Security International in Cleveland.

The pen pistol is breach loaded by unscrewing the top and dropping in a tear gas cartridge or .22 bullet cartridge, slender end down. The bullet shape of the pen pistol prevents it from being loaded incorrectly.

After the .22 cartridge is dropped in, the top is screwed back on, and from that point on, it's loaded. The trigger is a large ball bearing on the side of the cap. To activate the gun, the spring-loaded internal hammer is cocked by pulling back on the knob on top of the pistol until it stops. To fire, the pen clip is rotated to expose the ball bearing. After the pistol is pointed to the target, the ball bearing is pressed. Internally, the ball bearing releases the coiled spring that strikes the hammer onto the cartridge's primer cap, which ignites the enclosed gunpowder and expels the bullet. To reload, unscrew the pen, withdraw the spent cartridge, and put in a fresh one.

The pen clip is not only part of the disguise, but it is also the gun's main safety feature because it blocks the ball bearing from being depressed accidentally. With a loaded pen pistol in a pocket already, a gun enthusiast such as Denhardt could arm and fire the novelty weapon with his eyes closed—with just one turn of the pen clip—and in the dark, Denhardt practically did. Pointing the pen pistol away from his body, with his arm straight, Denhardt discharged the weapon toward the field across the road. His body blocked Baker from view, and he never broke stride walking back to his car.

Baker started down his driveway with trepidation. On the far end of his focus, he had just started to make out the silhouette of a large man's head and shoulders moving from the east toward the Chevrolet. Just a second or so after making out that it was a human form nearing the car, Baker was startled for a third time that evening. A second shot went off, but this one was nowhere near as ominous as the first. The difference between how the two sounded might be best described this way. When the M1917 was chosen by the U.S. Army as the sidearm of choice for the troops, it was because the munitions experts at the Pentagon considered it a "man stopper." Because of its low noise and light recoil, the .22 is the caliber of choice for Boy Scouts going for merit badges. The sound of the second shot did not travel far. The Carpenter brothers on the Parker farm next door only heard one shot. Mrs. Baker never heard a second shot, either. Inside the farmhouse, even Trixie only seemed to notice the first shot.

"General, is that you?" Baker called out after the second, weaker shot.

"Yes," Denhardt confirmed as he move toward the back of his car.

"Did you hear that gun?" Baker said, referring to the first shot.

"Yes, I did, did you?" Denhardt said as the two men moved closer to each other in the dark.

Denhardt took a step closer to Baker, friendly for the first time tonight. Baker noted that Denhardt looked frightened. "Yes, wasn't that second shot fearful?"

Baker did not want to be disagreeable, but he thought the two did not compare, so he rejoined, "Yes, it was—and the first one, too."

Denhardt then said emphatically, "The lady that was with me went up the road to pick up her glove.... There were a gun in my car!" At this, Denhardt opened the driver-side door and looked at the front seat and the glovebox. "The gun is gone!" exclaimed Denhardt. "Do you have a flashlight?"

"Yes, sir," said Baker.

"Well, get it, and let's look for her!" Baker thought the general seemed perfectly capable of looking for the woman himself, but he was happy to get him some light.

"I will get you a lantern," Baker said as he turned and went up toward the house.

Denhardt said, still processing his disassociated experience, "My, my, ain't it awful? She was the finest woman I ever knew." Baker thought Dehardt's use of the past tense sounded odd, and the whole sentence seemed sort of premature. As a narcissist/sociopath, Denhardt had no trouble killing Verna Garr Taylor, though he had a problem trying to *sound like a guy who didn't.* His tearless, wooden, word-for-word repetition of "My, my, ain't it awful? She was the finest woman I ever knew," would leave anybody who heard him confused all night.

Just as Baker made it inside the farmhouse to fetch a lantern, Hundley finally drove up with Shaver on the shoulder of the road facing Denhardt's car. Leaving the maroon coupe running with the headlights on so they would have something to work by, Shaver and Hundley were getting out and grabbing the battery to put it into Denhardt's car when Denhardt came up excitedly to the two men saying, "I heard two shots up the road." There were no greetings and no expression of gratitude from the general for having put them out so much, just this sudden blurting about two shots up the road.

Hundley and Shaver nodded but did not pay any attention to Denhardt because they did not really understand how that pertained to the installation of the battery. They thought he was just reporting the news, of sorts. Both men wanted to take care of the roadside emergency and get to their respective homes, but Denhardt persisted. Baker had gone inside, located the lantern, lit it, and returned when he heard the general pestering the men about going up the road and seeing about "the shots," not about Verna it was pointed out later, but "the shots."

"Let's go see about the shots." he said.

Shaver said incredulously, "Do you want to go now?"

"Yes," Denhardt said. "Boys, you've got to go up the road and look for her."

"Well, all right," Hundley said, so he and Shaver started getting into the coupe. Then Hundley opened the door again, stepped out, and said to the general, "You're coming with."

"Well, I will go," said Denhardt and he got in the back seat.

Hundley was confused by the lack of information. He really wasn't even sure what they were looking for—people with guns in the dark? Why? What were "the shots"? Who exactly was the "her" they were looking for? He had just assumed that Verna was in the Bakers' farmhouse, all toasty and warm.

"Mrs. Taylor went up that way, hunting for her glove," Denhardt explained to Hundley as they were driving up SR 22, but Hundley was still confused. "She was the finest woman I ever knew," Denhardt said several times. Was Mrs. Taylor hurt while she was glove hunting? Had she fired a gun? Why was he talking about her in the past tense? The three men drove all the way up to Browning's at the Sligo Road, then turned around and started to come back again, looking for Verna on both sides of SR 22 in the coupe's headlights.

"Well, we'll go back and put the battery in Mr. Denhardt's car, so we will have more light," Hundley said, laying out the plan as they got out of the coupe again at the Bakers' driveway.

While Hundley and Shaver were fixing the Chevrolet's battery, Denhardt grew insistent, "Boys, see about the woman first thing!" Hundley and Shaver ignored him, anyway, and just kept working. "There's no use in getting two cars," Denhardt said. "She must be *off* the road. She was the finest woman I ever knew."

It should be noted that at no point did Denhardt grab Baker's lantern and start to walk up and down the road to look for Verna himself, like a caring authentic fiancé. Instead, Denhardt was focused on getting other people to do it for him. Not because he was lazy or afraid, of course, but because somebody else finding Verna was central to his plan. If Denhardt himself found her, then it would have emphasized that he knew where to look. Instead, he was trying to play the part of the concerned fiancé, dependent on the good will of others in his time of emotional need. The problem for Denhardt was that he did not know how a concerned fiancé dependent on the good will of others sounded. That's why everything Denhardt said that night landed so flat, so detached. Denhardt spoke like he was reading cue cards in the dark.

To people like Denhardt, those who act as if they are the center of the world around whom all others revolve, it's genuinely frustrating when lesser beings do not follow their instructions. At first, after getting the lantern, Denhardt would have walked with Baker until he manipulated the farmer into finding Verna's body, thereby reinforcing the suicide narrative that Denhardt had decided to sell. When Hundley and Shaver showed up, Denhardt tried to get them ALL to go up the road to find Verna's body, but they were only willing to do it in their car, something Denhardt suspected would have been pointless because it would have been unlikely that the men would have seen the body from the roadway in the headlights. Compounding all of that was Denhardt's inability to persuade, manipulate, or command. Denhardt pushed the men through some imagined authority to go on foot to look for her body, but it did not take Shaver long to push back.

"Well, wait until we fix the car! We'll put the battery in, and we'll drive both cars up the road with the lights and see if we can find her," Shaver said, confronting the general.

Thinking about it for a minute, it occurred to Baker where Verna must be. Baker had reckoned to himself that if somebody were shot on the new road, they might roll down onto the old road. So, Baker accidentally saved Denhardt's alibi. "Men," Baker said, "I don't think you'll find this lady with the automobile. I believe that she is over in that old road."

Taking a minute to understand what Baker meant by "the old road" is crucial to knowing what happened next and why. Like a lot of places, the original roads of Kentucky were built along oxcart and carriage paths that had followed horse trails, deer paths, and the Native Americans who followed the deer. The first formal highways in Kentucky were not necessarily roads of intention, but perhaps literally "paths of least resistance" that added gravel or bricks to the contours of these well-worn trails. As transportation became more sophisticated, local and state governments accommodated the growing commerce by formalizing existing highways between major county seats, towns, and cities. Such is the case of Kentucky State Road 22. For many years, what had been designated as SR 22 was just a gravel and dirt road that meandered from Louisville through La Grange, New Castle, and beyond. That was "the old road."

In the early 1930s, following the same general direction of the old road, a straighter, properly engineered, two-lane highway was designated the new SR 22 upon completion. The graded roadway was built up in layers off the original elevation and slightly arced so that the shoulders sloped on both sides for drainage, safety, and longevity. The crowning innovation for the new SR 22 was a top layer mix of tar, cinders, and fine gravel in a process that was called "road metaling" at the time, from the Latin *metallum* for "quarry." In fact, the road surface back in the 1930s was often just referred to as "the metal" of the road. Today, it would just be called "blacktop" or, by its next recipe innovation, "asphalt." When it was decommissioned, the old SR 22 that ran parrallel to the new road in many places was allowed to go to seed.

If Baker were right, the reason why Verna would not be spotted from either car was that, in some places, the old road was four or even five feet lower than the new SR 22. Baker said to the men, "It will take a lantern to find that lady, for I believe that she will be found over in the old road." Denhardt's plan was coming together, although not by his design. There was a little difficulty getting the old car battery out and the new one in. As Shaver and Hundley were working, Denhardt and Baker kept talking about the missing woman.

At one point, Denhardt said to Shaver, "What do you think could have happened?"

Shaver shrugged and said, "I don't know."

"Well, I had a gun in the glovepocket of my car, and now it's gone. Did either of you see Mrs. Taylor as you drove up the road?"

"No," Shaver said.

"So, what do you think could have happened" Denhardt asked again like an instructor.

"Maybe Mrs. Taylor killed herself," Shaver said, and Denhardt agreed. The intrigue having been built up, when the men finished installing the new battery, the barber turned to the farmer and said, "Let's go see about the lady."

"I will go tell my wife," Baker said, "She is at the house by herself."

Baker handed Hundley the lantern as the farmer ran inside and back quickly. Shaver started down the left side of the road with his flashlight, and Hundley followed the right side of the road with the lantern, each looking down into the ditches. The old road paralleled SR 22 on Hundley's side. As Baker hurried to catch up with the two leaders, he passed Denhardt, who was hanging back by about twenty feet or more, walking slowly down the middle of the road, just waiting.

Baker and Hundley had paired up together, but Hundley was still carrying the lantern. As the ditch got deeper and further from the metal of the road, Hundley started down into the weeds.

"I don't think there is any use to get in the grass. Wait 'til we get up there." Baker pointed ahead. "I just feel she is over in this flat part of the old road." By this time, Denhardt was so far back that he could no longer be seen in the darkness. Almost exactly where Baker's hunch had predicted, about six hundred feet from his farmhouse, there she appeared, the pale visage of Verna Garr Taylor on her back, her gaze fixed upward, yards to the side of SR 22 down on the old road.

"Shaver, there she is!" shouted Hundley as he made his way down to Verna's body. The mechanic came over from the other side of the road, and he and Baker followed Hundley down to check on the beauty's condition. Denhardt walked slowly to the edge of the roadway, looking down. Supine, Verna's skin was already seemed waxy under the ghostly lights. She was flat on her back, with her coat open, her right leg straight, her left knee slightly drawn up, and to the right, an obvious, shiny crimson bloodstain under her left breast. Her chalk-white face stared upward to the stars, her right arm was splayed out slightly while her left arm was crooked at the elbow. Verna's right shoe was on, but her left shoe was resting in the space between her left elbow and her torso, not far from the blood on her dress. A .45 caliber revolver could be seen several feet up from her right hand on her right side, closer to her face on a kind of natural dirt shelf in the old road. Verna's left hand clutched a black leather glove firmly. Hundley looked up and stated to the general, "She were dead."

Denhardt stayed on the metal. "My, my, ain't that awful," was all he said nervously. All the men agreed it was. "That is my gun," Denhardt stated.

Hundley looked up at Denhardt and asked, "Who must I call?"

"Call Mr. Keightley, and call the coroner," directed Denhardt. Smith Keightley was a La Grange funeral home director and an old Garr family friend, and another funeral director, D.L. Ricketts, served as the official coroner for Henry County. The general murmured, "My, my, isn't it dreadful? Isn't it awful?"

Hundley asked, "Is there anybody else you think I should call?"

"No," was all Denhardt said. Not her daughters, not her mom, and certainly, God forbid, not her brothers.

"Yes, sir," said Hundley, climbing back up the sloping fill to the new road. "Well, I will go and call them." Hundley took a few hurried steps back toward his car when he turned and called back, "Y'all be sure to stay with the body, and don't leave it until I get back." Shaver, Baker, and Denhardt stood there for a few minutes before Baker said, "I'd better get back on home I don't like leaving my wife alone any longer if there's a killer at large in these parts."

Knowing that there was nothing left to do for Verna until the coroner arrived, Shaver followed alongside Baker's lantern as he began to walk briskly against the night air back to his farmhouse and the warmth of his wife. Denhardt had no interest in staying with the body, so he walked slowly back up toward his car. Within a hundred steps or so, however, Baker's flickering flame caught the glint of a silvery object directly ahead in the road. Shaver bent down and picked up a nearly full ring of keys and a non-functioning chromium flashlight and held it toward Denhardt, who was still a few steps behind.

"Chief or Colonel or whatever, is this your flashlight and switch keys?"

Denhardt then patted his overcoat as he came up to Shaver saying, "Where are my keys?"

"Here they are. They were laying in the road." The men were not even a quarter of the way back to the farmhouse. According to his testimony to the press later, Baker looked at the general then found a stick on the side of the road, jammed it into the dirt level to the spot in the road where Denhardt's keys and flashlight were found, looked at the general one more time, and went home to check on his scared wife and tell her the sad news.

Baker came out again to find Denhardt and Shaver standing near the general's car. It wasn't long before Hundley came racing up to the Baker house with Smith Keightley in an ambulance without the sirens going. Denhardt got in the cab in front, Shaver and Baker stood on the running boards, and the men took Keightley down to the old road where they found Verna's body. After they stopped, Denhardt and Keightley were getting out of the cab of the ambulance when Denhardt said very loudly and unprovoked, "I couldn't have killed her. I was too crazy about her!"

Shaver, Hundley, and Baker climbed down the embankment to assist Keightley while Denhardt stayed up by the ambulance. After first confirming that nobody had altered the crime scene in any way, Keightley placed a pillow under Verna's head, and the men helped pull a sheet over her body. It seemed like it took a long while for Coroner Ricketts to arrive, but that might have been because the cold of the night was seeping in.

"I were getting chilly," Baker said, trying to warm himself, standing vigil with the other men over Verna. To signal Ricketts, Keightley turned on a flood light. When he pulled his car over, Keightley walked up to Ricketts.

"Verna Garr has been shot."

Within a few minutes, the undertaker, the garageman, the barber, and Ricketts—a gaunt, sunken-cheeked, somewhat cadaverous-looking man—were preparing to put Verna on a stretcher. Ricketts took the names of everybody who had been in the original search party and then carelessly picked up the Smith & Wesson that lay a few feet from Verna's right hand but closer to her head. With the care of a professional, Ricketts examined the gun and determined that there were two spent shells and that the rest of the rounds were chambered but unfired.

"Would this be yours, General?" the coroner asked.

"That is my gun," Denhardt replied. "She was wearing a diamond ring. I wish you would see if that is still on her hand."

Keightley raised her left hand, the one that was clutching the glove, and said, "Yes, the ring is here."

"I wish you would take care of it," Denhardt asked.

"I will," affirmed Keightley.

Ricketts, Keightley, Hundley, and Shaver all carried Verna's body in the stretcher up the side of the road while Baker held the lantern.

"Mr. Ricketts, I would like a word with you," Denhardt said as the rest of the men managed the stretcher around to the back of the ambulance. Ricketts was too preoccupied to answer.

"Mr. Ricketts, I would like to talk to you," said Denhardt as the men swung the stretcher around.

"Just a minute," said Ricketts as they finished loading Verna's body into the back of the ambulance.

The entire time that his fiancée's body was being moved from the ditch in which she lay to the ambulance that would silently take her away, Denhardt never made any attempt to see the supposed love of his life once more, to smooth her hair, to kiss her forehead, to touch her hand. All the men noticed that Denhardt stood there watching the stretcher like a busy man waiting for a bus to pass so he could cross the street.

While Keightley and Ricketts secured Verna's stretcher firmly in the back, Denhardt turned to Baker and *apropos* of nothing, said, "Mrs. Taylor said that she would kill herself, but I paid no attention to it because I have said the same thing and so have you many times."

Baker replied, "No, I never did say I would kill myself that I can recall."

"Well, I heard her say that many times, and I have made that remark myself," Denhardt restated. Baker did not know what to say. After an awkward pause, Denhardt repeated, "She was the finest lady I ever knew."

With the ambulance door shut, Keightley and Ricketts came over to Denhardt and signaled him to walk over to Ricketts' car for privacy. All three men got into Ricketts' car, leaving Shaver, Hundley, and Baker standing around the back of the ambulance. Making conversation, Baker said, "Mr. Denhardt could not have killed that woman because I was with him when the last shot was fired." And for the second time that night, something that Baker said would save Denhardt's plan from certain ruin.

Inside Ricketts' car, Denhardt volunteered to Ricketts another unprompted denial to an accusation that nobody was vocalizing. "Mrs. Taylor killed herself. Why, I did not kill that woman--we were engaged to be married in a month. I did not kill her. I loved her too well." Denhardt wanted to make the proposition clear, so he repeated it a couple of times. Of course, the illogic of that statement is, had he not loved Verna so much, killing her might have been possible, but Denhardt's love for Verna was so great that it eliminated any motive for murder. "Just this afternoon, Verna had threatened to kill herself, and we even tussled over my gun, which I took away from her and locked in the glove pocket and locked the door," Denhardt explained.

Denhardt seemed weary and nervous to Keightley. Denhardt turned to Keightly and reminded him, "Remember, you promised to look out for that ring on her ring finger for me." The undertaker promised that nobody would take it under his watch. Around this time, Henry County Sheriff Evan Harrod and his deputies began to arrive.

One more odd conversation with Denhardt stayed with Keightley, although he did not recall it word for word. Sometime before Keightley left the scene, based on his family friendship with the Garrs, Denhardt asked, "What do you think the attitude of the Garr Boys will be toward y'all finding Verna dead in my presence—and shot? Do you think I ought to go home with the body or go to my farm?"

Keightley replied, "I would go to your farm and let Coroner Ricketts notify the family. How had Verna come to this?"

Denhardt said, "I told you, she had threatened to kill herself this afternoon, and I had taken the gun away from her."

"Well, if she loved you well enough to wear your ring," Keightly wondered, "she sure was leaving you in an awful spot."

Denhardt thought for a second and said, "She had promised to leave a note explaining everything."

"Well, evidently we will find that note at her house," Keightly reassured the general.

"I did not think so," he despaired. "We had argued, and she had given me back the ring. I made her take it back. The girls objected to their mother keeping company with me and kept nagging her, and Verna was tired and had threatened to kill herself. We had tussled over the gun before I took it away from her and locked it up. You know I didn't kill her. I loved her. We were to be married in a few weeks. I couldn't kill her."

Married in a few weeks? That was news to anybody who knew Verna. Then again, she kept her privacy.

In the last conversation between Ricketts and Denhardt that night, Ricketts assessed that Denhardt was sober and that he did not smell any alcohol on his breath at all. Denhardt said that the day had been very trying and that he was exhausted; he asked if he could go home. Ricketts said that it was okay, but that they likely would be stopping by for more questions in the morning.

Denhardt asked Keightley, "Could somebody drive my car to town for me?"

Keightley asked Shaver, "Would you take the general to town?" Another man named Lowell Talbot followed.

Verna's body was then transported to the McCarty and Ricketts Funeral Home for a cursory medical examination and the issuance of a COD.

While Harrod and his deputies fanned out over the area for the purposes of keeping the growing onlookers away and looking for any evidence, what was described as a large, bloody splotch was found on the road to the west of Denhardt's vehicle before the slight bend in SR 22. Not wanting to take any chances with it, Harrod ordered his deputies to grab a shovel and remove the entire piece of bloody roadway for testing later on.

Driving to Denhardt's farm, there was no conversation about the shooting. Close to Denhardt's farm, the road got muddy, and Shaver got Denhardt's car stuck. The general got out and had to walk the rest of the way up the long driveway to his house, carrying Verna's purse. Denhardt's car remained stuck in the mud until Saturday.

Yet Denhardt knew the worst was to come. If a possible indictment were not enough concern, the Garr Boys were about to be notified that their sister had been found dead on SR 22 with a bullet hole through her from Denhardt's gun. Northern Kentucky in the 1930s was a much different time and place than the Appalachian feuds of the Hatfields and McCoys just after the Civil War, but a latent belief in the virtues of a torchlit mob still throbbed just under the metropolitan veneer of social progress. As Cuba Shaver said, "The general sure looked nervous" as he drove him home that night. Hard to know which might be more nerve-wracking for Denhardt, the humiliation of a public trial or the intimidation of close-knit family of experienced hunters seeking justice for their sister.

Denhardt had a right to be nervous. He probably did not know that Verna's Aunt Mary Garr, worried about the general, came to this author's grandfather, Ed Hill, who had been a detective, and asked for his advice. "Get her away from him, Aunt Mary," Hill was known to have recommended, "He's a foul ball." As a result, the whole extended Garr family definitely knew that Verna planned to give back the ring to Denhardt that night. They were all waiting to know it was over. Instead of being relieved, however, the family was about to learn that Verna was dead.

Perhaps that's why Denhardt proceeded to get very, very drunk.

CHAPTER SIX

There are two ways to get a topnotch, trained hunting dog. The first way is to pick out a purebred puppy from the appropriate sporting group and train the dog yourself. The other way to get the best field-tested hunting dog is to buy one already completely, professionally trained from a reputable expert. Known for the quality and consistency of their dogs, Roy and Jack Garr were considered among the best trainers in the country. People who can afford the best will pay for the best. A "Garr dog" was almost a luxury brand, at the very least their champion hunting dogs demanded top dollar even in the Depression.

Roy, about forty-five when Verna was killed, was a "husky, tanned outdoor man" who lived on a farm three miles north of La Grange with his wife, Bettie Smallwood Garr. Tall and broad-shouldered, Roy was once described by *The Louisville Times* as "a mountain of a man" and that "no matter what size suit he wore, he would look bound by it." Roy had an almost boyish face, high cheekbones, and kindly blue eyes with a twinkle in the corner.

Jack, thirty-seven, had been living just over the river in Mount Washington, Ohio, with his wife Marguerite on his own farm. He had more chiseled features and a pretty good shock of black hair and "romantic coloring" to his face, said the *Times*. Considered good-looking but modest to the point of self-effacing, his skin, too, had the tone of a man who lived an outdoor life.

Roy and Jack traveled the country exhibiting their dogs and testing them in competitions. According *The Louisville Times*, the men were considered well-off in the midst of the Depression.

Before the Great War, Dr. E.S. "Doc" Garr, their older brother, was considered the most cosmopolitan of the three. "His deep eyes were dark socketed," one reporter described him. "He is more urbane in manner than his brothers and he has a flair for congeniality." He was a reader who could get lost in thought. He had been married to a school-teacher, the former Theresa Ross, but they were divorced, and she had custody of their three kids: Miriam, Stanton Ross, and Burke. Doc now lived on a small farm and looked after the Garr family matriarch just outside of La Grange.

More thin-faced and self-contained, Doc had branched out of the family business a bit by becoming a veterinarian, but it was not a stren-uous practice, mostly horses. Like Denhardt, Doc also served in World War I, but unlike the general, he didn't come home with a chest full of medals. Doc's war memento was "shell shock," a precursor of what is now called post-traumatic stress disorder. Many victims of shell shock were never unable to re-assimilate to society, but Doc fared better. He did suffer from bouts of nervousness, short-temperedness, and an in-ability to concentrate, but judging by the newspaper accounts at the time of Verna's murder, Doc benefitted from a lot of community sup-port and sympathy. Still, because of Doc's emotional instability, Roy had become the unofficial Garr *pater familias* despite his status as mid-dle brother.

Doc was the first of the Garr brothers to get the news that Verna was dead. Doc was over at Verna's house, as he often was, with Mary Pryor that night when the call came from Coroner Ricketts sometime around 11:45 p.m. Frances found out at the dance, almost exactly at the stroke of midnight. Roy was in Indianapolis on business when he was given the message. Jack was the first of the Garr brothers to find the spot where Verna's body was found, and he took Roy back there on Saturday morning at about the time that Verna's newly embalmed body had been brought to her house for the service the next day. Home funerals were most common then.

Along with Sheriff Walter E. Briggs of Oldham County, an incred-ulous Roy walked the entire scene, already convinced Denhardt had murdered his sister. With their shared knowledge of animal tracks, blood trails, and gunshot wounds from years of hunting, Roy and Sheriff Briggs reexamined the scene of a crime. With the benefit of the daylight, both men believed that they discovered a significant clue missed by the investigators the night before. Fifteen impressions of what appeared to be a woman's shoe of the style size and style worn by Verna appear to be backing up into the ditch before they abruptly stop.

To Roy and Briggs, this was distinctive marking of a prey in flight, trying to turn and run to avoid an armed predator—Verna backing away from Denhardt as he pointed a gun at her rib cage. The bullet entered just below her left breast, pierced her heart, and exited just below her right shoulder blade.

In Roy's reconstruction of the tragedy, the force of the large caliber bullet knocked Verna off her feet, onto her back where she died mercifully fast. In the process, her left shoe was knocked off, which Denhardt picked up and carelessly tossed upside down onto her body into the crook of her arm. In the minds of Roy and the sheriff, Denhardt then threw his gun next to Verna's right hand and called it a suicide. Hustling back to his car, Denhardt then met up with farmer Baker and initiated the charade he quickly rehearsed in his mind.

After the Garr Boys conferenced later, there was no doubt in the family that Verna had been murdered and that Denhardt would get away with it if he could sell his suicide story to the sheriff. The Garr Boys, ordinary if not prominent citizens, were determined to get justice for Verna within the existing legal systems. They knew it would not be a process without setbacks.

Reinforcements were in order.

Chapter Seven

B ecause the focus of the true crime magazines that followed Verna Garr Taylor's murder and trial so closely was on the work of law enforcement, the reporters often took dramatic liberties with the actual facts of a case in order to emphasize the heroics of the investigators. For example, although Henry County Sheriff Evan Harrod had been around a few suicides and murders, he was not an experienced, modern crime scene investigator. As the true crime magazines slanted it, though, when the 6'5" Harrod arrived on the scene of SR 22 the night of Verna's murder, he took charge of the investigation.

Harrod was the kind of man's man that true detective magazine readers liked. That's why he was presented as a Gary Cooper-like character—tall, strong, and taciturn—even though he was not the lead investigator in Verna's murder at all.

The man that should have gotten more play was early crime scene investigation pioneer Sargeant John Messmer, the forty-year-old founder of the Crime Detection Laboratory of the Louisville Police Department in 1934. Messmer was brought into the case in the first few hours of the investigation because, although Denhardt was working his spontaneous suicide scenario hard, there were too many red flags for another key member of the investigating team, Coroner Ricketts. Ricketts' willingness to bring in help from another jurisdiction changed the trajectory of the investigation. There would have been no case if Coroner Ricketts had simply listed "suicide" on Verna's official Commonwealth of Kentucky COD. Ricketts was egoless enough to be "Dr. Watson" to Messmer's "Sherlock Holmes," but magazine readers heard little about the crucial work of Coroner Ricketts either. Perhaps Rickets would have gotten more copy if there had been a *True Coroner* magazine or a *Crime Fighting Undertakers Monthly* on newsstands.

After Verna was taken to the McCarty-Ricketts Funeral Home in La Grange, Ricketts performed a cursory examination to determine whether there were two separate bullet wounds, one in front and one in back, or one shot straight through. The post-mortem had taken place in Oldham County, but because of where the body was found, the place of death was listed as Henry County on the COD. Special attention was paid to the bullet wound in Verna's chest, its position and angle. Neither the dress nor the slip underneath showed any signs of scorching around the bullet entrance, which would have been the sign of a close shot. It was confirmed that only one bullet had entered Verna's body, passed through her heart at an angle nearly impossible for a right-handed person such as Verna to fire, and then exited through her back. Because death was almost instantaneous, even if Verna had fired with her left hand, something a right-handed person would be unlikely to do, she would not have had time to drop the gun to her right and pick up the glove she was found holding in her left hand. Ricketts and Keightley also discovered a lengthy bruise, some six inches in diameter, on the inner portion of Verna's right thigh.

Harrod asked Ricketts, "Would you say that this is the sort of injury from an attack or an attempted rape?"

"I would," replied the coroner, and the plot thickened.

From the first night, there was only one way the investigation was headed. Having virtually eliminated Verna as the shooter, that left only one person who was on the road that night who could have fired Denhardt's .45, the only other person who even knew there was a gun in the car, the service revolver's owner, Henry H. Denhardt. Verna's clothes were bagged as evidence in a suspected case of "willful murder."

With the gratitude of the family, Keightley began the embalming process. He sutured the bullet hole closed and washed Verna's body, including her hands, with a mild soap solution. It would take ten hours before Verna's body would be ready for delivery to the Taylor house the next day for the home service.

Denhardt had been granted permission to leave the crime scene on on Friday night with the stipulation that he would make himself available for further questioning as the investigation continued. Ricketts would not wait long to hold Denhardt to his word. Denhardt, too, must have sensed that a fight was coming his way. Ricketts had shown Denhardt no deference, no reassuring wink between public servants that Verna's death would get just a *pro forma* investigation only to pacify the Garrs. If Denhardt had been gambling on Ricketts to be so confused by the staged suicide that he would just throw up his hands, play country dumb, and say, "I guess we'll never know what happened," he had underestimated Ricketts considerably.

Rather, when Denhardt had arrived home Friday night, still holding Verna's purse, he would have trudged up the half-mile-long, muddy driveway of his farm wondering whether the odds of him *not* being indicted were growing slimmer by the minute. Anticipating the worst, like any field commander, Denhardt had rallied his troops. The first call may have been to a childhood friend, Dr. Arthur T. McCormack, head of the State Department of Health and president-elect of the American Public Health Association, because first thing Saturday morning, acting as Denhardt's personal physician, Dr. McCormack put the sheriff's department and all public officials on notice. With all the gravity that his offices could provide, Dr. McCormack had issued his medical finding: "In view of his overwrought condition, I do not think it would be advisable for anybody to see him."

When Ricketts, Harrod, Henry County Deputy Sheriff Paul Stivers, and Verna's cousin by marriage, Mr. D. F. Lee (Bessie's husband), knocked on Denhardt's front door first thing Saturday morning, the coroner demonstrated how much he gave a damn about Dr. McCormack's "do not disturb" memo. The presence of Mr. Lee standing in for the Garr Boys was an intentional choice that signaled a desire to keep the meeting informational and non-confrontational.

At first, no one in the house responded. After the second knock, Miss Bertha, Denhardt's older, unmarried sister, finally came and unlocked the door. Her brother's biggest fan, Miss Bertha kept a scrapbook of his press clippings and accomplishments. She was very protective of her successful sibling. "My brother is quite ill and cannot be disturbed," Miss Bertha said stiffly.

"We are here on official business, pursuant to an understanding I had with General Denhardt last night, and it is a matter of necessity that we speak with him," Ricketts insisted. The coroner went on to explain Lee's role as a representative of the family. Miss Bertha still said "no" and locked the door. Ricketts, Harrod, Stivers, and Lee remained at the door, demanding entry. Miss Bertha then conferred with her brother. After some time had passed, Miss Bertha unlocked the door and allowed Ricketts and Lee to go up to Denhardt's bedroom.

According to Denhardt's own attorney's files, this is what happened next.

Miss Bertha took Sheriff Harrod and Deputy Stivers to a sitting area, where they made polite conversation. She told of how "delighted" the family had been at the impending marriage of the general and Verna and how sad they were to learn "how their plans had been thwarted by this occurrence." Upstairs, Ricketts and Lee entered Denhardt's bedroom to discover that "General Denhardt was very much intoxicated" and refused to get out of bed.

"I've come here to tell you the attitude of the Garr Boys, which you asked me about last night," Ricketts said. "I had a talk with them, and they seem to me to be very much wrought up, but I think I can handle them possibly. In the meantime, it's probably best for you, General, to stay away from La Grange. I think what would help here would be for you to talk things over with Mr. Lee, who has been entrusted to be the Garr family representative. Tell Mr. Lee what happened with their beloved Verna, and that will help all concerned. I'll leave you two alone."

Ricketts came to join the conversation with Miss Bertha, who asked about funeral plans. Ricketts said that he thought the service and the burial would be Monday. Just then, Miss Mary Cole, a teenage girl who was part of the tenant family who resided at the estate, came running to the setting room door, telling the men to come quick because there was a disturbance in the bedroom. When Ricketts, Harrod, and Stivers entered Denhardt's room, the general was beating on Lee. Harrod and Stivers restrained the very drunk Denhardt and slammed him to the bed while Denhardt continued to swing away at all of them. Quietly, Miss Bertha moved around to the head of her brother's bed and removed another handgun that had been underneath his pillow. Denhardt shouted that the contingent had no business there and that "they were merely there for the purpose of making publicity."

It did not take long for a man Harrod's size to pin Denhardt's arms behind his back. After calming down, the general then rolled over on his bed and cried loudly.

There was no mention of a suicide pact at this time. Not a word of Verna's demands that she and Denhardt run off and get married. To the Associated Press and *The New York Times* that same day, however, Miss

Bertha said that her brother had confirmed to her, "Mrs. Taylor took his .45 caliber pistol out of his car and walked up the road and then soon he heard two shots." She insinuated to the reporter what Denhardt had suggested the night before, that Mrs. Taylor's daughters were to blame because they "did not want her to marry." Miss Bertha added that "distress over this situation may have led Mrs. Taylor to kill herself."

About that same time in Louisville, Messmer was loading his case with the necessary equipment to make a paraffin wax mold on Verna's hands that would determine whether or not she had fired a weapon. Ideally, this test is performed shortly after the subject is accused of a shooting, but it can still be valid up to five days later and even under other adverse conditions, such as the subject being dead and washed. The chemistry behind it is complicated, but the explanation is simple.

When a weapon is fired, there is a momentary backward expulsion of hot gasses and microscopic debris from the cartridge that has just been ignited. Each weapon sends a distinct pattern of hot gas and particles toward the hands of the people holding the weapon. Because the gas flash is very hot but brief, it momentarily expands the skin pores near the weapon. Burnt, backward-flying gunpowder particles in the form of nitrates become embedded in those opened pores, but as soon as the skin cools—which is almost immediately—the expanded pores contract around the particles, where they remain benignly embedded for some time.

When a paraffin mold is made, pure, clean, colorless wax is melted and then brought to just above skin temperature so that there is no burning. The wax is then applied in layers. The heat from the wax expands the pores while the wax itself adheres to any embedded particles. When the wax cools completely, the molds are carefully split, packed, and taken to a lab. There, a special solution called a "re-agent" is applied that turns any nitrate particles embedded in the wax a noticeable dark blue. Just one or two tiny nitrate particles could indicate the firing of a weapon. At least, theoretically, a total lack of particles indicates that a weapon has not been fired with that bare hand. Because the pores have been closed since the skin cooled around the particle, mere washing of the hands will not eliminate the nitrates.

When Messmer arrived at Verna's house, the family had been in mourning for hours, but they understood what had to be done. The Garr Boys were gracious and grateful for any efforts to prove that their sister was murdered and disprove Denhardt's suggestion that Verna's own daughers had "stressed" her into such an irrational act. The very idea only compounded the family grief, but the Garrs were committed to working within the system to seek justice. By all reports, the Garrs wanted to see Denhardt dead for what he did; not at the end of a rope thrown over a tree, but rather, in Kentucky's electric chair. Because of the prominence of both the Denhardt and the Garr clans, Ricketts was determined to run a textbook investigation.

After Messmer had heated the wax bath solution to the proper temperature, both of Verna's hands were dipped several times to make sure they were completely coated before they were allowed to cool. Although Verna was found clutching a glove in her left hand, neither Messmer nor Ricketts wanted to leave anything to debate later on. After the molds cooled to room temperature, Messmer deftly split them and he returned to the McCarty-Ricketts Funeral Home with his complete lab kit Saturday sometime after 8:30 p.m.

With Ricketts observing, Messmer demonstrated the big difference between a county coroner's budget and a metropolitan police department crime lab. Messmer dabbed the molds of Verna's hand with the revealing solution and held them up to the light. They remained completely clear, no bluish dots. Microscopic analysis confirmed this. "The tests are negative," Messmer declared. "Mrs. Taylor did not fire the weapon that claimed her life. These molds would show if she had shot that gun within the past four or five days, and the bullet fired into heart was just twenty-four hours ago."

By proving with state-of-the-art science that Verna had not fired a weapon with either hand, the paraffin wax test only added to the belief that Verna did not take her own life. If she had fired the weapon, it still may not have made any sense, but the family could have accepted that. Nothing about Denhardt's behavior was consistent with his story, however, and his treatment of Mr. D. F. Lee earlier on Saturday only confirmed the stories that Denhardt was an arrogant drunk given to bursts of violence. Gathering the physical evidence from Denhardt would have to wait until sometime Monday, but the tests would still be valid. Ricketts, Messmer, and Harrod agreed to keep Verna's results away from reporters for the time being.

Within a few hours of Messmer putting another nail in Denhardt's coffin, Verna Garr Taylor was being remembered in church services all across Oldham and Henry counties. A small, intimate, private memorial was held in her own home where she was celebrated by her family and friends for her dedication as a wife, mother, and sister; lauded for her community service as an employer, woman of charity, and social leader. When that was done, at least two hundred people drove or walked to Valley of Rest Cemetery for a burial service conducted by Rev. W.B. Garriott from La Grange Methodist Church. Verna was laid to rest next to Barc.

Denhardt said he had wanted to be there for Verna but that Dr. McCormack had advised him against attending either Verna's memorial or the graveside service for fear of "worry or further excitement" in his fragile health. No flowers were sent from the Denhardt family either, but Miss Bertha alleged that this *faux pas* was the result of a conspiracy. She claimed that Ricketts intentionally had told her that Verna's services were scheduled for Monday. By the time the Denhardts learned differently, it was too late to get flowers to her home. Having remained stoic on Friday night and not attending either the memorial service or the funeral for Verna, Denhardt's streak of consecutive days without any public expression grief for Verna was unbroken.

Whether Ricketts had sabotaged the funeral bouquet plans or not, Miss Bertha's mood shifted dramatically to the negative the next time Ricketts, Keightley, and Deputy Clayton Renaker came to the Denhardt estate. The following Monday, November 9, at 2:30 p.m., Ricketts, Keightley, and Renaker returned to the estate where Denhardt had continued to seclude himself from public scrutiny. Messmer was still on the way from Louisville when the men arrived. Family friends provided support and light security to Denhardt because of a vague, rumored threat of Garr-led mob vengeance in the air. As far as Denhardt's supporters were concerned, if the general said it was a suicide, his word should be enough to close the case. From their cars to the Denhardt estate front door, Ricketts, Keightley, and Renaker passed through a gauntlet of stares.

Miss Bertha also believed that a man as important as her brother should be taken on his word. While Denhardt was getting ready to receive the gentlemen in his room, Miss Bertha sneered, "If the [Garr] family knew what we know about this, they would stop this investigation." The comment stuck with Ricketts, but he was more focused on the paraffin wax molds he needed to talk the general into allowing to take the bait.

Denhardt was wearing a royal blue robe over street clothes and laying on a chaise lounge when Ricketts, Keightley, and Renaker entered his room to notify him that there would be a coroner's inquest and that Denhardt was expected to attend. This time he was not drunk; no punches were thrown. That said, according to his defense attorney's own files, at first, the general did not cooperate. When Ricketts started talking about the need for the paraffin wax test to show one way or another if he had fired a gun recently, Denhardt declined. Ricketts was fixing to leave when, on further reflection, the general signaled that he wanted to confer with Deputy Renaker.

Renaker reasoned quietly to Denhardt, "They've already taken molds of Mrs. Taylor's hands, and they need to take yours now for comparison. It'll either clear you or convict you." Renaker said that Messmer would explain the whole process when he got in from the car with his kit and added, "We cannot make you, but this refusal to do it would look pretty bad."

Denhardt relented confidently. "I will allow you to make the mold because I have not fired a gun in six months." Messmer explained the process and the wax was applied without any further drama. When the paraffin molds were completed, safely packed away, and ready for transport, Ricketts asked where the suit the general had worn the night of Verna's death was. The general said, "I'm wearing it."

"Do you still have Mrs. Taylor's pocket book?" Ricketts asked.

"I do," Denhardt said and sent somebody to find Miss Bertha, who relayed the pocketbook back with all of its belongings intact.

"Did you wear an overcoat on Friday night?" Ricketts queried.

"Yes," Denhardt pointed to the hat rack in the corner. "There it hangs, on the rack."

"Can we examine that overcoat?" Ricketts asked politely, and Denhardt walked over and handed it to Ricketts. The five men held it up, looked at it in the afternoon light of the room, said nothing, left the coat with Denhardt, and then said their good-byes at the front door as they departed. It was not until they had already left his house and were halfway across his yard when Ricketts reconsidered leaving the potential evidence there.

"Wait a minute, I'm going back to get that overcoat," Ricketts said as he quickly returned to ask Denhardt to allow the county to take his coat into evidence.

"All right, but I've got to go to Taylorsville in the next day or two, and I'll need my coat to wear down there," Denhardt demurred.

To Ricketts, that seemed understandable, but he felt he really needed to examine the coat under brighter lights before determining that it did not contain anything useful. He also did not want to give Denhardt a chance to clean it now that he knew they wanted it.

"If that's all the objection you have," Ricketts said, "you can have my overcoat, and I'll take this one," Ricketts offered. And the general agreed to try it on.

"Yes, I believe I can wear it," Denhardt said. The swap would have gone through, but Denhardt instead decided, "No, never mind. I have another overcoat here I think I can make out with. It's not very cold yet. It's a little light one, but I think I can make out with that."

"Let's go get the coat," Ricketts said, and the two men went back into the house. In handing over his brown overcoat to Ricketts, however, Denhardt put his hand on the coroner's should and said, "Ricketts, don't let anyone put blood on this coat because there's none on it now."

Ricketts assured him, "We're not going to let anybody put anything on this coat that isn't on it now, but since you mention blood, let's go out in the yard and see what's on this coat."

This exchange was significant, of course, because up until this point, *nobody had said anything about looking for blood on the coat.* The coroner, the funeral director, the policeman, and the deputy had all looked at the coat and said nothing. Plus, Denhardt's warning was obvious, as well. Despite the unblemished reputations of Ricketts, Keightley, Messmer, and Renaker, Denhardt seemed willing to insinuate that any unfavorable evidence against him would be either planted or manufactured.

Ricketts and Denhardt walked outside to the lawn with the coat held in front. Once in the sunshine, Denhardt and the four investigators looked at his coat and saw many drops, drips, and smears of dried blood on the brown overcoat. Denhardt himself scratched at one spot lightly, started to say something, but never finished. He handed them the coat and walked back into his house. Unlike Saturday morning when Denhardt was fighting, cursing and crying, after scratching at that spot on his coat, Denhardt had been rendered speechless.

Later that afternoon, Messmer performed the tests on Denhardt's wax molds and confirmed what all had suspected: Denhardt had been less than truthful when he said it had been six months since he had fired a gun. The tests showed nitrate contact within the last few days. More damning, the nitrate specks in the paraffin mold of Denhardt's right hand were concentrated between his right thumb and forefinger, exactly where Messmer had expected them to be after he had done tests with lab assistants firing Denhardt's gun. The scientific evidence showed that, based on the dispersal of the nitrates, Denhardt had not just fired any weapon within the last few days, more than likely, he had fired a .45 caliber Smith & Wesson M1917 service revolver.

Coroner D.L. Ricketts scheduled an official inquest at the Pendleton Schoolhouse near the shooting for Thursday, November 12, 1936 at 2:30 p.m. Because Denhardt was the main witness to the events leading up to Verna's death, the coroner's inquest would be the perfect opportunity for him to tell the whole world all about his last day together with the beloved woman he claimed he was just weeks from marrying. A coronor's inquest would be the easiest way to clear everything up about her death, once and for all.

Assuming, of course, that Denhardt had any interest in making anything about Verna's death any clearer to anybody.

Chapter Eight

A Kentucky town like New Castle does not get that much excitement. That's part of its charm. Even today, there is a unique character to Henry County that makes it feel quainter, sleepier than its neighbors, Oldham and Shelby counties. For example, you won't see a McDonald's or a Burger King in New Castle—or any chain store for that matter. The main business in historic downtown New Castle is the business of Henry County, same as it ever was. The Henry County Courthouse accounts for all the storefront law offices and bail bondsmen locations in the area.

Downtown New Castle is not just historic in terms of its layout and turn-of-the-last-century architecture, it feels like a town caught in a time warp. I'm sure things have changed since Coroner D. L. Ricketts held an inquest here in 1936 to investigate the death of Verna Garr Taylor, but not much.

Nothing wrong with the people, though. If you're looking for a friendly bite to eat, Buddy's Place, a good "meat-and-three" place. For Yankee readers, a "meat and three" is a plate lunch with the special meat of the day (pulled pork, barb-b-cue chicken, meat loaf, etc.) and your choice of three sides, such as mac 'n' cheese, sliced apples, and cornbread. If you're eating alone and the place is busy, you'll make a new friend when somebody pulls up a chair to your table.

Nationally recognized author, poet, and activist Wendell Berry lives in Henry County and boasts on the town's website, "Our history makes us what we are today, and our future depends on our past." Another way to say that is the past is the present *and* the future in Henry County. I heard him speak once when I was in seminary. Wendell Berry is a gentle, interesting, and articulate man whose father was a key part of Denhardt's legal team. It is because of John Marshall Berry and the generous donation by the Berry Center in New Castle that historians and researchers have access to the Denhardt trial transcript, the examining trial, and so many memoranda, letters, and notes. The Berry family remains very influential in New Castle.

By comparison to New Castle, for better or worse, La Grange feels like a modern, small city. Downtown La Grange also makes an effort to preserve its original historic character with the help of an active and sophisticated historical society, but it also has a rather unique feature: train tracks that run lengthwise through the town square, right up Main Street. Up to thirty times a day, traffic comes to a halt while a freight train blows its horn and drives slowly down the middle of the town like it's looking for a parking space. La Grange is one of only two places left in the U.S. with this configuration.

If you talk to lifelong residents of La Grange or New Castle, they'd tell you that it's always been that way. La Grange/Oldham County is only a few miles closer to Louisville, but it has always been more metropolitan than New Castle/Henry County.

Even today in the Henry County Courthouse, one climbs the same iron staircase that Denhardt would have climbed to get to the courtroom. The room itself is smaller than it was then, as Henry County added an interior wall along the back of the original courtroom in order to create new work spaces on the other side. The wood tone is lighter, it seems, the ceilings have been dropped for new fluorescent fixtures, and the layout has changed, but many of the same framed photos of previous circuit judges accent the walls of the main courtroom at the Henry County Courthouse, just like they did in 1936 on the afternoon of November 12, 1936, when the good people of Kentucky (and some of the bad ones) filled every seat in the courtroom, the hallways, and the courthouse lawns outside an hour before the coroner's inquest was to begin. Newspaper men from all over the country were there. Who killed Verna Garr Taylor was the only thing people were talking about in Bluegrass Country.

A coroner's inquest is both similar to, and quite different from, a trial. The verdict of a coroner's inquest would *not* be a finding of guilt with regard to an individual, but only a finding of fact surrounding a sudden or unexplained death. The potential verdicts in most coroner's inquests would be "death by natural causes," "accidental death," "suicide," "murder," or "death by misadventure," which is defined as an unlucky event or a mishap, frequently while doing something stupid. Accidental recreational drug overdoses are sometimes listed as "misadventure." Most cases of people peacefully dying of natural causes in their beds would never warrant an inquest, but the death of some drunk guy lighting fireworks off his head might require further investigation to determine whether it was murder, suicide, or misadventure.

At an inquest, witnesses to any aspect of the death being investigated are compelled to testify. Even if the testimony can make a witness look bad—such as a bystander who did nothing at a fire to help victims—a coroner can incarcerate an uncooperative witness on the grounds of "contempt of inquest" if they refuse to testify. In a case with as many moving parts as the death of Verna Garr Taylor, an inquest would be an expeditious way to determine whether a victim was murdered or committed suicide. Denhardt was not on trial, but as a witness who claimed unique knowledge of the victim's state of mind the night she died, his testimony was crucial. Because Denhardt previously had expressed a willingness to share this experience to authorities on other official occasions, testifying to his recollections under oath seemed like something he wanted to do.

In fact, Denhardt himself was responsible for the coroner's inquest into Verna's death being moved to the Henry County Courthouse from the originally scheduled location, the old Pendleton Schoolhouse off SR 22, right where Denhardt's car had stalled in the first place. Given the buzz about the inquest, Denhardt personally had asked for the larger space so that the interested public could see the issue resolved more comfortably. Henry County officials conferred on the venue change on Tuesday morning, November 10. The deciding factor may have been a concern for rumored violence by the people in La Grange. As the *Henry County Local* newspaper reported on November 13, 1936, "public unrest in La Grange over Mrs. Taylor's death was discussed in connection with the shift of the scene." In other words, Denhardt wanted the inquest to be held as far away from La Grange as possible. Coroner Ricketts announced that he would honor the general's request. It was a wise thing that he did.

The standing room only crowd of about a thousand people was surprisingly orderly. Sheriff Harrod walked through and summoned six Henry County citizens to comprise the coroner's inquest jury per Kentucky law. It's easy to imagine how exciting that must have been. One minute you're waiting in line for the opening of the hottest ticket in town, and the next thing you know, you have been asked to be in the chorus. The six men—James Ethington, Charles Moore, L.R. Brown, Will Ebersbaker, James Young, and Claud Knight—were impanelled and sworn in in preparation for the arrival of the key players and the star witness. A court stenographer was ready to record every word. There would not be many of them.

From Shelby County, Captain H.B. Kinsolving represented the Commonwealth of Kentucky. Sheriff Harrod took his seat next to Coroner Ricketts as the courtroom quieted down.

Denhardt entered punctually at 2:30 p.m., appearing at ease, followed by his entourage: Miss Bertha and Jesse Denhardt, the general's brother and publishing partner in the *Bowling Green Times-Journal*, from whom reportedly the general had been alienated. The *Louisville Times* described Denhardt as a "commanding figure in this drab and ancient room with its towering ceilings, smoked walls, and askew pictures of jurists that had gone before." Seated next to the family was Dr. McCormack and Denhardt's team of attorneys: Berry, state legislator Rodes K. Myers from Bowling Green, and Beckham Overstreet of Louisville. Ricketts grabbed his gavel and banged the proceedings to order. Ten witnesses had been called and were all present. The atmosphere was thick with anticipation. In just a matter of minutes, it seemed, everybody would finally know how the Prettiest Woman in Two Counties had been taken from them.

Ricketts called Denhardt as the first witness. Denardt's composure left him. It was reported that his facial muscles twitched and his hands fluttered nervously, but Denhardt did not answer the coroner's call. He said nothing. After a few seconds of awkward silence, Denhardt's lawyers unveiled the legal strategy they had hoped would kill the coroner's case while it still slept in the crib.

Standing, Berry said, "Your Honor, we object to General Denhardt being called as a witness because of his constitutional rights."

Kinsolving then also stood and said, "Your Honor, if Mr. Denhardt is willing to testify knowing his constitutional rights, he has a right to do so even though his counsel objects, and I ask the coroner to ask him if wants to testify."

Ricketts looked at the general curiously and said, "Mr. Denhardt, are you willing to testify in this case?"

Denhardt responded haltingly, "I would like to very much, but my counsel insists that I shall not for reasons best known to my counsel."

Then, Ricketts attempted to clarify. "Do you want to testify?"

"I would like to very much," he replied tentatively. "But my counsel insists that I shall not and begged me for several hours and begged me last night that I should not testify, against my desire."

"Then," said Ricketts, "you absolutely refuse to testify."

"I am not refusing, but my counsel is objecting. If I had my way, I would tell it, but my counsel tells me not to, and I therefore decline to testify."

"That's beside the point. Will you testify?" asked the coroner emphatically.

"I am declining on advice of counsel—over my protest."

The inquest was barely a minute old when Kinsolving had had it with the semantic gamesmanship. Kinsolving announced that it would be futile to proceed. "Denhardt was the only person present when Mrs. Taylor was killed," he snapped. "I move that the inquest be moved to an indefinite date."

But Denhardt's lawyers immediately pressed for the inquest to continue. There was a huddle at Ricket's table with all the lawyers. The back-and-forth ended when Kinsolving glanced over at Sheriff Harrod and nodded. As Berry pushed Ricketts to deny Kinsolving's move to postpone, Harrod stood up and moved over next to Denhardt and touched him on the shoulder as the entire courtroom listened. With his voice resonating deeply through the crowd, the sheriff said, "General Denhardt, I have a warrant for your arrest."

The gallery of the court cheered and hollered.

The chain of events happened so fast the significance deserves a review. First, Denhardt went out of his way to request a larger auditorium to bring in as many people as possible to witness the inquest. Why? Neither he nor his attorneys ever expressed a motive for moving the inquest other than some uncharacteristic civic concern for a larger crowd's "comfort." More likely, they were afraid of a lynching. A small schoolhouse provided scant protection from this supposed, rumored Garr-led mob of vigilantes. But since Denhardt's lawyers were planning on preventing the general's cooperation while still insisting that the inquest continue, perhaps, to them, a larger audience might mean greater public pressure on the coroner to finish the proceeding.

Possibly, Denhardt's advisors saw a large crowd as a chance to intimidate Ricketts with Denhardt's popularity in Henry County—but that kind of backfired. From another perspective, there could have been a strategy in place to influence the potential jury pool of Henry County citizens or establish the grounds for a change of venue if the lawyers did not like the way the proceeding was going. The Denhardt defense team had been planning already for a change of venue for the trial, so any way they could make it seem that their client was unsafe was to their advantage. Whatever it was, with his three attorneys and Denhardt's own experienced legal mind involved, if it had been to Denhardt's advantage to keep the inquest in a one room schoolhouse, it's doubtful they would have requested the move. Regardless, it was a move that had little concern for the comfort of the gallery.

It is also possible that Denhardt sincerely wanted to testify at the inquest, but his lawyers forbade him. By invoking his constitutional right against self-incrimination, Denhardt's lawyers were willing to give the impression that *they* thought Denhardt was legally vulnerable if he told the truth while the defendant himself insisted that he would "tell it," whatever the "it" was, and clear everything up. The general's ego probably made it difficult for him to shrink from a fight, but he humbled himself to seek refuge in his legal counsel. Because a witness can be punished legally for refusing to testify at a coroner's inquest, however, Denhardt's lawyers may have insisted that he not use that word, instead referring to his refusal as "declining." Perhaps it was just a PR move, but maybe his lawyers determined that only if the witness officially *refuses* can he or she be held in contempt at a coroner's inquest.

Perhaps by objecting to the indefinite postponement and trying to force Ricketts to continue the inquest, Denhardt's attorneys also were trying to get a sneak preview of the testimony they would be up against if the case did go to trial, but without having their client commit to anything under oath. Kinsolving appeared to recognize this possibility right away. By pressing Ricketts to see the inquest through, the best case scenario for Denhardt would be that, after having starved the inquiry of its primary witness, the jury would have decided it could not find for murder and instead rule Verna's death a suicide or a death by misadventure. If so, Denhardt would have walked without another day in court.

Were Denhardt's lawyers surprised that Sheriff Harrod had a warrant for Denhardt's arrest in his back pocket all along? Maybe Dr. McCormack's presence in the courtroom was not just an indication that Denhardt might need a doctor's attention for his "grief." Denhardt's childhood friend was also a very rich man. If Denhardt had not expected some trouble, it is doubtful he would have brought so many lawyers. Perhaps the better question would be whether Harrod or Ricketts were surprised that Denhardt refused to cooperate, despite his public position as the "aggrieved lover" searching for answers? The coded "nod" between the attorney for the Commonwealth and the sheriff suggested that they had suspected some type of ruse was afoot and planned for it accordingly.

"Quiet, please!" Harrod admonished the gallery as he handed Denhardt the arrest warrant. Denhardt barely glanced at it as he passed it to his attorneys. Looking over the document, Denhardt's attorneys demanded that their client be brought before a county magistrate judge immediately.

After the sheriff instructed the crowd to remain in their seats and maintain decorum until all of the officials had left through the courtroom's back entrance, Harrod and his deputies escorted Denhardt's party to the waiting chambers of County Judge A.S. "Sid" Morgan. "Please remain in your seats for two to three minutes until the group has a chance to reach the judge's chambers. Inquest adjourned," pronounced Ricketts as he rapped his gavel once and followed. Only after the officials were gone did the crowd burst into excited speculation.

It may have been a short hearing, but it was dramatic. Gavel-to-gavel, it had taken fewer then fifteen minutes for Sheriff Harrod to serve the warrant that had been sworn out by Doc earlier in the day. Swearing out a felony warrant as a citizen is a unique, fairly antiquated feature to criminal law. It dates back to England, but it was common into the twentieth century in a few Southern states. It works like this. Instead of waiting for the police to investigate a case and then waiting for a prosecutor to decide whether to bring a person to trial, a citizen could fill out some forms listing the criminal complaint, take an oath that swears to the truth of the charges, and then ask a magistrate to issue a warrant for that person's arrest, which would then be executed by the police. Through a subsequent examining trial, a judge then would determine whether the case should be sent to a grand jury. The warrant had been Harrod, Kinsolving, and Ricketts' hedge against Denhardt's ability to manipulate the legal system, like the time he famously hid from his indictments for vote tampering until the governor could arrange a pardon.

Inside Judge Morgan's chambers, Harrod produced the warrant.

"The affiant, Dr. E.S. Garr, states that H.H. Denhardt did, in Henry County, on the 6th Day of November, 1936, shoot and kill one Verna Taylor with a pistol or other deadly weapon loaded with leaden ball and other hard substance from which said shooting the said Verna Garr Taylor did then and there die within a year and a day. Dr. E.S. Garr." The warrant was notarized by Elizabeth Rouse and dated November 12, 1936.

Locked in Judge Morgan's chambers away from the public and the press, Denhardt and his legal team did their best to get the Garr warrant cancelled or dismissed. Thirty minutes later, however, Judge Morgan ruled that he himself would preside over Denhardt's examining trial on November 20, and until that time, Denhardt would be held in jail on the charge of murder. Bond was to be set at $25,000, roughly the equivalent of half a million dollars today. Before the hour had passed, though, Denhardt was free to go, the bond having been met with a pledge of real estate from Dr. McCormack.

Back upstairs, the courtroom was now about two-thirds empty when Coroner Ricketts came back in and rapped his gavel again. "Possibly," he said humorously, "you people would like to know what has happened. Denhardt has been arrested and is now in the county judge's office where bond is being fixed."

Dr. McCormack's official medical opinion was that Denhardt's Oldham County farm was not conducive to the general's recovery from the physical and emotional strain of having lost his fiancée. Taking up residence at Dr. McCormack's mansion in Louisville would not only be therapeutic, but it would also provide preventative medical care as well. For example, staying out of the vicinity of La Grange meant Dr. McCormack would not have to remove any bullets from Denhardt's back again. *Time* magazine reported that, for at least part of the time, Denhardt actually was luxuriating at his favorite hotel in Louisville, under the care of a private nurse who administered the strong sedatives Dr. McCormack was prescribing to keep his temper down.

Despite the medication, in the November 30 edition of *Time* magazine with Marlene Dietrich on the cover, Denhardt reacted to the news that it was human blood on the road far away from where the body was found by barking loudly, "Damn what the coroner says!"

As Denhardt hurried out of the courthouse past the still large crowds, he continued to deny that he had refused to testify under oath. He did answer reporters' questions, though "Did you kill Mrs. Taylor" was met with "I am not a killer," "I loved her too much," and "the engagement was still on!" "Why did you refuse to testify, General?" was another question shouted in different forms from waiting reporters. "If they would let me testify," Denhardt yelled back, "I would tell them damn quick who killed her!"

Of course, at any time, Denhardt could have yelled out "damn quick" the name of the person who he said had killed Verna because nobody was stopping him. If Denhardt had named somebody, being a key witness to the event, the sheriff would have been obligated to investigate. In the time it took him to say he *could* do it, he could have *done* it already. The "they" to which he refers were his own attorneys. Why would his own lawyers want him to be prosecuted when their client could clear up the matter with one uttered name? There was no reason to wait eight days until the examining trial.

Perhaps his lawyers only wanted the illusion of a menace as a legal ruse, a red herring that they could use to create doubt in the minds of the jury just long enough to get Denhardt off the hook. If Denhardt had told law enforcement the name of the person who killed Verna and the investigators found that it was all smoke and mirrors, that would be that. Instead, by waiting until the actual trial and insinuating that somebody else were to blame other than Denhardt during the proceedings, the defense could use the hint of another person to redirect attention away from its client. Very likely, the defense already had a fall guy in mind.

Denhardt's insinuation that some unnamed third party was ultimately responsible for Verna's death—coupled with Miss Bertha's contrary claim to the press that Verna destroyed herself as a way of getting back at her family for standing in the way of the marriage—exposed the extent that the Denhardt team was willing to foster confusion inside and out of the courts. Through the change of venue request, the refusal to testify, and the attempt to force the inquest to reach a conclusion anyway, a strategy of manipulating the legal system was beginning to emerge: deny, deflect, and delay. Denhardt's lawyers seemed willing to say anything, even if they contradicted themselves. For example, while they decried the role of rumor in the prosecution of their client, the Denhardt defense team was actively involved in the promotion of the ugliest of insinuations about Verna.

With regard to Miss Bertha's statement, "If the [Garr] family knew what we know about this, they would stop the investigation," Ricketts learned that the defense was preparing to put *the dead victim* on trial by implying many people might have wanted to kill her and/or she was crazy. Attorney Beckham Overstreet confirmed to Ricketts that the defense had learned through gossip that Verna was pregnant at the time of her death, and they were working with that information to create a defense.

Perhaps coincidentally, over at his Louisville police crime lab, Messmer was concerned about the quality of the autopsy performed the night of Verna's murder. Even though only a minimal amount of evidence would be presented at an examining trial, with three smart criminal attorneys working for the defendant, the prosecution was preparing for surprise attacks. The Commonwealth was going to get one bite at that apple, so they had to make sure that all of the forensic testing of Verna's body told the same story: Verna could not have killed herself, and she was not pregnant.

To seal the deal for the prosecution, the tests also needed to prove that the killer stood near her, used a gun just like Denhardt's only once, and that when she had been shot through the heart, Verna could not have walked from the blood splotch near where the road bends to the wet, grassy area on the old road where her body was found.

The more Ricketts thought about it, the more he knew this would mean something dreadful for the grieving Garr family. Verna would have to be exhumed, and another more detailed autopsy performed on her violated body almost immediately. Messmer and Ricketts knew that even families anxious for a conviction are prone to deny the exhumation of a loved one because it's too upsetting. Furthermore, given what the authorities witnessed at the coroner's inquest, there were real concerns that if Denhardt's sophisticated defense team found out about the exhumation, they could find a way to get in the middle of the process, disrupt the exhumation petition, find a Denhardt-friendly judge to slap an injunction on it until her body decomposed further, or demand to be present during the new autopsy in such a way as to limit or skew the results. Not only did Ricketts need to persuade the Garr family to dig up Verna's casket, there was no time to waste.

With the examining trial still eights days away, Ricketts had to approach the right member of the Garr family to sign a top secret order of exhumation, disinter Verna's casket from Valley of Rest Cemetery, transport it to the morgue at McCarty-Ricketts, arrange for experts to perform new and invasive tests on the corpse, put everything back together again just the way it was, and get Verna reburied before any of Denhardt's well-connected lawyers could either stop the second autopsy or insist on being present. Added to that awful task, would be the murder of one innocent Kentucky hog.

CHAPTER NINE

The only thing the Garr family wanted less than pulling Verna back out of the ground was for Denhardt to avoid responsibility for putting her there in the first place. "It's like this," Messmer was quoted as explaining to the family in a group meeting with Ricketts and Harrod, "we have the two location points there beside the Baker farm. The first, that spot at the bend in the highway where we took up the bloodstained paving. We assume Mrs. Taylor was shot there because of the bleeding. The second, the old-road hollow where her body was found... So, we've got to know, did Mrs. Taylor die instantly as the nature of her wound suggests, or could she conceivably have walked or staggered (that distance)?"

Harrod added for emphasis, "And if she had walked that far, she'd have left a trail of blood every foot of the way."

Respecting just how wily Denhardt was, and how an experienced attorney has a lot of tricks to get guilty men free, Roy Garr accepted the explanation of the evidential windfall possible from a more detailed autopsy, plus the need to head off any further trashing of Verna's reputation by confirming that she was not pregnant. Maintaining a chain of secrecy, Roy Garr wrote the request for the exhumation on behalf of the family. Messmer signed and filed the affidavit in Oldham County, stating that Verna's death resulted from unlawful means and required disinterment. Oldham County Coroner Kos Gividen ordered the exhumation to take place after dusk on November 13.

It must have been hard to disturb such a peaceful, flower-covered gravesite. Promptly after 7 p.m., Verna's casket was removed, placed in a hearse flanked by seven law enforcement vehicles, and transported to the blackened windows of the McCarty-Ricketts Funeral Home. Once inside, Verna was taken to the basement, and everybody acted quickly. Two prominent Kentucky physicians, Drs. John T. Walsh and Herbert

B. Blaydes, performed the new autopsy, but their independent conclusions mirrored the original cursory exam. Verna had died as a result of a single .45 caliber bullet through the heart: "Death came to her instantaneously, being a matter of no more than thirty seconds at the most." The bullet had entered just below her left breast, six centimeters from the midline of the body between the sixth and seventh ribs, with an upward trajectory of thirty-three degrees, and exited just below her right shoulder blade. These were not separate bullet wounds. Fragments of Verna's rib bone were imbedded behind the skin of her exit wound. There were two spent casings in the six-shot revolver, but only one bullet passed through Verna's heart, through the thoracic aorta, through the lower third of the right lung, then deflected to her right slightly after nicking her spinal column.

As for the issue of Verna's pregnancy, much was at stake when the lower abdomen was opened during the autopsy. If Verna had been pregnant at the time of her death, it would have done considerable damage to her reputation as a proper widow who was putting her toe back in the waters of romance after her tragic loss five years earlier. A pregnancy would have opened the door for Denhardt to either make the claim "I never would have killed her—she was carrying my baby!" or "It was somebody else's child, and they came to kill her for being with me!" Theoretically, Denhardt could have attempted the "I killed her in a moment of passion when she told me she was pregnant!" angle, as well. If the pregnancy could be determined to be advanced before their time together, Denhardt also could have asserted that the killer was a jealous former lover, or even that she was committing suicide because of the social shame of being unwed and pregnant.

What Drs. Walsh and Blaydes found was that Verna's uterus, left ovary, and tubes had been removed years ago, apparently without family knowledge. All she had left was a normal right ovary. Being forty-years-old with just one ovary could suggest perimenopause, or early menopause or other physical symptoms that could result in sleeplessness, mood swings, and increased headaches, but never pregnancy. Verna's own body was able to repel Denhardt's first attack on her character. Future offensives by the Denhardt team would be better designed to be less easily disproven.

Walsh and Blaydes further carefully studied the characteristics of the bullet hole and determined that the revolver discharging the fatal bullet had been held at a distance from Mrs. Taylor consistent with murder, not suicide. Powder specks around the hole suggested the presence of only expelled *unburned* gunpowder grains into the tissues of the entrance wound, but no microscopic analysis was done. There were also only two or three black threads from her dress that had been caught in the wound. A closer shot, it was suggested, would have brought more of the fabrics into the chest cavity.

Walsh, Blaydes, Ricketts, Messmer, Briggs, and Harrod then attempted to determine the likely distance that the murder weapon was held by studying how much "ballooning" had transpired around the wound and concluded that the gun that had fired the fatal shot was not at contact point or even near contact point with Verna's skin. This next forensic test would be performed on a nameless Chester White breed of hog.

Earlier that day, the doctors had ordered the hog killed, his blood drained, and his hide shaved. Swatches from Verna's actual clothing and underclothing were layered on top of the hog's skin in the same order the bullet had pierced her clothes that night. Using Denhardt's actual service revolver, shots were fired into the carcass from various distances. Comparing Verna's entrance wound to the series of various distances shot into the test animal, it was unanimously decided that Denhardt's Smith & Wesson could not have been any closer than nine inches when fired and, based on the ballooning patterns, more likely eighteen inches away.

More calculations demonstrated that because Denhardt's .45 was eleven inches long from the end of the pistol grip to the tip of the five-and-a-half inch barrel, the trigger had to have been about fifteen inches away from the body when pulled. Verna's arms were measured to be twenty-six inches long. Holding a two-and-a-quarter-pound gun that long a distance of at least nine inches from the left side of the body while still being able to pull the trigger with a left-to-right, upward trajectory would be *nearly* impossible with one's left hand. On the other hand— the right hand to be specific—not only would it have been a *physical impossibility* to fire a gun in a traditional manner, it begs the question why would somebody intent on killing themselves contort the gun into such a bizarre, unreliable position to begin with?

If, as Denhardt had repeated, Verna had said, "I can't stand living any longer like this, but when I do kill myself, I will leave a note explaining how you had nothing to do with it," why wouldn't she just hold the gun up to her heart and pull the trigger? Why not do it in front of witnesses like George Baker or Barney Browning to ensure the exoneration of the man for whom she was supposedly sacrificing herself?

Walsh and Blaydes also reviewed the previous autopsy's conclusion with regard to the six inch diameter bruise and scratches on Verna's inner right thigh. Their finding confirmed that this profound, intimate bruise was created soon before death.

Anticipating the most vigorous possible defense when this case came to trial, Ricketts asked the doctors what would be the most convincing way to present this evidence to a jury? The doctors felt that preserving the skin samples themselves could demonstrate the facts of Verna's killing to even a skeptical court, so they cut away her flesh from around the entrance and exit wounds. The doctors then preserved the nearly identical wounds that they created on the hog in question.

With dignity and gratitude, Verna's body was then re-dressed by Ricketts and Keightley, returned to her casket, and reburied at Valley of Rest Cemetery. This time though, according to the story that has been told in the family for generations, when Verna was buried the second time, the grave was left unmarked to prevent it from becoming a tourist attraction. It would be decades before the family felt it was time to mark her grave once more.

Overall, the night was considered a triumph of forensic police science and reason. Adding to the fact that Denhardt had recently fired a gun with the exact same nitrate pattern of his .45 revolver while Verna had not fired any gun at all, it was concluded that a distance of nine inches with an eleven inch gun fired into the left side with the right hand was beyond even the range of hypothetical possibility for suicide—unless some smart lawyers could find a new way to hold and fire a gun.

The secret exhumation of Verna Garr Taylor went over about as well with Denhardt's attorneys as expected. As the *New York Times* reported on November, 14, 1936, "Autopsy Performed in Kentucky Slaying: Body of Mrs. Taylor Exhumed—Counsel for Gen. Denhardt Voices Surprise." That was putting it mildly.

Notified of the exhumation later that night by a reporter for the *Louisville Courier-Journal*, attorney Overtreet told the press that had the defense had been thinking about doing an exhumation first and they would have sought representation at the tests had it known of the plans of the investigators. Overstreet would not say whether the defense would demand a second exhumation of their own before the general's examining trial on November 20, but held that open as an option. Denhardt's legal team did file a motion with the Kentucky Board of Appeals, demanding that the Commonwealth reveal all of its physical evidence to the defense before the examining trial, but their motion was denied.

Denhardt continued to hide out comfortably at Dr. McCormack's mansion in Louisville. Captain Kinsolving, Sergeant Messmer, Coroner Ricketts, and Sheriff Harrod spent the days leading up to the examining trial making sure their case was in order. This time, the prosecution's case would be handled by both Kinsolving and the Commonwealth's Attorney James F. Thomas of Henry County, but also present were J. Wirt Turner and J. Ballard Clark, both family friends and local attorneys.

Despite its more ominous name, an examining trial is just a preliminary hearing or, in other jurisdictions, something referred to as a "probable cause" inquiry, one that will determine whether a defendant will be held until a grand jury decides if the defendant indeed will have to be tried. This part of the process prevents felony warrants that have no merit from going forward to a grand jury. This means that an examining trial is more procedural than evidentiary, but there is a judge and witnesses involved, and no one can ever be sure what could happen. Everybody expected that Denhardt's lawyers would attempt some legal wrangling to derail the prosecution. Nobody expected as many people to come by.

On Friday, November 20, in and around the same courthouse that struggled to accommodate the almost one thousand in the gallery and on the lawn of the coroner's inquest, five thousand people came to catch a glimpse of Denhardt's examining trial. Six state policemen had been requested in advance, and Harrod had as many men as he could deputize, but as it turned out, there was no real need for crowd control. Eight-hundred-fifty people showed up two hours early to get a seat in the courtroom as others were admitted but forced to stand. Those that could not get into the courtroom staked out a spot on the stairs and in the hallway. The estimated four thousand people on the Henry County Courthouse lawns were in a fairly festive mood and seemed content to mill about in order to be among the first to hear the news from inside. Automobiles of all types brought spectators from every corner of Bluegrass Country, and they packed the public square. Coffee and sandwich stands were set up again on the courthouse lawn.

In its issue that week, this is how *Time* magazine broke down the examining trial:

> 'The truth of the matter is that Mrs. Taylor was begging the General to marry her. He will tell the truth about this when the day of his trial comes,' said a Denhardt lawyer. 'Mrs. Taylor's daughters,' countered Coroner Ricketts, 'are prepared to testify that their mother told them the General had threatened her several times when she tried to break off their affair. The Taylor daughters will say that the General told their mother, 'If you don't marry me, you won't marry anyone!''

The examining trial would not disappoint the throngs. Promptly at 10 a.m., Denhardt entered the court. His arrival touched off a barrage of lightbulb flashes from the press photographers, a display of "fireworks" that reportedly lasted for five minutes. The hot, smoking, used flashbulbs were tossed into a bushel basket on the press table just as fast as the photographers could reload. Judge Morgan waited patiently for a few minutes, but with no end in sight, the judge finally ordered the photography to stop. One more photo popped with a light. Judge Morgan looked sternly at the press table and told Sheriff Harrod to remove the next man "who so much as sets off a bulb."

A visibly agitated Denhardt took his seat next to attorney Myers, who had been accompanied this time by his wife. While waiting for the proceedings to begin, Denhardt chatted with another lawyer and old friend at his table, G.D. Milliken, Sr., also of Bowling Green. At 10:10 a.m., Judge Morgan brought the room to order and asked the bailiff to lock the courtroom. After some pleasantries, Harrod called for the witnesses: Barney Browning, filling station owner, the farmers Mr. and Mrs. George Baker, Smith Keightley who had prepared the body, J.B. Hundley, the barber who found the body, and Drs. Herbert Blaydes and J.T. Walsh. Also summoned was Robert Thompson, a man whose name was unfamiliar to almost everybody connected to the case. He turned out to be an assistant in Messmer's crime lab.

Myers stood and announced, "Your Honor, the defense has no witnesses in the courtroom at this time," a statement that caused a flutter in the crowd. If Denhardt were sitting in the courtroom but not listed as a witness, the move was considered a sign that the general would not be testifying. Once all the witnesses were accounted for, Judge Morgan swore them in together. At the conclusion of their oath, Myers asked that all witnesses be removed from court and segregated from each other so that each would be unaware of the other's testimony.

Commonwealth's Attorney Thomas was directed to state the case against the defendant. Thomas bluntly accused Denhardt of murdering Verna Garr Taylor because she had changed her mind about marrying him and had wanted to end the engagement. He then called for his first witness, Barney Browning. Browning took the stand and explained how Verna had come into his filling station, how he and George Baker had tried to help. Denhardt watched the witness closely. Since the defense chose not to ask any questions of the witness themselves, the filling station owner was excused, and George Baker was brought in to continue the story.

Baker confirmed his role in the stalled car committee and that Denhardt did not speak, just looked out the window or stared straight ahead. Since the battery on Denhardt's car was completely dead, there were no lights of any kind. Hundley was there trying to help when Baker had returned with his car and his wife. Hundley had pushed Denhardt's car up as far as the road, but their bumpers had locked. The men worked to separate the cars. Hundley volunteered to drive Mrs. Taylor and the general back to La Grange, Baker said, and for the first time that he had heard, suddenly Denhardt spoke: "I do not want my car on the road without any lights."

Baker testified about the first shot--"I were scared"--and how after an unknown number of minutes, Baker went outside and started the walk to the stalled car in the driveway. "I could see Mr. Denhardt," the farmer said. "I heard a little gun go off. It sounded like a little pop gun or at best a .22. That's when Denhardt said to me, 'A lady was with me and went up the road to look for her glove.' As I watched him, he reached in the car, I judged for a gun, and Denhardt said, 'The gun is gone.'"

To aid in the search for Mrs. Taylor, farmer Baker went into his house for a lantern. Hundley testified about getting the mechanic, and when he came back to the car, Hundley had brought Cuba Shaver and a battery.

"How would you describe the general's condition?" Kinsolving asked.

"He seemed very frightened," Baker offered. "Then Denhardt said, 'Ain't that awful? My, my, she was the finest woman I ever knew.' He muttered that many times. 'Ain't that awful? My, my, she was the finest woman I ever knew.'"

Baker said that then Denhardt ordered Hundley and Shaver to drive up the road and look for Mrs. Taylor, but Hundley and Shaver wanted to repair the car first. Baker testified that Denhardt then commanded, "Boys, see about this woman first," and when they finally did, Denhardt hung back until he heard Hundley say, "She were dead." He added, "General Denhardt come up about that time behind us. 'Ain't that awful,' he said. Of course we all felt that way too." Baker specified that Denhardt never left the road, never approached the body. Denhardt ordered Hundley to call the coroner.

Most of the witnesses were excused without any cross-examination.

Hundley told the same story of finding the body first and the others coming up from behind him. It was pretty obvious "she were dead. And that's when Denhardt said to me out of nowhere, 'You know I couldn't have killed her. I was too crazy about her.' Not long after that," Hundley testified, "Baker said to me, 'Mr. Denhardt could not have killed that woman because I was with him when the last shot was fired.'" The prosecution let that stand, and the defense did not ask any questions so the barber was excused.

Undertaker Keightley identified the revolver in court as the one on the scene and confirmed the "bullet entered Mrs. Taylor's body under her left breast," and there were "two exploded and four unexploded cartridges" in the gun. Keightley talked about his unusual conversations with Denhardt, too: "'She had threatened to kill herself that afternoon, and we had a little wrestle before I took the gun away from her. Why, I wouldn't kill that woman. We were engaged. We were to be married.' Denhardt repeated that many times."

Dr. Blaydes was one of the few prosecution witnesses who was cross-examined. His testimony reflected his autopsy findings, however, he did seem to waver on the question of whether there was evidence of burned gunpowder—implying a closer shot—in Verna's wounds. By equivocating, he opened a door for the defense.

As was the prosecution's prerogative, no physical evidence was presented. This agitated the defense as they had hoped to get a better idea about what the Louisville Police Department Crime Lab had discovered. At the close of the Commonwealth's case, Myers immediately made a motion to dismiss the charges and discharge the defendant, and Judge Morgan agreed to hear the motion.

"We, as defense counsel, want to thank you for your patient attention to the evidence in this case. We also want to express to you the belief that we think that you desire to be fair and right and just. We think that the sincerity of that belief was evidenced by the fact that, although we realized Your Honor was related to the decedent, we did not make attempt—"

Judge Morgan stopped Myers dead in his tracks. "Let me interrupt you. I am not related whether by blood or marriage."

"Well, I was misinformed, Your Honor. I beg your pardon. I was misinformed by co-counsel," Myers stammered.

"I am responsible for that information," admitted Berry.

"I just wanted to set the attorney right," said the judge.

"He's practically the only one in this room that isn't related to her," whispered one wag in the gallery.

Myers gathered his thoughts, paused, and went on. "But being of that impression, we were still willing for you to sit in this case.

"Now then, before an examining court can hold any person to answer any charge that a grand jury might bring against him, two things are essential for you to believe. First, that an offense has been committed in the County of Henry. Second, that there are reasonable grounds for believing that the defendant has been connected in some way with the offense by the evidence that is heard by you in open court by witnesses who have been sworn—not by rumor or by newspaper articles—but only by the testimony that came from the mouths of witnesses that testified in your presence."

From there, for the next several minutes, Myers went through all the witnesses' statements to point out that the witnesses never claim that an offense had taken place in Henry County. Myers highlighted farmer Baker's comment to Hundley: "Mr. Denhardt could not have killed that woman because I was with him when the last shot was fired."

"Whoever had that revolver fired both shots," Myers argued. "She could not have been dead and fired the second and not any question about two being fired, so whoever had that revolver fired both of those shots because that revolver was found there above her on the highway, within four or five feet of the body."

A little later in his motion, Myers spun Dr. Blaydes testimony pretty easily to suggest that the doctor was saying there were powder burns consistent with a shot close to the body, and then he started to make his case by connecting them: "You put that testimony together with Mr. Baker that 'I know Denhardt didn't fire the shot because I was with him when the second shot was fired.' We do know that two shots were fired because there were two empty hulls. The hulls are there for Your Honor to observe, and not the slightest bit different, not the slightest bit of corrosion to show that it remained there longer than the other as result of having been fired and left in the chamber, both alike, both empty cartridges.

"Suicide doesn't mean an offense committed in Henry County. There isn't any testimony, not one scintilla of evidence showing that any human being had that gun in possession except herself... She was a prominent reputable citizen of Oldham County. He was a man who had attained prominence in the World War, as lieutenant governor and adjutant general. The newspapers have made of this case a mountain, and if it had happened in some remote county where the decedent and the other parties scrutinized were of no prominence or happened in your county under the same circumstances with people of no prominence, had not been played up, people would look at it fairly, justly, and at the cold facts. Happening, as it did, two shots fired as they were, one loud, another muffled, powder burns on the body and inside the wound. There would have been no further steps taken."

Myers then spoke to the lack of motive established by the Commonwealth. The defense's position is that no evidence or testimony brought forth established "premeditation and with malice of forethought," a necessary requirement for a murder charge. "Where is the evidence of any motive that General Denhardt would want to take the life of this woman?" Myers went on to ask, "Were they having a fuss? Was she in fear? Was she trying to get away from him? No."

No evidence or testimony that established premeditation is one thing, but as it was related by the witnesses, Denhardt himself had said that they had a fight, that she tried to give the ring back, and that she wanted to get home. Browning, Baker, and Hundley testified that it was

Verna who wanted to get the car fixed and get going. Myers had one criteria for the exhibition of fear, that Verna would have vocalized her need to escape to somebody else around her.

Myers concluded, "So, we ask Your Honor as a Court, as one who, I know, wants to do right, we ask you to say, regardless of the headlines of the newspapers, regardless of rumors that have persisted in the atmosphere, regardless of one thing carried as announcements in the afternoon papers and denied in the morning papers, that regardless of that, you would say, 'When I was sworn in as County Judge of Henry County, I held up my right hand, and I swore to try those cases that came before me according to the law and according to the evidence that I heard, and in this case, the evidence that came before me was not sufficient to me to give reasonable grounds for believing an offense was committed in Henry County or that the defendant was connected therewith.' The evidence warrants that finding, the law warrants that finding... There is no testimony, no witness that has testified today that has said a single word from which there can be deduced any belief that there is a reasonable cause for believing that anything happened, except Mrs. Taylor took her own life and that General Denhardt is not connected with it. I thank you."

In response to that motion, Judge Morgan signaled to the prosecution, "Proceed with the argument."

Commonwealth's Attorney Thomas stood to refute Myers statements. "May it please Your Honor, I want to say in the outset that we agree with the distinguished counsel for the defense, we also think you are a good judge. If they can throw bouquets, so can we. We think you are a good judge, but whether a good judge or a bad judge has nothing to do with the facts of this case."

Thomas then took on Myers' arguments, point by point. He agreed that the case had gotten a lot of publicity and had been the subject of irresponsible speculation in newspapers, but Thomas scoffed at the argument that Denhardt was only being prosecuted because he was a prominent person. Thomas shot back, "I will venture the assumption—and we have got as much as to assume as he does—that if some man down here in the country who had a wife, and if that wife was found dead with his gun, regardless of the circumstances, since last Saturday, that man would have been in the Henry County Jail. I have been county attorney of this county for seven years, and no man has ever yet been charged with murder—except Denhardt—that didn't go to jail."

First, there was just a smattering of applause, but it grew until the entire courtroom crowd broke out in shouts, hoots, and cheers. The judge rose from his chair and rapped the court back to order with his gavel and admonished the gallery, saying, "One more time like this, and I'll clear the courtroom. I won't have that in my court." But Thomas had made his point. According to Kentucky law of the time, nobody charged with murder in the first degree can be given bail, but Denhardt was.

"Now, let's see, Mr. Myers tells you that Baker said, 'He couldn't have shot her. I was with him when the second shot was fired.' I say to Your Honor that Baker didn't say no such thing, J.B. Hundley made that statement, and Baker never made it under oath from this witness chair."

Myers corrected himself, explaining that he should have said that Hundley said Baker said it about Denhardt.

"I did not interrupt him," Thomas said to the judge. "I will ask the same courtesy." Myers acknowledged the rebuke. Thomas continued:

No, let's see what we can deduce from this case. Let's see what the physical facts are in it, not the statement of any person. Let's examine the attitude of this man charged with murder. What is the first thing that Denhardt said to Baker when he came out of the house after the shot was fired? He said, 'She was a fine lady.' Before he found her body, 'she was a fine lady.' General Denardt is an educated man, he knows the difference between 'is' and 'was.' When he said, 'she was a fine lady,' he used the past tense, and he knew she was dead. Otherwise, why would he say she *was* a fine lady? Because from his statement, for all he knew, she was up the road, looking for a glove or doing something else. They told you there was two shots fired from that gun that night. The only real evidence they have is Mr. Myers' unsupported statement that there is no corrosion on one shell that shows it had been fired sooner. Well, I don't know, I'm not an expert. No expert testified as to that, but what does Baker say? Baker says the first shot was loud, like something big, a big pistol or a shotgun, the second shot was like from a pop gun or a .22 rifle, and he don't say from this witness stand it was muffled! He just says it wasn't as loud. Why assume that two shots were fired just because two shots were in the chamber. Maybe he carried that gun on a blank cartridge. A lot of people do who know something about firearms, either carry a gun on an empty chamber or a blank cartridge. Why? To stop the probability of it accidentally discharging. This man has been in the army. He knows all about firearms.

Thomas proceeded to dismantle the suicide theory based on the ridiculous contortion of a woman with short arms shooting herself using a long, heavy gun pointed to the right under her left breast. Thomas pantomimed this action to the judge saying, "What do you think?"

But Thomas' most colorful moment came when he passionately mocked Denhardt for his obsession about getting Verna's ring back. "And another thing. They tell you that General Denhardt could not have shot her, 'Why, he was in love her! He was going to marry her!' Well, what's the first thing he said when they find her dead body laying down there in the ditch? 'Take care of my ring.' Jesus Christ, Judge, a man in love with a woman—why, he would have rushed down there and taken her in his arms. He wouldn't have cared anything about a diamond ring or ten diamond rings."

Kinsolving had his own rebuttal to the defense motion for discharge— he went through the testimony one more time—but it was probably overkill, so to speak. After all the lawyers were done talking, Judge Morgan just said, "Very good, gentleman. Anything further?"

Mr. Berry said, "That is all."

Then, casually, after however long all that lawyering took, Judge Morgan said, "Motion overruled." Denhardt would be held over until a grand jury could meet on the matter. Pending the grand jury's decision, which likely would be a rubber stamp at this point, a trial date would be set. If the defense did not know it for sure then, they were smart enough to suspect that from this point forward, all of their efforts would have to be put in defending Denhardt against a murder conviction. If the news for Denhardt were not bad enough, Judge Morgan also refused—or perhaps the word is 'declined'—to renew the general's $25,000 bond. Judge Morgan was revoking that which he himself had allowed the defendant at the end the coroner's inquest.

For the next few weeks at least, Denhardt would not be allowed to post bond in exchange for his liberty. Denhardt was then handed over to Sheriff Harrod, but with an usual stipulation from Judge Morgan. In recognition of the inflamed sentiments against the general that had encouraged Coroner Rickets to move his inquest further away from

La Grange, Judge Morgan ruled that Harrod was to make arrangements to have the prisoner housed at the Jefferson County jail in Louisville until the next phase of his trial. The precaution was being taken, the judged noted, because violent hostility toward Denhardt in Oldham County clearly was rising, as well as in Henry County, and the Henry County jail was too frail to withstand a mob of vigilantes.

Harrod reassured a *Time* reporter that "[b]ecause of the intense feeling against the General, and the murmuring of some of Mrs. Taylor's kinfolk, we are preparing for any emergency. We are going to be ready to repel any attempt against the General's life."

In light of the judge's order, Harrod decided to wait a couple hours for the crowds to dissipate before transporting the prisoner. Denhardt was then brought down to the street. State police vehicles were lined up both in front of and behind Harrod and Denhardt in the sheriff's car before they left for Louisville. It was reported that Denhardt remained in good spirits during the drive, exhibiting no particular concerns, at least until the procession approached the jail in Louisville. The reality of it all must finally have sunk in then. When he was handed over officially to Jailer Martin J. Connors, Denhardt's glib, carefree attitude was gone. Behind bars, this former prosecutor, himself a former judge, and a former strikebreaking general who knew brutality only as he wielded it on others, might have wondered whether he would have been safer at a gun range with the Garr Boys. Processed, stripped of his fine clothes and comforts, and ushered into a cell by Deputy Jailer E.J. Columbus, Denhardt, it seemed to observers, was struck by how far he had fallen. In jail, Denhardt passed a restless first night but then put down a hearty breakfast in the morning.

In exchange for a chance to push his "I loved her too much to kill her" defense with a *Time* reporter, Denhardt agreed to be photographed examining the first-ever issue of *LIFE* magazine. On November 21, a *Chicago Tribune* reporter witnessed Denhardt getting more comfortable in the limelight of the Jefferson County Jail. "I am not a killer, and I had no purpose or intention of killing (Mrs. Taylor)," Denhardt said to the *Trib*, "and I wouldn't have had it happen for anything in the world."

In La Grange, there was a spirit of jubilation. Denhardt finally was behind bars and headed to trial. For all the rumors about a Garr-led mob of vigilantes, history shows that the Garr family was determined to follow a more modern path. Putting their faith in forensic science and the legal system, the Garr Boys were cooperating fully with the Commonwealth to bring a killer to justice. There was one more reason for the family to smile. As reported by *The New York Times* and papers across the country, Mary Pryor and Allen Brown got married. It was not, of course, the original plan, but if Mary Pryor was being forced to move through her grief, she and Allen decided they might as well move through it together. Both Verna's absence and her presence were felt all day of the wedding.

Meanwhile, Denhardt's legal team of Overstreet, Myers, Berry, and a new science legal specialist, W. Clark Otte from Louisville, set to free the general from the Jefferson County Jail on a writ of *habeas corpus*. After nineteen days in county lock-up, Denhardt was brought before Circuit Judge Charles C. Marshall in New Castle on December 9, 1936. Citing that Denhardt was no more a danger to society now than when he had been granted bond before, the writ of *habeas corpus* argued that even if Judge Morgan had the general's safety in mind, he had erred by refusing to allow Denhardt to post bond. As part of its argument to the court, the defense had subpoenaed select prosecution witnesses from the crime lab, which was a clever move. These subpeonas could have forced the Commonwealth to reveal the results of the blood tests on Denhardt's overcoat and on the highway pavement earlier than it wanted. The Commonwealth chose to keep its evidence under wraps and let Denhardt walk. Judge Marshall ruled in the defense's favor, and once more, Dr. McCormack secured Denhardt's liberty in exchange for property.

Another bold defense move was attempted on January 16, 1937, just a few days before the grand jury was expected to meet. By design, grand juries only hear evidence from the prosecution's side. In front of the news media and legal witnesses, Denhardt signed an affidavit voluntarily waiving his constitutional rights and promised to answer any question put to him by the Henry County Grand Jury. As part of this gambit, Denhardt offered to bring "reputable authorities upon the subject of blood technique and forensic ballistics." The affidavit went on to claim that a nationally recognized authority had tested and determined the blood spot found on the SR 22 to be non-human blood. Denhardt's affidavit was a fairly extensive survey of all the people who thought him to be innocent and falsely accused. In some ways, it was a legal "Trojan horse," a chance to get behind enemy lines and thwart his indictment before it could be issued...

If Denhardt's legal affidavit is any indication, his grand jury testimony would have been a unique narrative. In this, Verna's bad headache and general despondency were the only potential motives given for her suicide. No mention of her daughters or any other family interference, and nothing was said about that mysterious third party even though Denhardt had promised "If they would let me testify, I would tell them damn quick who killed her." Denhardt prepared the affadavit himself, but he did not name Verna's supposed killers as he claimed he would. In this written testimony, Denhardt said, "He heard the first shot, and that after that was heard, he found that his revolver, which Mrs. Taylor knew was always in the glove compartment, had also disappeared. Then for the first time affiant states that he felt the worst had happened. The second shot followed when affiant was in the presence of Mr. Baker; it was a muffled shot." When Denhardt signed it, it became a legal document. Interestingly, Denhardt readily admitted he always carried his revolver in his glove box, but later he would change that under oath, too.

Without stating a reason, the grand jury declined his offer.

Being secret proceedings, all that went on in the Henry County Grand Jury room is not known, but *The Louisville Courier-Journal* reported that Mary Pryor and Frances had testified about "conversations in which they said '(Denhardt) had threatened (Mother).'"

As expected, on January 19, 1937, a Henry County grand jury returned a "True Bill," that is, an indictment for "willful murder." The decision of the twelve member grand jury was unanimous. The murder one trial was scheduled to start six days later on Monday, January 25. Further violating the Kentucky law requiring people charged with murder in the first degree to be jailed before a trial, Denhardt remained free. An enterprising reporter tracked down Denhardt, sitting with a beer and a female companion across the street from the Henry County Courthouse, and told him the grand jury had just indicted him. "Oh, have they?" the general replied coolly. "Well, see my attorneys." After that, Denhahrdt went back to sipping his beer and eyeing his friend.

The stage was set for the sequel. The general would strike back.

CHAPTER TEN

At least in public, John Marshall Berry went to his grave professing Denhardt's innocence. Judging by Berry's own files, however, Denhardt's legal team knew from personal experience the general was a scheming, dishonest, dishonorable, arrogant, violent drunk capable of using and assaulting people, and then thinking nothing of it. In fact, if pressed outside of the bounds of attorney-client privilege, the entire Denhardt legal team might have agreed with the prosecution team that Denhardt was not a good man, that he was bellicose, belligerent, and prone to erupt in physical force to exert his power. In the end, Denhardt's lawyers might even have concluded that Denhardt was a habitual liar who could not be trusted, but oddly, they all drew a line at saying he was a killer. Instead, the intelligent, reasonable men in Denhardt's camp insisted that Verna Garr Taylor just decided one day to kill herself in the most bizarre way possible.

At the same time that Berry and his colleagues were paying operatives to investigate any rumors that could further put the victim's reputation on trial to defend their client, Berry's collection of memos, correspondence, and briefs associated with the trial reveals that Denhardt's own lawyers, one by one, were reduced to threatening their client in an attempt to control his ugly behavior.

The first lawyer to butt heads with Denhardt was Beckham Overstreet. In a letter to Berry dated December 16, 1936, just one week after getting Denhardt freed on a writ of *habeas corpus.* Overstreet resigned from the case. Overstreet begins the letter by acknowledging with gratitude the support of colleagues Myers and Milliken in his effort to be paid for services rendered so that he could close the chapter on his representation of Denhardt. Per Overstreet, both Myers and Milliken regretted Overstreet's withdrawal but understood why. Without going into any detail about what had happened, Overstreet wrote angrily, "I never was in all my practice for the twenty-six years treated by a client like General Denhardt has treated me, and I do not propose to tolerate it any longer. No one has a nicer practice than mine... That being true, why should I be continually assaulted and offended by a client?"

Whatever it was that happened between Denhardt and Overstreet, the use of "continually" suggests the assault was not an isolated incident. Overstreet goes on to threaten a lawsuit against Denhardt if he was not paid immediately for his representation and emphasizes that testifying to his treatment at the hands of Denhardt "would be a substantial hurt to his cause." The letter then warns that "insults and assaults are suffered to shield and protect the cause of my client," but essentially, if he were not paid, there would be no public relations protection for Denhardt in Overstreet's civil suit to recover his fees. Denhardt needed to pay up or be exposed.

Overstreet was not the only one concerned about Denhardt's lack of payment for his mounting legal bills. In Berry's files, there is a bundle of correspondence regarding compensation. For example, in a letter dated December 17, 1936, Berry forwarded the business card of a Louisville real estate agent who was interested in the purchase of Denhardt's farm. By chance, Denhardt's land values had increased because the Kentucky legislature had approved the building of a new penal farm in Oldham County. While Berry avoided a direct conflict of interest, he vouched for this realtor and laid out how this sale would be a providential way for Denhardt to finance the expensive trial ahead.

On December 18, 1936, Berry writes to Myers with several concerns. First, he speaks candidly about driving to Sparta, Kentucky, to "run down a rumor" about Verna, but it did not lead anywhere. Berry uses a kind of code to Myers when he says, "It appears that the dangerous element in the case has some possibilities, and I am encouraged in so far as the case itself is concerned but am very much discouraged and annoyed by our client's condition and conduct." Exactly what the "dangerous element" to which Berry refers is difficult to decode for certain, but there is little doubt that Denhardt's "condition and conduct" referred to the general's frequent drunken mendaciousness. To that, Berry explains in the same letter, "Last night General Denhardt was in Shelbyville at a restaurant eating a lunch and drinking some beer. He was engaged in conversation and made a dam fool of himself."

In the court of public opinion, the defense had been making Denhardt out as a war hero, a dedicated public servant, and a victim of unsubstantiated rumors and a hostile press, but this argument evaporates if Denhardt truly is the mean, explosive drunk who everybody says he is. "Not only must his mouth be stopped," Berry demands, "but he must be removed from this locality if you and Judge Miligan [I think he meant their colleague and Denhardt's hometown friend, G.D. Milliken] can devise any way to do it." The general had only been freed for nine days, but Berry knew "his persistence along the line of his present behavior will defeat every otherwise successful effort his attorneys can possibly make."

There is no way of knowing for sure what Denhardt was running his mouth about, but it must have been so awful that Berry wanted the general *physically removed* from Shelby County. The media had reported already that Denhardt was known to get drunk and tell stories defiling Verna's virtue. Perhaps the subtext for that concern was also Denhardt's behind-the-scenes legal efforts to get the trial moved to Shelby County. What's the point in successfully getting a change of venue if the county seat where you end up hates you more than the one you left?

On December 19, 1936, probably before Myers received Berry's letter warning of their client's misconduct, Myers wrote to Denhardt, encouraging his client to accept the offer of $110 per acre for his farm in Oldham County from the realtor Berry had recommended. The Commonwealth was ready to buy, the sale was nearly a done deal, and the general would get $88,000 for his acreage, worth about $1.5 million today. Not bad for a tenant farm that just happened to be exactly where the Commonwealth wanted to be put a new prison (coincidence or a leftover political favor?). At this point, none of the lawyers had been paid for Denhardt's legal work, and hard costs incurred by the attorneys were being reimbursed sporadically, if at all. Denhardt's lawyers were losing money by representing him. With one stroke of a pen, Denhardt could pay his attorney's fees and be set financially for life.

One of the most disturbing paragraphs in all Berry's private correspondence is in an early letter between Berry and Denhardt that refers to the "secret angle" of their defense and the funds needed to explore it. Berry was concerned about public backlash against Denhardt and his lawyers if this "secret angle" were to be connected to them in any way. To prevent damage to the reputations of Berry, Myers, and Otte, Denhardt would need to commit adequate funds for an operative with the discreet sensibilities to dig up this kind of dirt.

"The secret angle of the case should now be investigated exhaustedly and the investigation cannot be made by any person known to be identified with your defense," wrote Berry to Denhardt. Whatever the "secret angle" was, Berry knew would be just as important for his image as an ethical attorney as it would for Denhardt's cause in the press:

> . . . it must be done secretedly and undercover. Such investigation will require the services of one skilled and experienced in such work and who will require adequate pay for his time and for his service. It has occurred to me, therefore, that I should recommend that you provide and place in Mr. Otte's hands an adequate sum of money to pay such person as we may deem competent to start work immediately upon this investigation.

So, while publicly complaining about the rumors swirling about their client—many of which his defense lawyers were learning to their chagrin to be true—the defense wanted to pay somebody off the books to uncover every possible embarrasing inuendo about the victim. Berry concludes, "And as you know, we have not scratched the surface of this phase."

What could this "secret angle" have been? Perhaps all we have to go on was the "real story" of November 6, 1936, which Denhardt was more than willing to share to a friendly ear over a beer or three. In saloons and restaurants, Denhardt loved being the center of attention and having people buy him drinks. In return, he would become increasingly verbose about the "real story" of the night in question, both to entertain, it seems, and also to vent his frustrations.

The Garr Boys were the face of those frustrations. Denhardt could not resort to physical threats over the Garr Boys as he had done with others in the past. Denhardt had no rank, no economic leverage over the Garr family—he had no way to hurt or intimidate them. The thing they loved most, Verna Garr Taylor, had already been taken from them, so the only pressure point Denhardt had left on the Garrs was this "real story" about what happened to Verna on SR 22. More admired in death than she may have been in life, perhaps, Verna was being venerated all over Kentucky and the country through the press. If the Garrs could not protect Verna physically anymore, then they could at least protect her legacy. This was the weakness in the family defenses that Denhardt could exploit, so Verna's virtue became his point of attack in conversation. This is how he could make the Garrs pay for his misery. Denhardt would not be bested.

As his January trial date approached, Denhardt's battle plan was to share his manufactured gossip privately and have others spread the rumors for him. This was attested in the first attack on Verna from Miss Bertha, who compounded the pain of Verna's daughters by making them responsible for her suicide. It started as a thought-seed the night of Verna's death, but it was more of a side comment. With the help of the Associated Press, Miss Bertha actually appeared to taunt the Garr family by saying Frances and Mary Pryor were to blame because they "did not want her to marry."

Repeatedly, Denhardt asserted there was a secret side to Verna to which only he was privy. If Verna was described as a composed, successful, independent woman, Denhardt's version of Verna would be one that was emotionally unstable, clueless, and needy. If the neighbors revered her as a model mother devoted to her daughters, Denhardt would paint her as libidinous woman who could not wait to be rid of children. Even the storied love between Verna and Barc was fair game for Denhardt. Contrary to public opinion, Denhardt would not only claim that Verna no longer grieved for Barclay but that Denhardt was the only man she thought was worth dying for. When Barc died, according to Denhardt, Verna found a way to go on, but at the very thought of losing Denhardt because of family interference, Verna lost the very will to live.

Never mind that this contradicted Denhardt's own frequent, sober *bon mots* that "Verna was such a sweet woman, sensible, refined, and highly educated." This was the Verna everybody else knew, too, but why would a sweet, sensible, refined, highly educated woman decide on the spur of the moment to kill herself? Over time, various versions of the "the untold story" of that night were spread around Northern Kentucky. The following is one of the earliest versions, reportedly told in a bar, printed in a couple of true crime magazines.

Verna and Denhardt were going to Louisville for lunch, bridge, errands, shopping, and fun when Verna asked if she could look in on her client at the Kentucky Military Institute. She'd been gone for a while, but when she came out, it appeared as though she had been crying. Sitting in the car on the side of the road, Denhardt asked kindly, "Is there anything the matter?"

"Oh, Henry," Verna blurted out. "I have a terrible confession to make to you. That's why I was gone so long. I found a place in there where I could be alone, and I tried to think the thing out. I hardly know how to begin."

"There, there," the general said, as he put his arm around Verna's trembling shoulders. "It can't be as bad as that, my loved one."

"Oh, you have no idea how bad it is!" Verna cried. "You are the most wonderful person in existence outside of God himself—and to think that I have done this to you... ."

"Done what, my dearest?" Denhardt tenderly prompted.

With appropriate solemnity, Verna explained that her daughters and her brothers were interfering with their marriage plans, and it was tearing her apart. She did not know what to do. She professed her love to him but added that her family expected so much from her that she feared it would eventually come between them. Denhardt, in need of a bracing swig of good Kentucky bourbon, reached into his car's glove compartment for his flask, and that's when the real trouble started. Between the roadmaps and the bourbon glinted Denhardt's blue-black .45 service revolver. Sensing she had found a panacea for her problems, Verna began to reach for the dark metal gun. Before she could grab it, Denhardt snatched her hand.

"Come now, Verna," he commanded. "We'll have none of that."

Flinging her arms around Denhardt's neck, Verna proclaimed, "Oh, Henry, you're too good for me, I want to die. I don't want to live and look again into your honest eyes!" Denhardt was an even better man than she could ever have hoped for, she proclaimed madly. "[L]et us both die! Today! Let's die together!"

A suicide pact? But Denhardt did not want Verna to die, and he did not want to die himself, he wanted a chance to enjoy what life still had in store for them. It did not seem hard, at first, to talk Verna out of her hysteria with promises of their happily-ever-after.

"Well, then, let us be married right away—today. Let's go now and find a justice of the peace. That would take care of the problem. Nobody could stop us then. Come, my love, let's get married this afternoon."

Denhardt was not sure which plan sounded crazier, suicide or elopement! Denhardt took Verna's hand with a smile and said, "Now, wouldn't that look silly for a couple people our age running off and finding a preacher like a couple of kids that *had* to get married? It just wouldn't look right. Besides, all our friends would be so disappointed that they couldn't be there," the general claimed he said.

Verna persisted. One way or another, she said, she wanted the general for herself. After canceling plans with others and spending the day with Verna trying to reassure her that he would stand by her through her family turmoil, Verna broke down and admitted that, in the end, it did not really matter because everywhere she went, she carried a death sentence that also put others in harm's way. Through her sobs, Verna explained that one of her employees, twenty-six-year-old Chester Woolfolk, had misconstrued her kindness to him and was convinced that they were meant to be together. Verna assured Denhardt that her affection for Ches was all very innocent. Chester dropped off the day's receipts to her home in the evening and had given one of her girls saxophone lessons. From that, Chester had gotten the wrong impression and went mad when he heard about Denhardt's proposal to Verna.

"Chester Woolfolk told me that if I persisted in marrying you, he would kill me, anyway. If you take me home tonight, I'll be dead in fifteen minutes. I love my children, my mother, and, most importantly, you, but I am tired of living. I'll make sure to leave a note explaining everything." Based on his years as a county judge, a soldier, and a commander in the battlefield, Denhardt thought he recognized the signs of somebody having a nervous breakdown. Verna's crying fits, the talk of suicide, the rambling logic—he'd seen it all before.

Fearing for her life from her jealous employee, clinging to the hope that she could be married soon to the man she loved, and still recovering from her bad headache, Verna told Denhardt she was going to keep on driving. Instead of turning left onto the main road that would have taken them north into La Grange, she steered eastward into the rural, night air on SR 22 toward Henry County. There, they found a nice quiet spot in the parking lot of an old schoolhouse and sat together quietly while the whole world melted away. Verna seemed to gain control of her erratic impulses. Verna renewed her request that they show the world how committed they were to being together for eternity, through death or until death did them part.

"I'm tired of my daughters' interference and my brothers' meddling!" Verna exclaimed. "If my daughters or my brothers do not understand, then I just did not want to live."

But Denhardt kept encouraging her to just stick to their plan of tying the knot with all their friends and family in a few days' time, objections be damned, and then they could handle the dastardly Chester Woolfolk together. Looking back on it, as he would tell those in rapt attention at the bar, he realized that her mind had been made up and that even his love was not enough to withstand the pressure she was experiencing from her daughters and her brothers and her fear of Chester Woolfolk. He would take to his grave his regrets that he was so trusting of her smiles. He was tricked into leaving her alone with his keys and his gun in his locked glove compartment. She disappeared into the night, killing herself to spare him the horror of seeing it in his car.

Was this the kind of story that forced Berry to write, "Last night General Denhardt was in Shelbyville at a restaurant eating a lunch and drinking some beer. He was engaged in conversation and made a dam fool of himself"? Was this "secret story" the same as the "secret angle" being pursued by Otte's very private eye? Unlike the coroner's inquest when "they" would not let him testify, Denhardt promised at his trial in just a few days, he finally would tell the world who was responsible for Verna's death, as the expression goes, "come hell or high water."

About that high water thing...

CHAPTER ELEVEN

In the month January in 1937, it rained all but eight days along the Ohio River in Kentucky. Because it had already snowed and thawed a few times by New Year's Day, the Ohio River was already swollen by January 5. The first flood warnings only concerned the lower-lying areas along the river. When the heavy precipitation started January 13, however, it pounded everywhere for eleven straight days. Just between January 21 and January 22, the Ohio rose over six feet.

Certain parts of Louisville had always been seasonally susceptible to flooding. In 1884, for example, at the bend of the river where parts of the city are surrounded by the Ohio on three sides, the record for the number of feet above flood stage was nineteen. But by January 24, just one day before Denhardt's trial for willful murder was to begin, the Ohio was *thirty* feet above flood stage. When the river crested on January 27, it rose to *fifty-seven* feet above normal. By then, 70% of Louisville was underwater. Hundreds of people were killed, and 175,000 residents were forced to evacuate the city with only a few minutes' notice in some cases.

My mother, Ann Garr Hill Punnett Artze Brown, was one of those flood refugees. To Verna, my mother was a first cousin, once removed. Even though she was not quite six-years-old during the Great Ohio River Flood, my mother remembers it vividly.

"At first I wasn't aware there might be a dangerous threat somewhere in my world. Mom and Dad were aware, though. Adults with an anxious family turned to radio news more than usual. There were more calls to and from relatives and friends. Dad explained to me that water from the Ohio River was rising and pouring over its banks. We shouldn't worry, he told me. Low-lying areas of Louisville often flooded after heavy rains, in historic Shippingport and Portland, but not in our very large area near Broadway. Not our house. The West End would be safe."

But it wasn't. Of all the cities along the Ohio River, from Pittsburgh to Cairo, Illinois, the cold, whipping rains of January slapped Louisville the hardest. In today's dollars, the Great Ohio Flood of 1937 caused $4 billion in damage to the Commonwealth alone. Even those who did not live in Louisville or along the river were effected by the disruption to the economy. An incalculable number of people saw everything they ever had, including barns full of livestock, just washed away. Beginning on January 25, Denhardt's trial date was scheduled and rescheduled several times until life returned to normal in Northern Kentucky.

New Castle-based attorney Berry used the opportunity to collect sworn affidavits from forty-seven Henry Countians who claimed Denhardt would never get a fair trial there. The large crowds that Denhardt himself had encouraged by demanding a bigger site for the coroner's inquest and later for the examining trial were used as evidence that angry mobs were out to get him. Furthermore, Berry argued a change of venue was necessary because a local merchant had displayed a similar Smith & Wesson M1917 service revolver in his window, thereby prejudicing the potential jury pool.

The trial date was set for Monday, April 19, 1937, at the Henry County Courthouse. The Commonwealth was expected to ask for the death penalty. The possibility that a former lieutenant governor, an active general in the National Guard, and a prominent figure in Kentucky politics for forty years could be executed by the very government he had served was front page news all over the country. Would a jury of country folk be too starstruck to believe that somebody as educated and distinguished as Denhardt was just another cold-blooded killer? Would Denhardt be viewed as a victim of love or Verna as a victim of anger? As the date approached, the showdown was set not just between two legal teams but also between the defense's cynical suicide theory and the prosecution's newfangled crime science-derived evidence.

But the other questions that also had people wondering were, "Will we ever hear a word out of the Garr Boys?" "Will Denhardt testify in his own defense?" They would not have to wait long.

On the morning of the trial, Denhardt rode into town, fresh from a Florida vacation while his lawyers toiled. In a white shirt, a trendy polka-dot tie, and a flattering blue serge suit, Denhardt looked fit and rested. His tan skin, quick smile, and casual demeanor gave the impression not of a man facing a capital murder conviction, but of a man without a care in the world.

Did Denhardt know something the prosecution didn't? There had been only one other death penalty case in Henry County in its 139-year history. Just before the Civil War, a black maid had been convicted of killing a white baby. In the history of the Commonwealth of Kentucky, no political official of his Denhardt's stature had ever been executed for any reason.

But this was Verna Garr Taylor, and too many people spoke of her as a treasure who had been stolen from the whole community, not just one family. "Only one defect is rumored in her stoutness of character," wrote *The Louisville Times*, "that is a report yet to be established. She wore General Denhardt's engagement ring. She admitted to friends, some say, that she was affianced to him, but that she had no intention of marrying him. This would scarcely be cricket, to say the least. It is a perilous game when a mature player tosses lighted matches at an inflammable adversary."

There may be some truth to that. At very least, the part about Denhardt's combustibility.

CHAPTER TWELVE

Reporters and historians alike have referred to the opening of the Denhardt trial on April 19, 1937 as a "near circus" atmosphere. They had a point. Judge Charles C. Marshall was the perfect ringmaster, through every pre-trial motion and defense argument, Denhardt's troupe of elite attorneys had proven themselves skilled tightrope walkers over flaming pits of logic, and the public prosecutors had the difficult task of juggling the instability of early forensic crime science evidence.

And, of course, there was a well-known clown.

For eight days, the Henry County Courthouse grounds were transformed into a midway. There were crowd-pleasing performers such as roaming snake charmers and singers, and food vendors, such as the women of the local Baptist church selling all types of refreshments. Just as they had for the examining trial on November 20, more than five thousand people lined up to get a seat in the big top, so to speak. This time, however, Henry County was better prepared. New Castle's only hotel had been booked for weeks, but visiting press could find rooms for a fee from one of the county seat's five hundred local residents or rough it a nearby mobile home park. The state police were brought in to handle the snarl of cars, trucks, saddle horses, and farm wagons, and local restaurants stocked up with plenty of food for the influx of tourists.

As Jane Dixon of *The Louisville Times* reported,

> Folks who haven't met each other for years are 'parley-vooing' and taking a squint at the out-landers who are here for the duration of the trial. The chief attraction on the green is our own *Times* trailer which the men who are writing stories for you have christened, 'By Liner'... A snake

Indian medicine show on the green gave our trailer a run for first place in attractions... Your correspondent bought a box of luck rabbit's foot salve. Nothing to use it on now but if what we think is going to happen actually happens in the courtroom, we'll need it to take the prints of people's elbows out of our ribs.

By and large, the festivities remained peaceful, albeit with a few testy moments. Famously, a photographer from the *Chicago Daily News* almost got decked by Judge Marshall when the newspaperman bumped the jurist in a crowed hallway. The judge threw a punch, but it did not land. He later apologized for blowing his cool but still kept the reporters on a short leash.

Once more, at the defense table sat a relaxed Denhardt. "They shouldn't try me here," he said "discreetly" to a newspaper man sitting near, always pushing for how unfair the world was treating him. "This place is hostile."

Denhardt was surrounded by attorneys Myers, Berry, and Otte, alongside whom Denhardt had served in "the Great War"—or as it was often still referred to then—"the Overseas War." In fact, in the press of the day, much was made of the fact that both Denhardt and Commonwealth's Attorney Kinsolving were respected "Overseas veterans." This fact about Captain Kinsolving may have been promoted intentionally to the press as a way of equalizing the general's status as a decorated war hero. Military service played a big role in the perception of one's betters in Bluegrass Country.

In places like Oldham and Henry counties, everybody kind of knows everybody—and might even be related to them. Because of their local family longevity, the Garrs were referred to in the newspapers as "Bluegrass aristocrats." This was certainly tongue-in-cheek, but being a prominent family meant having solid business and social connections. For example, Kinsolving had been friends with the Garr family for years and this made him passionate in his prosecution of Denhardt. Kinsolving knew from personal experience how preposterous it was for Verna to leave girls entering young womanhood parentless over an older man who she had known for just a few months.

For the Commonwealth, Kinsolving and Thomas were assisted by two outside lawyers hired by the Garr family as special prosecutors,

Wirt Turner of La Grange once more, brought in by Mary Pryor and Frances to represent their interests, and J. Ballard Clark of New Castle, hired by Doc, Roy, and Jack.

As the trial was called to order, in the finest tradition of Southern jurisprudence, Judge Marshall spat out all of his chewing tobacco before he made some opening remarks about his expectations for such a large crowd and what the week's schedule looked like. As jury selection was to begin, Judge Marshall signaled to the prosecution and defense that this would be the last time to have any pre-trial motions considered. A quid of fresh chewing tobacco then went back in as the judge leaned back. Not to be inhospitable, at the end of every courtroom pew bench there were cuspidors for the spectators, as well.

Off to the side of the judge, safely outside spitting distance, was Henry County Court stenographer, Madelyn Baldwin. Researchers and historians everywhere dream of a woman like Ms. Baldwin, somebody who could preserve word-for-word what was said in both Denhardt's examining trial and his willful murder trial. For decades, the transcripts for these proceedings were thought to be lost. When the transcripts were rediscovered recently in the Berry family archives, they were donated to the Berry Center in New Castle and then to the Filson Historical Society in Louisville, but all of this amazing detail would been lost if it were not for what the *Courier-Journal* described as "Madelyn's small, well-cared-for hands."

"Your Honor," Myers spoke up, "at this time, the defense asks for a continuance on the grounds that important witnesses, such as J.B. Hundley, are absent today. He's the witness who found Mrs. Taylor's body."

Hundley was out with the flu. A photo of a sick Hundley in his pajamas in bed was published in the *Courier-Journal* on April 22. Constant requests for changes of venue or delays appeared to be an intentional defense strategy. *Front Page Detective* assessed the Denhardt defense tactic aptly: "Every postponement the defense could gain was so much more in their favor. For whether it is for justice or no, popular sentiment and inflamed newspaper stories have a great deal to do with the psychological background of a murder trial. The colder the story got and the more people in general forgot about it, the less likely there was to be a resurgence of popular anger."

"The motion is denied," said Judge Marshall. "This trial has been delayed enough due to the flooding. Anything else?"

"Your Honor," Myers continued, "the defense asks for dismissal of the case on the grounds that a court stenographer was in the grand jury room during the investigation." Of course, this would have been Madelyn Baldwin. Stenographers are allowed in the grand jury in an official capacity, but spectators are not permitted. The defense inferred that Ms. Baldwin had been spying on the proceedings to give the Commonwealth an advantage. Judge Marshall overruled the motion because an affidavit was produced showing she took no notes and passed along no information.

"Your Honor," announced Kinsolving as he turned around and glanced to the first bench of the gallery where Verna's daughters and brothers were seated, "before jury selection begins, after careful consideration, in the willful murder case of the Commonwealth of Kentucky vs. Henry H. Denhardt, we will be seeking the death penalty."

With that, the jury selection process began. Tobacco planting season was right around the corner in Kentucky, so it took a few days to get enough reluctant, sunburned men to forgo their fields long enough to impanel the jury of eleven tobacco farmers and one filling station operator (not Browning). For spectators, the parade of potential jurors was more of a casual affair. Women brought knitting and mothers brought babies. After debate and deliberation, the twelve jurors were chosen and sworn in by 6:30 p.m., Thursday, April 22, but they were expected back early the next morning before the trial started for preparation. The jury consisted of Newton Price, Joe Henderson, Levi Thurman, Pryor Martin, James Bryant, Richard Adcock, Carl Chilton, Lefron Ransdell, Linden Cofer, Martin Hall, Wesley Hall, and Urban Hames. Only 168 days after shooting Verna on SR 22, Denhardt was facing the electric chair.

But Denhardt was no common killer. As a former prosecutor, county judge, and defense attorney, he knew how little it took to create reasonable doubt—and how much more vexing *unreasonable* doubt could be to a jury. As a soldier and a field commander, Denhardt could simultaneously attack and think dimensionally, to move forward and watch his flank, to make quick decisions on his feet that would take concentrated premeditation in a less-experienced man. As a lifelong politician, Denhardt was skilled at garnering support from others, even while he had only his own best interests at heart. Starting the next morning, the prosecution was going to try to build a cage around him, without knowing that Denhardt had escape hatches in place long before Verna's blood dried.

Anticipating that April 23 would be the day that testimony would begin, the line for the gallery formed extra early that beautiful spring morning. The people who got a seat took no chances that they would lose it during a recess, so a basket and rope system was improvised to send drinks and food from the lawn up to the gallery.

"Well, gentlemen, let's call the case of 'Commonwealth against Denhardt,'" Judge Marshall said, and the court quickly came to order.

Kinsolving laid out the framework of the prosecution's case.

"May it please the court and you gentlemen of the jury, ordinarily in the trial of a case such as this one, where there will be a number of witnesses introduced, possibly over a period of some days, in order to be better enabled to understand the proof and purposes for which it is offered at the time a witness takes the stand, it is usually proper and necessary for you gentlemen to have a short résumé, so to speak, of the evidence upon which the Commonwealth proposes to rely for a conviction in the case."

Kinsolving proceeded to describe Verna Garr Taylor, as:

> a woman of unusual ability, unusual personality, a friendly, vivacious, lovable and companionable person, not given to melancholia or moods, going from depression to one of exhilaration, or anything of the kind; but that her temper and her demeanor and her character and her personality were more or less those of a normal, enthusiastic, companionable, lovable person, and that she endeared herself to everybody who knew her in the community where she lived and those with whom she came in contact.

His biography of Verna transitioned into the many ways that she had been investing in the business, planning a future, and enjoying her daughters and the thought of marriages and grandchildren to come. Kinsolving went through the arc of her day, from the girls at breakfast to Denhardt's arrival, Mildred's errand, the stop at the laundry, the flue maintenance, the uneventful trip to KMI, the flat tire, and the cancellation of lunch and bridge. The afternoon errands were then covered: the Walgreens lunch, the business follow-up, and the chance meeting with

Ballard Clarke. Kinsolving pre-sold the testimony of Browning, the Bakers, Hundley, Shaver, Keightley, Ricketts, and more. Some big promises were made by Kinsolving with regard to the forensic evidence, like the paraffin wax tests, the "sparkograph photography" of the backward dispersal of the burned gunpowder, the FBI's participation, the blood tests, and so much more. Kinsolving spoke at such length and in so much detail that he was frequently interrupted by objections from the defense on the grounds that Kinsolving was attempting to put details into the minds of the jury without anybody having testified to them yet.

He concluded, "And when you gentlemen have heard the evidence in this case we believe, and confidently, that that will be your conclusion and that your punishment will be meted out justly under the proof as it is given you."

Judge Marshall asked the defense if it wished to state its case at this time, and Myers said, "No, sir. We reserve the statement." With that, the Commonwealth called its first witness, Roy Stewart, the boiler specialist with the L&N Railroad who had consulted with Verna at the laundry on November 5, 1936, the night before she died. Verna's disposition was as cheerful as it ever was, Stewart told the jury.

The newly minted Mrs. Allen Brown, Verna's recently married daughter Mary Pryor, was next on the stand. She was with Verna the morning of November 6, when she and her sister had breakfast with their mother for the last time. When Denhardt had come to pick her up, "Mother left the house that day just as happy as she could be," Mary Pryor said in her soft, slow drawl. "Mother has never been known to be moody, morose, or melancholy."

Kinsolving pressed Mary Pryor on whether at any time recently before her mother's death there had been any disagreements or fusses between her mother and the general. "Yes, there were," Mary Pryor said before the defense objected. She later continued, "I was in the next room. It was on a Sunday night. I could tell from the tone of voices that there was an argument. In fact, there was a great deal of storming around in the room on the part of General Denhardt, which I heard. Then I heard my mother say, 'Well, you can leave.'"

Mary Pryor also said that she was never sure if her mother was actually engaged, but that she often wore the ring around the house.

On cross-examination, defense lawyer Otte seemed to congratulate Mary Pryor on her marriage, but then pointed out how unusual it was that her new husband was just nineteen and that they got married so fast after her mother's death. "Mrs. Brown, did your mother oppose your marriage to Mr. Brown because he was so much younger than you?"

"She did not," Mary Pryor refuted. "In fact, she had been planning our marriage."

On redirect, Kinsolving asked whether any member of her household objected to her mother's marriage to General Denhardt, but the defense objected to the question, and the judge sustained it.

Frances also testified that her mother was her usual happy self that morning, but she also testified that when she spoke with her mother on the phone at around 6:15 p.m., Verna had said she had a headache and could not chaperone the dance. She said that sometimes her mom had headaches but not more than every couple of weeks. In cross-examination, the curious subject of whether Verna kept some of the general's clothes in their house was raised. Frances knew nothing about it. On redirect, Kinsolving established that some clothes had been dry cleaned in Louisville, and sometimes they were dropped off at their house, not the laundry.

After establishing Verna's typical, sunny mood was as stable as ever the week of—and the morning of—her death, Kinsolving began to chart the rest of the encounters Verna had that day. After Denhardt picked Verna up to go into Louisville, there was Mildred Connell, then Mrs. D.F. Lee of Ivanhoe Court, Mr. Gorman from the bank, J. Ballard Clarke, Barney Browning, Mr. and Mrs. George Baker, the Carpenter brothers, lead-footed driver Bernard Shephard and his wife, Hundley, and Shaver. Baker's comment that "Mr. Denhardt could not have killed that woman because I was with him when the last shot was fired" became officially part of the record from his own lips, despite the best efforts of the prosecution to contextualize it.

La Grange residents Charles Powell and his son, Roy, friends of Denhardt's, were called by the prosecution to testify about Denhardt's ownership of a pen pistol. On a visit to the Denhardt farm last summer, the general bragged about owning a small, pen-shaped pistol in his collection of firearms. Charlie said, "He just said he had this gun, had a fountain pen gun, and I made the remark, 'What was it for?' or something like that. And he said, 'In case of emergencies,' see, something like that. Said, 'Shoot a man,' or something like that. That's the way I understood it."

Ballard Clarke for the prosecution stressed, "Said he had a fountain pen gun that was used in case of emergencies?"

"Yes, sir," said Charlie Powell.

"Did he demonstrate how to use it?"

"No, sir," but then Charlie clarified. "He said, 'when you are close on the person,' see. That's the way I understand it. That other person wouldn't know what it was for, see, he'd think you was after your pen or something."

"About what time was this, that you had this conversation?" Clarke asked.

"That was summer last year." Charlie was certain of that.

"The summer of 1936?"

"Yes, sir."

Otte objected, and Judge Marshall sustained, and Otte insisted that the elder Powell's testimony be stricken from the record as immaterial with no connection to this case whatsoever. Son Roy's similar testimony was also stricken from the record, and the jury was admonished not to consider it. The only portion of either witness testimony that was allowed to remain was "I heard Denhardt say he had a fountain pen pistol."

Over all, the defense never denied that Denhardt owned a pen pistol, and frankly, as hated as Denhardt was throughout Kentucky, who could blame him? For his pugnacious use of force to end labor disputes with steelworkers and coalminers, Denhardt was the subject of standing vendettas in several Kentucky counties, not to mention again he'd already been shot once in his hometown just for being an ass. A tenant farm landlord and a rich retiree like Denhardt might have also felt like a target simply because it was the Depression, an often violent era of haves and have-nots. Highway robberies happened along desolate country roads that Denhardt traveled all the time—even SR 22. Chances were if somebody had a nice car, they had money to steal. Denhardt's Chevrolet Master Sedan was one of the top-selling luxury cars of that era. An old service revolver in his glove compartment and a pen pistol in his vest might have felt like necessary accoutrement for a man of leisure who still had to keep one eye out for trouble.

Next, Sheriff Walter Briggs of Oldham County was called to the stand, and everybody wondered whether Roy Garr would be next. Briggs testified that he, Sheriff Harrod, and Deputy Stivers went to the site where the body was found on the morning of November 7 and found twenty or so heel indentations in the soft ground next to the road metal. He said those impressions appeared to come from Verna's shoe heels. Briggs said the area where they were found was about three feet wide. Jack had been out there already, too.

Roy himself, then, did indeed follow the sheriff to the stand, one of the few times Roy ever spoke about Verna's death in public. For the press, this meant they were about to get more than just a statement from a Garr family member. It's not that the Garr Boys were not considered neighborly, by the way, they just were not media-friendly. They were hardly anti-social. According to the press reports of the time, they knew everybody, but they kept to themselves. Their grief for Verna was private. Their efforts to see justice done were not for public discussion. They had a lot to say—they just didn't say it out loud to strangers. The Garrs, by nature, did not seek the limelight.

There would come a time when the Garr Boys would need to warm up to the press and one female reporter in particular, but when it came to Denhardt's trial, they preferred to trust in the law. Speaking for the family, Roy had said to the press recently, "We all feel pretty bad, of course, but it's got to be straightened out. If everyone who gets on to that witness chair will only tell the truth, it'll get straightened out somehow."

One public statement all three Garr brothers made every day was the simple act of sitting with Mary Pryor and Frances in the front row behind the prosecution, directly across from Denhardt. Sometimes, Doc would go sit by himself in one of the window seats. The Garr Boys spoke little to each other in court, though. Reporters watching Doc, Roy, or Jack long enough might have seen one of them exchange a glance to the others or communicate through barely noticeable coded gestures characteristic of people inseparable since childhood.

In court, the Garr Boys never stopped staring at Denhardt. They took bathroom breaks in relays so that there was always at least one of them staring at the general. During the trial recesses, the Garr Boys went around town together and were content to spend time with each other's families on the weekends, as well. As willing as the brothers were to talk socially in public on the streets of New Castle, photographers knew better than to ask the Garr Boys to pose for photographs.

Readers were so interested in what the quiet Garr Boys had to say, though, one trial reporter from the *other* Bowling Green newspaper (the one the Denhardts *did not* own) made notes as to how each of them sounded when they talked. Since being shell-shocked in the Great War, Doc, the oldest, spoke softly. The reporter described Doc as "firm-mouthed and sallow of complexion." Jack, the youngest, pale with rosy cheeks, was "chunkily built who spoke with a slight impediment." Roy, the middle brother, was put as more rugged, bigger framed than the other two, with a distinct Kentucky drawl.

The court went silent when Roy was sworn in as a witness.

Ballard Clarke led the direct examination.

"Mr. Garr, you live in La Grange?"

"Yes, sir."

"How long have you lived in that community?"

"About twenty-three years."

"What is your business?"

"I am a farmer."

"Are you in any other line of business?" Clarke asked.

"I handle bird dogs, yes, sir."

"How did you locate the spot where Verna's body was found?"

"Well, Jack and I went up there, and he knew where it was found. He had been up there previously."

After some objections to his testimony, Roy was allowed to answer Clarke's question about what he found in the soft ground.

"Well, they were heel marks there."

"About how many?"

"Well." Roy thought for a second. "There was five or six—five or six double heel marks."

"How were they related to each other?" Clarke asked.

"Well, each pair were apparently even, you know, and they looked like they had stepped back about a foot each time."

There was a lot of haggling between the prosecution and the defense on Roy's testimony. Roy described a much larger area where the heel prints were found than Briggs did, and he got in a lot of testimony from a "common experience" about the nature of the shoe prints as opposed to an expert opinion.

Unable to answer Clarke's questions clearly, Roy stood up and displayed the fearful reverse steps of a woman backing up on just her heels in the pattern of somebody retreating from a menace. As he narrated, Roy was careful to point out the position and spacing of the shoe prints that he and the sheriff observed, but his body language illustrated the prosecution's theory of an aggressive Denhardt. It was a very visual, dramatic moment that drove the defense lawyers crazy. Judge Marshall overruled the defense's objections.

Undertaker and Garr family friend Smith Keightley was called to the stand and sworn in next. Kinsolving went over all the key points in Keightley's role that night. The defense objected to Keightley's characterization that "Denhardt seemed weary and nervous," but he was allowed to talk about Denhardt's concern for what the attitude of the Garr Boys would be toward finding their dead sister in his presence. Keightly reaffirmed his examination trial testimony that Denhardt spoke freely about his heroic role in wrestling his gun away from her when she threatened to kill herself. Denhardt said they had argued and she had talked that afternoon of giving back the ring. Keightley also testified in detail about how Keightley himself washed her body and washed around where the bullet entered Verna's body. "There was a slight dark discoloration around the wound, and this wet sponge and soap immediately cleared that up around that point."

To the naked eye, Keightley said there were no signs of carbon residue in the wound and no signs of scorching on her clothing.

Over an objection from the defense that Verna's clothing had zero substantive probative value but would only be inflammatory, with the court's permission, the prosecution removed from a drab tan leather satchel various physical exhibits, such as Denhardt's service revolver, the defendant's overcoat, and all of the clothing worn by Verna the night of her death. A bullet hole and bloodstain was visible under the left breast of the slip and on the back. Mary Pryor and Francis gripped each other tightly, but neither the girls nor any of the Garr Boys sitting nearby shrunk from seeing the exhibits. Kinsolving asked Keightley whether he could identify each article of clothing.

"Mr. Keightley, I will ask you to examine this black crepe dress and tell the jury whether or not that is the dress worn by Mrs. Verna Garr Taylor when you found her body on the road and took it to your undertaking establishment?"

"Yes, sir, this is the dress," Keightley said.

The dress was then put into evidence. In succession, everything that Verna was wearing was given to Keightley to examine, shown to the jury, and then put into evidence. Seeing Verna's last coat, black dress, black toque hat, pink satin slip, silk "step-ins," and her opera slippers displayed to the jury and the court gallery took an excruciatingly long time for the family.

In cross-examination, however, Keightley's testimony proved less valuable. Under pressure from Myers, he had to admit he had very little experience with powder burns and could not tell on his own whether marks around the wound had been caused by burned or unburned gunpowder. His recollections about his conversations with Denhardt drew blood, perhaps, but otherwise his testimony was a wash for the prosecution.

The spring day that had started with blue skies and chirping birds in the open courthouse windows had turned ominous as the afternoon progressed. The horizon was hardening into a solid dark jade front, and it was moving their way.

Coroner Ricketts followed Keightley, both chronologically and thematically. Ricketts put Denhardt's gun into evidence as the "heavy army gun" he collected at the scene, talked about the chain of evidence, recapitulated some key points from previous testimony, and talked about being the first one to find the inner thigh bruise on Verna. He confirmed that washing the body likely removed important evidence of discoloration around Verna's gunshot wound. He also told the story about fetching Denhardt's overcoat from his estate the following Monday and how Denhardt and said to him, "Ricketts, don't let any one put blood on this coat. There isn't any on it now." Ricketts told of the entire group bringing the coat outside.

"Was there any blood on that coat at that time?" Kinsolving questioned.

"There was," Ricketts proclaimed.

When asked if he could demonstrate where it was, Ricketts said, "I can show you better standing up."

After an objection, however, the judge agreed with the defense that Ricketts was not qualified to determine that it was blood on the coat or its origin. The prosecution then agreed to not use the word "blood" but to refer to what Ricketts and the others saw as "spots." Problem was, no matter how many times Kinsolving attempted to correct him, Ricketts kept saying "blood" instead of "spots." He did not appear to understand the legal distinction.

When Judge Marshall stepped in to try to sort out the confusion, he said to Ricketts, "Well, now, Mr. Ricketts, you are not an expert as to blood."

"Well, blood spots!" Ricketts fired back.

This drew a large laugh from the gallery and an admonishment from the judge that the people present were not being solemn enough considering that a man's life was at stake: "I again tell you that is not an exhibition, nor is it being conducted for your entertainment or amusement." Judge Marshall threatened to clear the whole court again if anybody laughed. "Hear this," he told the crowd, "you'd better keep quiet."

But who couldn't laugh when, right in the middle of cross-examination a little while later, Ricketts just suddenly stood up straight from the witness chair?

"What do you want to do now?" asked Otte, confused.

"What do I want to do?" said Ricketts, standing in the witness box.

"Yes."

"I just got up to rest," Ricketts said.

"I thought you wanted to look at the coat again," said Otte.

"I will if you want me to to."

"No."

It had been only a decent start for the prosecution, it seemed. In cross-examination, the defense had tarnished Ricketts' testimony about the blood on the coat, which ones were spots, drops, drips, and smears, and how the evidence in general may have been mishandled. In the minds of the jurors, there was blood on the general's coat until further notice, but it just was not clear yet whether it was Verna's or not. Deputy Renakar had confirmed major parts of the story as testified, including explanations of the "the spots that could have been blood."

Over the next hour, thunder provided a low rumbling backdrop to the testimony of Dr. Blaydes, who established details of the autopsy and the "ballooning" effect of the skin around a wound from the gas expelled by the exploding bullet. Blaydes explained how ballooning outside the wound and inside the wound is different, how the latter can happen only when the weapon is close, six to nine inches, and how he found no particles inside the wound. He was adamant, based on all that he saw, that Verna's was not a "point of contact" gunshot.

In cross-examination, however, Berry brought up Dr. Blaydes testimony at the examining trial and how he equivocated on whether there was evidence of carbon deposits under the skin, just inside the wound. The doctor attempt to rehabilitate that answer by explaining he was confused at the time and had since had a chance to research the effect of formaldehyde on tissues. For those new to the concepts of forensic crime science in 1937, it all must have come off as very tentative.

At the end, Berry even got a little rough with Dr. Blaydes.

"Doctor, I will ask you if, at the autopsy or post-mortem, you took out a part of the outer layers of the skin?"

"I did."

The thunder was no longer incidental. A major thunderstorm was now centered just over the metal roof of the Henry County Court-house, the rumbling so loud it was becoming increasingly difficult to hear the witness.

"Around the point of entrance of that bullet on Mrs. Taylor's body and had them sent to Dr. A. J. Miller of the Louisville City Hospital for microscopic examination?

Dr. Blaydes seemed defensive as he drifted quiet saying. "I wasn't certain about the character of the staining..."

"Answer the question, Doctor," directed the judge.

"I cut those out and gave them to Mr. Messmer to be examined microscopically."

"*You* didn't examine them, did you, Doctor?"

"Only ocularly."

"You made your testimony on the examining trial from the examination you have made at the autopsy?"

"What I knew about it at the time," stammered Dr. Blaydes.

Berry moved closer. "And since that time, you have made no further examination or analysis of the evidence?"

"No" he said weakly. "But I read the report of Mr. Messmer—"

The judge stopped the cross-examination right there with, "That is an incompetent answer."

In just a few minutes, the dark green skies had turned black, and the lightening and the rain scattered the Kentuckians on the lawn who were still trying to catch every word inside. A half hour later, court would have recessed for the weekend anyway, but now the court windows were slammed shut as the brick courthouse shuddered from the storm. Large hail rat-tat-tatted the floor to ceiling windows. The tin roof of the Henry County Courthouse sounded like it was getting pelted by flying dumptruck gravel. Not only was it already late in the day, but suddenly it was also almost impossible to hear anything other than the pounding hail. The judge asked each side how many days they would still need to present their case, and each answered "two to three." Judge Marshall sent flood-skittish Kentuckians home early, and the trial was adjourned until Monday morning at 9 a.m.

The unrelenting winds of that storm damaged New Castle trees and property, but the big damage to the Commonwealth's case so far was getting a prosecution witness to state, "Denhardt couldn't have done it because I was with him when the second shot was fired" and for Dr. Blaydes to appear un-authoritative.

Their biggest challenge was yet to come, however. There were two spent cartridges in the Denhardt's .45 service revolver. There were two shots fired. There was only one gun found at the scene and one hole in Verna's body. George Baker had never wavered in testifying that the two shots sounded completely different, that the second "pop shot" sounded like a .22, not a muffled "man stopper," but the explanation for how "2+2 = murder" was not intuitive. The prosecution would have the weekend to regroup and to establish definitively how they would explain to the jury how Verna could not have fired that gun.

As the *Chicago Tribune* described on April 23, when the bulk of the trial started, the general had "his arm draped over the top of his broad bald head, lolling back in his chair... seeming unperturbed at the ordeal he must meet." At the end of day two, his easy smile bordered on smug. Denhardt knew his big scene was coming soon, and while the prosecution tried to make their complex case simpler, Denhardt would have the weekend to rehearse his tears.

Chapter Thirteen

If the gods seemed as if they were trying to drown out the prosecution on Friday, Monday's clear skies signaled better fortunes. Dr. Walsh, the younger of the two doctors who performed the autopsy, did everything right. Dr. Blaydes might have come off as doddering or ill-prepared, but Walsh picked up his fumble and started running with it. Walsh realigned the significance of previous testimony about Verna's wounds but reemphasized that Denhardt's gun was held too far away from Verna's body at an angle for her to have created that wound pattern herself. The skin from Verna's left breast entrance wound and some of the results from the "test hog" clarified for the jury the issue of hot gas expelled from the end of the gun and the resulting ballooning effect in and around a bullet hole.

Ballistics expert Clyde T. Erwin, from the Peters Cartridge Company of King's Mill, Ohio, showed the jury a series of "sparkographs," or black and white shadow images of Denhardt's revolver firing in "slow-motion." The sparkographs illustrated the backward dispersion of the gunpowder of a .45 Smith & Wesson M1917 service revolver and why this pattern was visible in Denhardt's paraffin wax test. Erwin was a gunpowder expert who, nonetheless, got side-railed in cross-examination about the difference between the gunpowder composition in the .45 caliber cartridges in Denhardt's gun and the grains they used in the .45 caliber cartridges for the test. Both .45 shells were made by Remington, but the *exact* cartridge model is no longer available—the general had an old box. They were identical as far as Remington was concerned, but not acceptable per the defense.

In chambers, the defense successfully fought to keep out the opinion of crime lab expert Dr. A.J. Miller who had concluded the service revolver could have been no closer than eighteen inches, not nine inches.

Sergeant Messmer told the story of the paraffin wax tests that had been performed on both Verna and Denhardt, how the tests were negative for the former having fired a weapon and positive for the latter. F.C. Buckmaster, a Pittsburgh chemist, backed up Messmer by explaining how the nitrate patterns showed Denhardt had definitely used a gun like his own revolver around the time that Verna was shot. In cross-examination, however, Buckmaster was asked to read an FBI bulletin that had been issued in October of 1935, which warned that paraffin wax tests were of limited value. On redirect, Buckmaster explained that while J. Edgar Hoover was right in being concerned by paraffin tests in 1935, the science had improved quickly since then and were considered much more reliable just a year later.

In response to that FBI memo, Kinsolving called Smith Keightley's wife to the stand to relate an experiment that was done with her and Denhardt's gun on April 20. After firing Denhardt's pistol twice into the ground, Mrs. Keightly's hands were washed with the same soap solution that her husband's funeral home used to prepare Verna. Then, paraffin wax molds of her hands were taken and sent to Messmer for analysis. Despite the washing, Messmer found traces of nitrates near Keightley's wife's knuckles, proving that just washing Verna's hands in preparation for burial would not have removed the evidence.

Although Kinsolving allowed the question of paraffin wax reliability to stand on its own, it should be noted that the FBI actually was most concerned that nitrate tests did not always pick up the presence of spent gunpowder on the hands of people who had been observed to have fired a weapon. There were *zero times* in the FBI tests where nitrates appeared on people who had not fired weapons; rather, sometimes the wax failed to pick it up in people who had. The other concern was that people who fired a weapon and then washed their hands with vinegar would test negative for nitrates. This is why a paraffin wax test was not considered reliable when it came to suspects--it was mostly the fear of ruling out somebody who should *not* be ruled out more than the fear of falsely accusing somebody who had not fired a gun.

E.R. Donaldson, a serologist for the FBI in Washington, flew in by request from the Commonwealth to reiterate the significance of the blood evidence on Denhardt's coat and Verna's dress. Both samples were "group A" blood–40% of the population has this blood group–but it was true that it was impossible to tell if it was Verna's or Denhardt's blood or both because they were both of the same type. The defense asked the serologist about the amounts of blood that were tested, and he conceded that there was not much. In cross-examination, the serologist admitted that given the small amount of blood present, all the trickles and smudges on Denhardt's coat could have come from a cut finger or a shaving cut, of which the general may not have even been aware. When pressed further, the FBI lab man had to admit, yes, all of the specks of blood on Denhardt's coat could have been the general's. The court was reminded, of course, it was Denhardt himself who said to Ricketts when he confiscated his coat for testing, "Don't let any one put blood on it because there's none on it now."

Perhaps the best success the prosecution had with rehabilitating an important part of its case against Denhardt was the appearance of Clarence Roberts, an eighteen-year-old neighbor boy who testified that he was a frequent visitor at Denhardt's farm, owing to his association with Carl Cole, the son of a tenant of the general. At one point a few weeks before Verna's murder, Cole took his friend into Denhardt's living room to marvel at the collection of firearms the general had. It was there in Denhardt's home that Cole showed Clarence Roberts the general's pen pistol and even demonstrated how it was loaded and fired.

Shortly before Verna's death, Clarence Roberts said that he saw the pen pistol again, this time actually in Denhardt's vest pocket. Had the judge allowed the testimony of Charlie and Roy Powell to stand, Roberts' story might have been more effective.

The biggest disappointment for the prosecution had to be the failure of the scientific evidence to get any traction. Both Denhardt and Verna were of the same blood type, so it was impossible then to determine what was Verna's and what was Denhardt's. What was supposedly to be a "ta-da" moment for Kinsolving turned into a greased pig contest. Of the almost nine hundred pages in the court transcript, about four hundred of them have to do with the forensic evidence, most dealing with aspects of the gunshot tests. In the battle of experts, the best that could be said is that it was a draw, and when one is talking about sending a prominent citizen to the electric chair, a draw is a loss for the prosecution.

There were several witnesses over the first few days of the second week of the trial, and many more confusing moments about crime science sliced thinly as the prosecution and defense went back and forth on the strength of the Commonwealth's evidence and testimony. According to the press, public opinion seemed to reflect pre-held beliefs. If you thought the general was guilty going into the trial, you likely remained convinced based on all the crazy things he'd said, but if you thought he was the victim of a political witch hunt, then the criminal science testimony just sounded like so much techno-voodoo contrived to put an innocent man to death.

In *The Louisville Times*, Jane Dixon's chronicle read,

> The experts are testifying, and expert testimony always is something to make strong men moan and weak men babble into their beards. Expert No. 1 spends hours proving how expert he is and just when we begin to believe he does know everything about whatever it is he has on the fire, along comes Expert No. 2 on the other side and spends an equal number of hours making a monkey out of Expert No. 1.

When Kinsolving finally rested the Commonwealth's case against Denhardt on April 28, 1937, the prosecutor honestly felt he had fulfilled his stated objectives of proving beyond a reasonable doubt that Verna Garr Taylor had intended to break off her engagement, that Denhardt had fired a gun, that the victim had not fired one, that she was shot while retreating from a threat, and that Denhardt had the victim's blood on him, even though he claimed he had come nowhere near the body. Unfortuantely, Kinsolving might have been the only one that felt there was no reasonable doubt about executing a man based on this case.

In the judge's chambers, based on his belief that the prosecution had not met its burden of proof, Myers called for a directed verdict of "not guilty." Usually, it's a motion that is quickly dismissed without much deliberation, but Judge Marshall gave it some serious thought before denying it. The gallery had to wonder, though, whether the prosecution's case was so weak it would not be worth the risk to put Denhardt on the witness stand.

The trial continued on April 29, a morning of recalled witnesses to start the defense. Myers and Berry chipped away at some finer points of Kinsolving's case but also set the stage for Denhardt's testimony by recalling J. Ballard Clarke, the special counsel for the prosecution, and Roy Garr. It seemed the sole purpose of Berry's re-cross-examination of Clarke was just to get him to say, Verna "told me she had a very bad headache."

When Myers recalled Roy to the stand, the line of questioning may have seemed irrelevant, but its purpose was clear: further attack Verna through implication.

Myers began, "Mr. Garr, what are the initials of your brother who goes by the name of 'Doctor'?"

"Dr. E.S. Garr," replied Roy.

"How old is he?"

"Well, I think forty-seven, I think. Or forty-six. Forty-seven."

"He is six or seven years older than your sister, Mrs. Taylor?"

"I think he was, yes, sir," said Roy.

"Has he ever been confined in a private or public sanatarium for the treatment of mental derangement or disease?"

"Well," Roy began slowly with his Kentucky drawl, "he never was confined, I would say. He went to a sanatarium once that I know of for a nervous breakdown, a slight nervous breakdown."

"How long was he there that time?"

"Well, I just don't remember. Possibly two weeks or ten days? Or two weeks. I just don't remember for certain.

"Then did he have to go back again?" Myers asked.

"Well, this happened right after the war," Roy said. "He was in the war and he was shell-shocked and—"

"My question is, did he have to go back again?"

"Well, I think he did," Roy said. "I think he went back again for possibly a week."

"How long did he stay there that time?"

"I just don't remember, but possibly a week. I just don't remember," Roy said and then he was excused.

The cornerstone of Denhardt's defense had always been that Verna had spontaneously committed suicide, even while convincing her fiancé that she was just fine. To some degree, this plays off the sexist belief that women are emotional time bombs who are one bad day away from sticking their head in an oven. The defense's re-examination of Roy Garr was intended to kick it up a notch: The *whole family* was prone to mental illness.

On the morning of April 29, at 10:00 a.m., by mutual agreement be-tween the Commonwealth and the defense, the jury was escorted from the Henry County Courthouse to walk the death scene. Under close supervision and away from any sightseers who were prevented from coming near, the jury was shown the grounds themselves, encouraged to get a better idea about distances in the chain of events that ended in the killing Verna Garr Taylor. The jury was fed and back in the court-room by 1 p.m. in order for the defense to begin its case.

For starters, Myers waved his right to an opening statement. By all appearances, the defense was not impressed with the Commonwealth's case. In their cross-examinations and recalls of witnesses, none of Kin-solving's scientific evidence had gone unchallenged and much of the expert witness testimony had become confusing to anybody but other expert witnesses. When it was the defense's turn, Myers, Otte, and Berry had been rehearsing Denhardt's testimony with him. They knew they had a talented storyteller and the power of narrative on their side.

For years, scholars have studied just what it is about a great sto-ry—fiction or non-fiction—that seems to be so much more effective in communicating information than just a static recitation of facts. One aspect of these studies focuses on what is termed "transportation theory," and it explores the tripartite nature of a good story: attention, imagery, and feelings. When a story is told well, it holds the listen-ers' attention, stimulates the imagination, and conveys feelings. This in turn encourages the listeners to be absorbed into another world and see themselves as the characters in the story. The fastest way to trans-port people to your side of a cause is to tell them a great story that holds their attention with images and feelings. The simple difference may be that transportation theory explains why we put up walls to prevent others from imposing themselves on our world, while a good story brings us willingly into theirs.

Trials are long. Facts are facts. After so many expert witnesses and so much bickering, Denhardt's jury was probably ready for story time. As a former prosecutor, judge, defense lawyer, battlefield leader, pub-lisher, and politician, Denhardt understood the power of narrative to win others to his point of view by convincing them to relate to his experiences and emotions.

On Thursday afternoon, fresh from the jury's field trip, with thou-sands of people still hanging on every word from the courtroom and

Miss Bertha in attendance for the first time during the trial, the defense called Henry H. Denhardt.

The Garr Boys continued to stare at Denhardt as he took the oath on the Bible and sat down. Which story was he going to tell? Would he claim he had no idea why she committed suicide? Would he cruelly blame her death again on her grieving daughters? Would he concoct a new story entirely? Denhardt tried not to look at Mary Pryor and Frances, but whenever his curiosity got to him or his strolling lawyer put the Garr Boys in his line of sight, Doc, Roy, and Jack were ready to meet his gaze with focused relentlessness. Including cross-examination, Denhardt testified for three hours and seventeen minutes. Any time that he thought he might be talking himself out of prison and into a long happy life, though, all he had to do was glance over at the Garr Boys to be reminded that justice for Verna might never be decided by a court.

Following the lead of his attorneys, he told his life story but focused on his accomplishments rather than his childhood, growing up the son of a German cobbler. He studied hard enough to get into Ogden College and Cumberland University. He answered his country's call to service, came back, and finished his degree, and then went on to law school. His success was highlighted as the fulfillment of his sense of Kentucky pride and national duty. He talked about his war record and his rise in ranks and emphasized his time as a lieutenant governor and the head of the Kentucky National Guard, which he had helped organize.

Under the guidance of his attorney, Denhardt cherry-picked his résumé and presented himself as a loyal brother, a committed member of the community, and a romantic.

Denhardt shared his "this is how we fell in love" story about Verna, a folksy retelling within the bounds of Southern propriety. Doc had contacted Denhardt when he heard that he might be interested in a rental property in La Grange. The Garr family had one, and it ended up being Verna who gave Denhardt the tour of the house. Looking at it again, this time with Miss Bertha, Verna and Denhardt struck up a friendly conversation. Denhardt's courtesy call to turn down the property resulted in a porch visit, a drive in the car, and, soon, dinner at the Louisville Country Club. The friendship resulting in sweet letters going back and forth when Denhardt went on annual maneuvers and

Verna made a trip to see her sister in New York. He read several of those on the stand.

Their relationship had developed to the point that frequent letters were replaced by daily phone calls, even long distance check-ins when he was out of town to Bowling Green and Russellville.

"I wrote her one letter on that trip, which she received, and told me so afterwards. She said it was the sweetest letter she had ever gotten in her life, that she had taken it to bed with her at night and re-read it... and that she wanted always to keep it," Denhardt boasted.

According to Denhardt, after helping him pick out the ring (he said the setting was platinum), Denhardt proposed marriage, and Verna accepted on August 30. "It was definitely understood. There was no question about it." Per Denhardt, just seventy-eight days after he came to sit on her porch, he and Verna were engaged.

"After the engagement, General, did you continue to go to see her as often as she would let you come?" asked Myers.

"Well, I went to see her almost every day, either at the home or at the laundry. If I didn't have an opportunity of going at night, I would drive to the laundry in the daytime, and she would come out and talk to me. If I was out of town, I would telephone her."

"Now, after the engagement, did she and you make any plans about what you would do after you were married?"

"Yes, we did," Denhardt said confidently.

"What were they?"

"Well, we discussed where we would live. She, at first, opposed living in La Grange, and she said she wanted to get away. She preferred Shelbyville. I preferred Anchorage or PeWee Valley, but finally we determined to compromise and live on my farm in Oldham County. We first planned to build a house on the farm, a new house. The old one is quite old and needs a lot of repair... We both determined that we would remodel the old house and make it our home."

"Your sister was to have a separate apartment?"

"Well, yes, the wing where she now lives or where we did live," Denhardt said.

"When, General, was it understood by you and Mrs. Taylor that you would be married, or approximately when?"

"Well, I left that entirely with her. I wanted her to take time and be sure of herself, and I always told her that she would have to name the date, that I would not push her into it. I didn't want anything of that sort. When we first became engaged, she said, 'In the spring.' Of course, I didn't want to put it off that long, and I tried to persuade her, in a way, but always ended by saying that, 'I want you to fix the time.' Of her own volition and accord, she then moved it up to Christmas. Then later, she moved it to Thanksgiving. Then later, her sister was going to visit her from Missouri. I think she was due to come on the Monday after Mrs. Taylor died on Friday night. It was agreed by her or rather fixed by her as the date of our marriage was to take place either while her sister was here or immediately after she left."

Asked about Verna's other sister, Denhardt talked about his friendship with Juanita that had developed when they were always together during Juanita's last visit. The general testified that he had received a letter from her.

"In the testimony of Mrs. Brown, one of the daughters of Mrs. Taylor, she testified that on a Sunday several weeks prior to her death, that there was some argument there at the home on some Sunday night several weeks prior. She said you were storming. Was there any storming done there by you?"

"I don't recall any storming," Denhardt protested innocently.

"Was there an argument between you and Mrs. Taylor?"

"Mrs. Taylor and I had a little tilt. It wasn't any serious one, and it ended in a few minutes, and we separated as usual that night. There was no breaking off, and no one ordered me to leave the house. No one ever did order me to leave the house. I was a welcome guest."

Myers submitted a letter postmarked October 14 from Juanita that Denhardt had showed to Verna. Denhardt said that Verna "read it. She chided me a bit about my friendship for Juanita. I regarded it merely as—I didn't take it seriously at all. We did talk about it, and there was nothing to it. I didn't think it was any fuss or anything of that sort."

"Had Mrs. Taylor expressed any jealousy over Juanita before?"

"Oh, frequently, yes. She asked me not to be so friendly with Juanita and didn't like Juanita—well, Juanita was very vivacious, very talkative, a very fine woman, and we talked a good deal, and Verna didn't like for me to do that any great deal, but I regarded that as trivial, and it was not of a serious nature."

"Is that the only argument you and Mrs. Taylor had, if you would call that an argument?"

"Well, that is all of any consequence that I recall," Denhardt said dismissively. "She didn't want me to see my wife or telephone her when I went to Bowling Green, and I promised not to. I had always gone to see her. We were on friendly terms. She was always glad to see me and is now, and Mrs. Taylor understood that, and she didn't want me to do that, and I promised her not to."

The testimony then shifted to the evening of November 5, after Denhardt had returned from a day of business in Louisville.

"As I was driving into town, I saw the laundry truck come out from the laundry, from that street which leads to the laundry. Mrs. Taylor rolled down the window and said, 'Henry, what are you going to do? What are you doing?'" Verna was in the passenger seat. Chester Woolfolk was driving.

Denhardt promised, "I'm coming over to see you after a while," and she agreed.

Giving Verna some time to have her supper, Denhardt came over to find Verna in a highly distressed state.

"Mrs. Taylor was very nervous and and in an unhappy frame of mind. She talked for some bit, and she told me that Ches was jealous of me. I said, 'Jealous of me?' She said, 'Yes.' Well, I said, 'Why?' She said, "Well, he likes me." And she said he trembled like a leaf and got as pale as a sheet every time I came near or telephoned. That was surprising to me, and I so stated, and she said he had been acting queerly for several weeks and had worried a great deal. I said, 'Well, of course I know you don't care anything about him.' She said, 'No, except as a friend.' She liked the boy. He had been a faithful worker for her, had been very kind in his treatment of her, and she felt sorry for him. He had come over to the house occasionally and had played cards in the kitchen, and he would drive her to Louisville, and she used his car, but her feeling for him was only that of kindness as an elderly woman would feel toward a younger man. She told me he was just twenty-six-years-old. We talked of that a few minutes that night, not long. I didn't pay any serious attention to it. I thought nothing especially of it."

"In that conversation, General, did Mrs. Taylor happen to mention if she were showing the ring that day?"

"She said the girls in the laundry had, in some way, heard of the ring and that they had gotten after her that afternoon, asked her to show it to them. She said that she hadn't worn it at the laundry to any extent, if at all, and kept it pinned to her dress inside. They got after her, so she told me, and she took the ring out and showed it to them and stated that she had told them that we were about to be married. She said some of them, or at least one of them, cried, and the others were happy for her... [S]he said that she had not showed it to Ches, that Ches didn't see it, but that Ches had heard about it during the afternoon and that he had gotten serious about it. The conversation that night was more or less casual... We dropped the matter, and we had a pleasant evening together, and I left, as usual, with the usual greeting."

"What was that?"

"Well, Mrs. Taylor was a very religious, good woman. She went to church and taught a Sunday School class up until, I think, maybe she quit some months before... She had a wonderful influence over me and tried to help me in every way. I thought, and still think, and will always think, she was one of the best women I ever knew, and I loved her because she was so good. We never left at night without saying, 'God bless you,' and we always agreed to and did pray for each other, and we would, of course, express our love for each other, and we kissed goodnight."

As Denhardt continued his testimony, his timeline followed along previously attested lines. According to the general, however, Verna had decided pretty early that she did not want to lunch and play bridge with her best friend and cousin and left her short a fourth player.

"Mrs. Taylor told me she hadn't slept well the night before and that she had a very severe headache, one of her usual headaches that she had been suffering with... She was nervous and hadn't slept, so she said, and that was her condition. She said she didn't believe she could go, or would go, but she hadn't fully decided at that time."

Myers prodded. "Did you stop anywhere—stop at the Kentucky Military Institute on the way into town?"

"We did. We stopped there every Friday... She came out after some time and told me she had had some little matters to straighten up—shortages, claimed shortages—and it had taken a little longer. But she said, 'While I was in there I stood by the window and looked out, and I saw you walking around.' In that conversation, which extended down the road, she said she was deeply troubled, worried very greatly, because of the mistreatment accorded her the night before by Ches, that is was the first time he had ever mistreated her or been rude to her in any way, and it seemed to hurt her a great deal."

"Did she tell you what that mistreatment was over, General?"

"Well, about this ring, about my marrying Mrs. Taylor. He said he was not going to permit it... She talked on going down the road. She said she had always been kind to him, wanting to treat him as a good friend, that she felt that way, felt sorry for him in a way, and did not realize that he was so deeply in love with her until just weeks before when he had been showing his feelings or expressing his feelings... It was through no fault of hers that he fell in love with her, but he had, and was devotedly in love with her and very much wrought up over the fact that we were going to marry... and that's when he mistreated her."

"While you were having that conversation," Myers said encouragingly, "was anything said about the ring you had given her?"

"She said, 'Now, Henry, I haven't told you this because it meant nothing to me.' But, she said, 'He is acting so badly I don't know what he is going to do, and if this affects you any, I will give you your ring back.' I said, 'Of course, it doesn't affect me. I don't care how he feels toward you.' I asked her, 'Do you love me as you alway said you do?' She said, 'I certainly do.' I said, 'If you do, you keep the ring. We'll work out the Ches matter together. He isn't going to do anything, and I don't care what he does so long as you love me.' She insisted that she did. I said, 'Keep the ring.' And she did keep it."

In Denhardt's testimony, he went on to say that he begged Verna to go to her luncheon, but she refused. She had become instantly depressed, and he said, "I thought it would help relieve her feelings. She seemed pretty much depressed, and I thought it would help her to go and insisted that she go to the party... I got to the parking lot at the Pendennis Club, known as the Aetna Parking Lot, and we went and parked my car. She then, again, insisted that I go and telephone Mrs. Lee. I urged her again that she go, but she was firm in her decision not to go. It was late then, and I called attention to the fact that it might embarrass Mrs. Lee to break the bridge engagement at so late an hour, but she said she couldn't go, didn't feel like it, and just wouldn't go."

"General," demanded Myers, "did you try to keep Mrs. Taylor from going out to Mrs. Lee's, to that party?"

"I urged her to go to divert her mind from her fancied troubles."

"What had been her mental condition all the way into Louisville that morning?"

"Very depressed, very nervous, very much distraught over this Ches affair, over which she had no control and for which she was, in no way, responsible."

"After you called Mrs. Lee, did Mrs. Lee inquire from you how you were doing?"

"Mrs. Lee asked me how I felt, and I told Mrs. Lee I wasn't feeling well, either. That's about all—"

"Were you feeling badly that day?" Myers asked sympathetically.

"Well, I had just been over to Taylorsville on Wednesday, that snowy Wednesday, just the day after the election, and I had to drive through a snowstorm over there and contracted a cold and really wasn't well at all.

Denhardt testified that most of their talk was about Ches and how he had "misconstrued her kindness to him into feelings that she might be in love with him. She said she wasn't and had only been kind. She said nobody had ever said she was or suggested that she was except one lady." He talked about wanting to lunch at the Pendennis, but Verna refused to go. "She finally consented to go into Walgreens Drug Store. That is in the Seelbach. We went in there and sat in one of those little booths in there, and I had a sandwich or something, maybe two, but she wouldn't eat anything. She drank a cup of tea."

They went to the bank together but soon separated and agreed to meet up again at 4:30 at the Aetna Parking Lot. Denhardt got a shave and spent his time "loafing" and going to his various clubs and favorite hotel hang-outs.

Prompted by his attorney, Denhardt flashed back to earlier that morning to explain how Verna came to learn about the revolver in his glove compartment. While they had had a flat tire, Denhardt had been helping the garageman secure his punctured tire back in the trunk. When he returned to the front seat, Verna, who had gone fishing in his glovebox and found his gun, was toying with his pistol in her lap. Denhardt had explained that he had kept his pistol in his car because bad weather had prevented him from getting all the way up his almost mile-long driveway. He carried the pistol for protection for the long walk home every night.

"'What are you doing with the pistol, Verna?' She said, 'Well, I was just looking at it.' I said, 'You oughtn't to do that because I doubt you know anything about a gun,' and I put it away and locked the compartment. She said that sometimes she felt that she would kill herself. I said, 'That's foolish. You won't do it.' She said, 'I would if I had the courage of a distant relative who did shoot herself through the head. I would do the same thing. That's the way I feel now.' I dismissed it and told her she was joking, that it was a foolish remark to make and she didn't mean it, and I don't think she did mean it."

"Now, when you returned to the Aetna Parking Lot that Friday afternoon at 4:30 p.m., did you see Mrs. Taylor?"

"Well, when I approached the car, she was all plunked down in the car, just leaning up against the side of it, just in a thoroughly depressed state of mind. I talked to her and tried to cheer her up, tried to dispel whatever her mood or thoughts were, and we talked there for some bit."

Across Denhardt's timeline, he describes these long conversations that were taking place at all times, all focused on how horrible Verna felt about attracting the attention of Chester Woolfolk and how bad she felt about making Denhardt feel bad.

"Now, before you left Louisville," Myers asked, "did you have anybody to fix the spare tire that was flat on the back?"

"Yes, I purchased an inner tube after I got back to the car. I purchased an inner tube at a place just over there on Third Street, back of the club, and brought it over to this Aetna Parking place and took my car over to the little house where they repair tires and wash cars, and a Negro changed my tire for me—that is, put an inner tube in the tire that had been punctured."

"In order to unlock the trunk, did you take the key out of your car?"

"Oh, yes, I took my keys. The two of them were fastened together in a little leather case."

"Was anything said by Mrs. Taylor about that?"

"When I got back—I had walked back and unlocked the trunk—and when I walked back, she said, 'Henry, you don't have to do that. I'm not going to do anything.' I said, 'Of course, you are not. I hadn't a thought about it.' I told her I had to take the keys back there to unlock that trunk compartment, and we sat and talked while the tire was being changed.... She was in a very depressed state."

"While you were there talking with her, was your future marriage discussed?"

"We talked about, for some bit, about various things, and she said, 'Henry, let's go get married today!' And I said, 'Why, that wouldn't do.

We shouldn't do that. Anyhow, I haven't even a new suit of clothes to wear and then it would look foolish and funny for people as old as we are to suddenly marry without giving any special notice to anyone to attend.' We had agreed that Mrs. Lee was going to be one of the witnesses. We hadn't mentioned it to her, and I told her we had better wait. I told her it wouldn't be but a few days, anyhow, until her sister would come, and we could marry at that time. She said to me, 'Henry, if you don't marry me now, you don't intend to marry me.' I said, 'I intend to marry you. There is no question about my loving you. I will marry you...' I repeated that to her several times during the night when she would go over the fact that she didn't believe I would."

Denhardt's testimony revealed that it took ninety minutes to repair the inner tube, and by that time, Denhardt was hungry again. According to Denhardt, Verna refused to go to the Country Club or the Pendennis Club.

"We finally got to St. Matthews, and I said, 'Well, we must eat something.' She said she hadn't anything to eat all day except two cups of tea, one at breakfast and one at Walgreens, so I finally persuaded her to stop there at the Sada San Restaurant in St. Matthews to get something to eat."

"Now, before you went into the Sada San Restaurant, was anything said about taking a drink by anybody?" Myers led.

"Well, I was, as I told you, I had been sick most of the day and for several days. I had been aching and had a cold, and I said to her that I thought a drink would help me. I hadn't been doing that, on her account. I said, 'Now, I won't do it unless you consent.' She said, 'It's all right, you are entitled to one, and it might do you good, and I want you to have it.' So I said, 'Well, I'll have to go in and write a check. I haven't any cash with me.' She said, 'Don't do that. It's not necessary. I have a dollar here. A silver dollar, and I have been keeping that dollar for you.' She knew that I had a collection of old coins, and she was giving me this dollar for that collection, but she said she could get me another one, and she gave me that dollar! I went across the street to Bauer's place and bought half a pint of whiskey and took a drink. We went back to the Sada San Restaurant and went in, and she and I spent the other half-dollar for two lunches or dinners. We sat there and ate our lunch or dinner."

Denhardt then described how Verna was not in the mood to chaperone that night, her head hurt, so she reversed the telephone charges to her home. Her headache was terrible, but she got behind the wheel to drive them back to La Grange. She drove until she came to a spot on the side of the road where a farm had some milk cans in front, and they pulled over there.

"How long did you stay there?" Myers asked.

"Oh, I guess about fifteen minutes or half an hour. I don't know. I can't tell about the time very well."

"Did you have a conversation with her at that time?"

"Oh, yes," Denhardt recollected. "She told me that she would be dead in fifteen minutes after she got home, and I told her that that was foolish and that if she loved her children and her mother and me, as I knew she did, she would dismiss that foolish thought from her mind. We talked there for some time, and she finally dismissed it, except she said, 'If I do, I'm going to leave a note.' So, yeah, that was about all that happened. We sat there a good deal of time, saying nothing."

Finally getting back on the road, they had made it to La Grange but just before Verna would have turned left to go home, she suddenly went straight and said, "Let's go on up 22, take a little ride."

Myers needed clarity for the jury. "Who, if anyone, suggested not stopping in La Grange and driving up 22?"

"She did," the general said emphatically.

Denhardt's the one who takes credit for insisting it was time to turn the car around as they approached Browning's Filling Station. That's when the whole car just stopped. The lights went out, and it wouldn't work. Denhardt did not get up or go for help because "[s]he said I was sick, and she knew the people, or they knew her." He explained that he knew nothing of cars, had offered to pay for the help, and didn't feel the need to do any of the work. "When my car stops, I stop, for I haven't any knowledge of a car."

Denhardt said that, when Hundley offered to drive Verna to town, she refused.

"I asked Mrs. Taylor whether or not she wanted to go, and she said, 'No, let's wait out here...' I told Hundley that we would stay."

"While you were waiting for Hundley to return, was there any talk there between you?

"Well, Mrs. Taylor at that time made a suggestion that we both die together, and I remonstrated and told her, 'There's no reason in the world why you should die. You've got nothing to die for, and I don't un-

Verna Garr Taylor

GIRL LOSES LIFE IN HOTEL SHAFT

Coroner Delays Verdict As Body Found Atop Seelbach Elevator.

DEAD SEVERAL HOURS

Mrs. Patricia Wilson, 24, of 847 S. First, was found dead shortly before 8 a.m. Wednesday, lying atop a service elevator at the bottom of a shaft at the Seelbach Hotel.

Newspaper article describing the death of Mrs. Patricia Wilson, Louisville Courier-Journal, July 16, 1936.

The view of the tan elevator door in the distance from the omelette station, Oakroom Restaurant, Seelbach Hotel, 2015, where Patricia Wilson fell and was killed in 1936.

Fairview Cemetery, where Mrs. Patricia Wilson is buried in an unmarked grave, 2015. Next to her there is another anonymous woman, perhaps another prostitute.

I IAN AND THE OWNERS OF THE SEELBACH HOTEL PURCHASED A
HEADSTONE FOR PATRICIA WILSON - AFTER ALL THESE YEARS -

Verna Garr Taylor in happier times, ca. 1935, pictured in the latest bathing couture, form fitting tank top with an open back. Courtesy of Kentucky Historical Society.

Poster advertising Denhardt's efforts to organize the 3rd Kentucky Infantry during the ~~Spanish~~ BORDER
~~American~~ War, ca. 1916. WAR WITH PANCHO VILLA.

Henry H. Denhardt as adjutant general of the Commonwealth, 1935. Courtesy of the Kentucky Historical Society.

Browning's Filling Station on SR 22 between La Grange and New Castle, at the Sligo Road intersection.

A Chevrolet Master sedan similar to Denhardt's make and model parked in the same part of the Baker driveway.

Abandoned Baker farmhouse from the side porch, where Denhardt and Baker talked, 2015.

The Baker farmhouse, front, as it appears from the driveway today, abandoned, 2015.

The Faultless Pen Gun in stainless steel. It also came in the acid bathed blue-black, date unknown. Denhardt admitted to owning something like this.

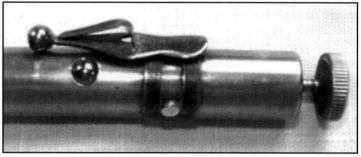

The plen clip is rotated to expose the ball bearing trigger, and the knob top is pulled back, coiling the spring. This pen pistol is ready to fire.

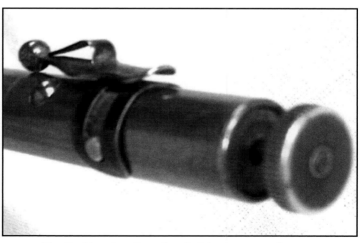

The Faultless Pen Gun, detail of the trigger mechanism.

View of SR 22 looking east toward the Sligo Road. Clearly visible after all these years is the road bed of the original highway to the right where people still drive their ATVs and tractors, 2015.

Verna Garr Taylor's murder pose was recreated often for newspapers and magazines, 1936.

Farmer George Baker demonstrates for the press the position and placement of Vern'as body, 1936.

THE GARR BROTHERS

Roy Garr, 1937

Jack Garr, 1937

Dr. E.S. "Doc" Garr, 1937, with the then still popular toothbrush mustache.

JACK, THE YOUNGEST BROTHER WHO INSISTED ON WALKING WITH HIS BROTHERS. THEY WOULD NOT ALLOW HIM TO SHOOT.
SUCH A SWEET PERSON, AND SO LOVED. WAS A RENOWN DOG TRAINER.

UGH. THEY THOUGHT THEY LOOKED SO DASHING IN THOSE AWFUL MUSTACHES...

ROY. THE MIDDLE BROTHER, WHO WAS IN CHARGE. ALSO A CELEBRATED DOG-TRAINER AROUND THE U.S. GOOD NATURED, WELL-RESPECTED.

STAUNTON, THE VETERINARIAN. "SHELL-SHOCKED" IN WWI. OLDEST BROTHER.

This unidentified photo from World War I inadvertently captured the image of the soldier in the lower left corner that some say typifies "the thousand yard stare" of shell shock.

Investigators near where Verna's body was found, looking westward on State Road 22 toward the Baker house and driveway, 1937. That flat area along the fence is what remained of the "Old 22" that ran parallel to the new road.

Photo with diagram of the death scene, November 1936. Verna's body was found where marked in the center left of the photo. Denhardt's car was parked in front of the Baker home, some 640 feet from where Verna lay. Courtesy of the Kentucky Historical Society.

Sgt. John Messmer and D.L. Ricketts, Henry County Coroner, 1937.

Historic downtown New Castle, Henry County seat, present day.

The home of Verna Garr Taylor, where a small, private memorial service was held.

Courtroom in Henry County Courthouse, present day. The wall to the left with the row of photos of past circuit judges was not there in 1936, allowing a much larger capacity for Coroner Ricketts' inquest into Verna Garr Taylor's death.

This is a .45 caliber cartridge for the M1917 Smith & Wesson service revolver. The lead bullet and the gun powder is inside the brass jacket. When the bullet is fired, the empty cartridge has to be removed by hand. A bullet just like this passed through Verna's heart, killing her almost instantly.

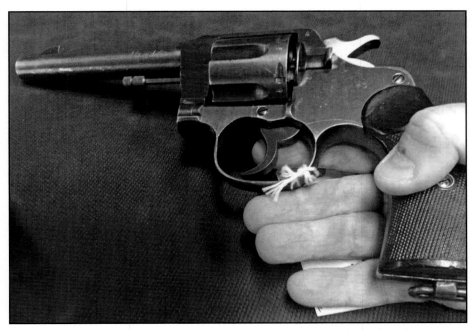

The Model 1917 service revolver was needed by the Pentagon in such numbers that the same gun was manufactured by both Smith & Wesson and Colt Manufacturing Co. The beauty of the design is the limited number of moving parts. There is no safety.

Historic downtown La Grange, Oldham County seat, present day.

MY MOTHER AND I TOOK THE "INTER-URBAN" CAR TO LAGRANGE
TO VISIT WITH AUNT MARY, VERNA'S MOTHER.
IT ALWAYS SEEMED SO STRANGE TO ME TO SEE TRAINS CHUGGING
DOWN THE MIDDLE OF MAIN STREET.

Verna's headstone in the Garr family portion of Valley of Rest Cemetery in La Grange, modern day, right next to Barclay Taylor forevermore.

Commonwealth Attorney James F. Thomas of Henry County, 1937.

Henry County Courthouse as it looked in 1937 and pretty much still looks today.

Defense attorney Rodes K. Myers arguing a point before Henry County Judge A.S. Morgan, November 1936. Courtesy of the Kentucky Historical Society.

Judge Morgan (left) in action, denying Denhardt counsel motions. Also pictured are (l-r) J. Ballard Clark actually holding his lapels like Southern lawyers do in movies, Overstreet, Thomas, and Myers, 1936.

Farmer George Baker, 1937

Denhardt is transferred to the Jefferson County Jail by Sheriff Evan Harrod (back) and an un-armed Kentucky State Trooper in front, Nov. 20, 1936.

Laundry employee, Chester Woolfolk, ca. 1937.

Aerial view of the West End of Louisville, January 27, 1937, when 70% of the city was under water. THE WEST END WAS WHERE I LIVED. I REMEMBER THE FLOOD VIVIDLY.

A photo that is both as iconic as it is ironic. The NAACP tried to make sure that Louisville's African-American community did not receive substandard relief efforts. Here, residents lined up for free food in the aftermath of the flood.

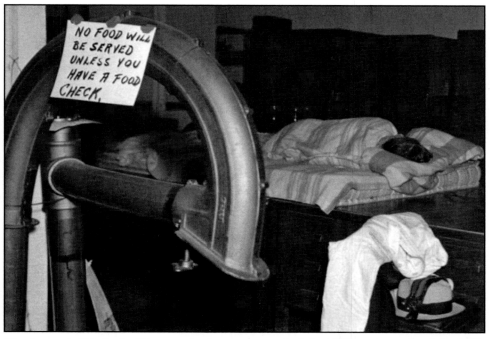

The sign reads, "No food will be served unless you have a food check." Governmental and charitable agencies stretched by the Depression struggled to meet the needs of 175,000 instant flood refugees.

By January 25, the flood waters and sewage back-up was rising so fast that even houses on knolls up from the street could only be reached by shallow-draft skiffs like this one.

WE LEFT IN A SMALL BOAT FROM OUR HOUSE ON A KNOLL. FLOOD WATER CAME INTO OUR BASEMENT, PUT OUT THE FURNACE, AND CREPT UP THE BASEMENT STAIRS, INTO OUR HOME.

After the flood waters receded, a horse that had been carried away by the Ohio River was found dead in a tree.

WPA workers were ordered by President Roosevelt to help with clearning the Louisville streets of sandbags, flood debris, sewage, and mud.

It was another full house, standing room only in the originally high-ceilinged Henry County courtroom, April 19, 1937.

Pictured l-r: Reporters Silliam O. Carver Jr., Hayden Moise Jr., and photographer Freddie Parker covering the Denhardt trial in the By Liner, a "motor trailer press-room" parked on the courthouse lawn, 1937.

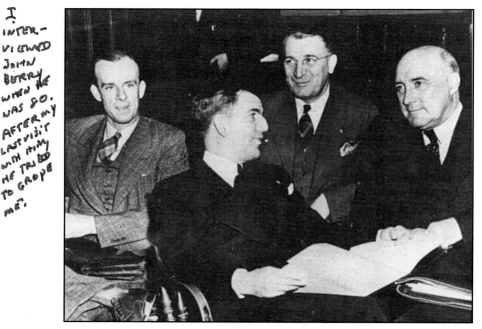

I INTER-VIEWED JOHN BERRY WHEN HE WAS 80. AFTER MY LAST VISIT WITH HIM HE TRIED TO GROPE ME?

Denhardt (at right) with members of his defense team, April 1937. Pictured l-r are John M. Berry, Rodes K. Myers and W. Clark Otte. Courtesy of the Kentucky Historical Society.

Wirt Turner, hired by Mary and Frances to help the prosecution, 1937.

New Castle lawyer and Garr family friend, J. Ballard Clark, 1937.

Large crowds gathered at the Henry County Courthouse, all vieing for a spot in the second floor courtroom. Courtesy of the Kentucky Historical Society.

Henry County court viewers hauling up some lunch from the lawn below where over 4,000 had gathered waiting for the last news, 1937.

Mrs. Taylor's Daughter Is Bride

LA GRANGE, Ky., Nov. 21 (Æ).— Miss Mary Pryor Taylor, 21-year-old daughter of Mrs. Verna Garr Taylor, who was found shot to death on Nov. 6, was married today at Shelbyville, Ky,. to Allen Hughes Brown, 22, of Jeffersonville, Ind.

The marriage was revealed by Mrs. Smith Keightley, friend of the Taylor family, who said the couple had been engaged for three years. Mr. Brown formerly lived in La Grange.

New York Times announcement of the wedding of Mary Pryor Taylor, Verna's daughter.

Frances Taylor, 17, and Mrs. Mary Pryor Brown, 22, Verna's daughters, bitterly resented Denhardt's claim that their mother had killed herself because of them, 1937. Both had dark blond hair. Other than Verna being brunette, many people remarked how much Mary Pryor favored Verna in appearance.

FRANCES AND HER AUNT JUANITA, VERNA'S SISTER, VISITED ME IN WINNETKA.

Denhardt as he appeared during the trial, April 1937. Courtesy of the Kentucky Historical Society.

I INTERVIEWED DENHARDTS NEPHEW IN THEIR HOMETOWN OF BOWLING GREEN, AND I SAW HIS GRAVE.

Denhardt holding the love letters from Verna he claimed supported his contention that she killed herself because of her feelings for him were so deep, April 29, 1937.

Members of the all-male jury consisting of eleven tobacco farmers and one filling station operator, walking out of the Henry County Courthouse on their way to visit the crime scene, April 29, 1937. Courtesy of the Kentucky Historical Society.

Verna's sister, Juanita, who visited often from Alford, NY, 1938.

MY MOTHER'S BEST FRIEND, JUANITA, VERNA'S SISTER. JUANITA STAYED WITH US OFTEN ON WEEKENDS WHILE I WAS GROWING UP. SHE WAS DELIGHTFUL! - AND SO BRIGHT. HER HUSBAND WAS DEAN OF THE SCHOOL OF CERAMICS AT ALFRED UNIVERSITY, NY.

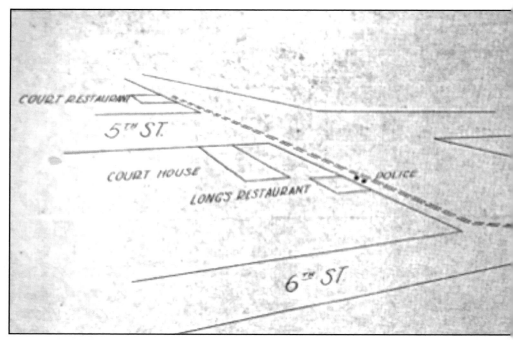

Graphic illustration of the path that Denhardt and Myers took coming back from the Court restaurant to the Armstrong Hotel. Dotted lines represent Denhardt's attempt to get to the hotel, and Myers escape up Main Street, 1937.

The body of Denhardt at the entrance to the Hotel Dining Room; a crowd watches in silence. Courtesy of the Kentucky Historical Society.

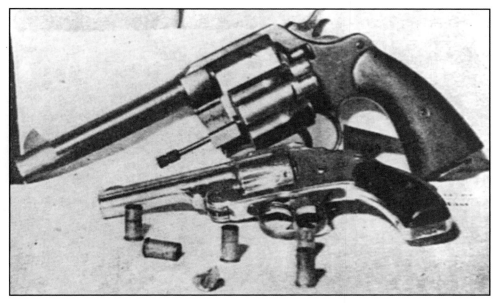

The actual guns that Doc and Roy used to kill Denhardt and many of the empty shells, 1937.

Harry Flood of the Armstrong Hotel posing with an unnamed Shelbyville bystander in recreating how Flood found the body of Denhardt, 1937.

Now unused and closed to the public, the original Shelby County Jail, right, where Doc, Roy and Jack were held in 1937, and the jailer's house, left, where the jailer and his family lived and prepared meals, 2015.

Now unused and closed to the public, the original Shelby County Jail cells where Doc, Roy and Jack were held in 1937, 2015.

The public viewing of Denhardt's body in the Bowling Green Armory, whether out of curiosity or grief, was well attended, 1937.

Denhardt's funeral was held in Bowling Green; three volleys fired by an honor guard concluded the funeral. Courtesy of the Kentucky Historical Society.

The Garr defense team, l-r: Gilbert, Doc, Clarke, Jack, Roy, and Todd. Notice the five o'clock shadow on the Garr Boys while they were being held in jail, 1937.

Autograph card for Miss Ohio 1955, Margie Garr. She signed with her proper name, Marguerite, named after her mother.

SUCH A DARLING GIRL! ~ ~~SO BOBBY~~ JACKIS DAUGHTER.
SHE & HER AUNT JUANITA CAME TO THE WEDDING ~ TEDS AND MINE.

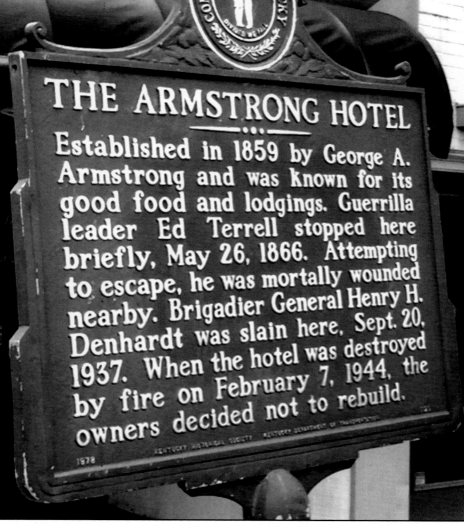

Historical marker, Main Street, Shelbyville, Ky., 2015.

derstand this talk, and as far as I am concerned, certainly I don't want to die, and you shouldn't want to die,'" Denhardt testified.

"And then she said, 'No, you don't deserve to die. You have been better to me than anybody in the world.' She said, 'This ring you gave me is the nicest thing I ever received in my life,' and she said, 'you, yourself, have been better to me than any person in the world.' She then kissed her ring then and reached over and put her arms around my neck and kissed me and said I was the best man that ever lived. That was her greeting, almost her last greeting to me. We sat there a short bit... ."

As Denhardt's words trembled and trailed off, those sitting closest to the witness stand thought they detected Denhardt's eyes misting up as the general thought about Verna's love for him as "the best man that ever lived." The room was quiet as Denhardt paused to collect himself. For a few seconds, all that could be heard was the passing traffic outside through the open windows and the general's gentle sniffles.

Then, according to several published reports, a raspy, guttural roar suddenly broke the silence of the room. Described by one writer in attendance as "a laugh so harsh and mirthless from the three Garr brothers on the front row bench" that it "chilled the spectators and stirred a sudden quaking in the general." And just as suddenly as the outburst started, it ceased as if on cue, leaving only the echo of the dark laugh in the high-ceilinged room. Through it all, the Garr Boys never stopped staring at Denhardt.

The defense table waited for an admonition from the bench, but none came. Judge Marshall may have thrown them a look, but no mention of it exists in the court record. Unlike the previous outbursts in the court, Judge Marshall said nothing. The prosecution certainly was not going to object. So, with the echo having evaporated up to the metal roof and the sound of the cars underneath the window back, on his own, unnerved, Denhardt pulled himself together and picked up where he left off.

"We sat there a short bit, and I talked to her and tried to persuade her out of any notion. She seemed much more cheerful and brighter, and I even suggested that we go on to the dance when we got to town and watch the children dance, and she said maybe she might. We sat there fifteen or twenty minutes, maybe, and in that, I thought I had quieted her. She seemed to be quieter after that little outburst of sentiment expressed to me, and I really thought she was in a good frame of mind, better than she had been all day."

Verna pressed Denhardt to check on the battery by asking the Bakers for a phone, and that's when Denhardt rolled out his latest edition of "what happened next."

Denhardt says that he approached Baker's side porch but got as far as the gate when he heard Verna say, "Henry! Henry!" So, Denhardt started on back. That's when Denhardt says that Baker came out, so he stopped right there, turned around, and asked for a phone. Denhardt insisted that even though Baker had already told the group by Browning's that the nearest phone was in Pendleton, he had not heard that. He also said that Baker was mistaken when he said that Denhardt came all the way up to the door. To reiterate, Denhardt called out "Verna! Verna!" but not loud enough for anybody else to hear. Just then, the Shepherds' car came flying around the bend and up the rise, slowed down, then took off down the highway. Shortly thereafter, the first shot rang out.

"Where were you, General, when that shot was fired?"

"I was at my car."

"When that shot was fired, what did you do?"

"Well, I—I felt that the worst had happened, and I was dazed at it and amazed and surprised. Immediately—after a second or two—I went toward Baker's house."

"As you approached Baker's house, did you see anybody?" Myers asked.

"Baker came out his door, his side door. I walked toward him, meeting him."

"Do you know where that walnut tree is located there in his yard?"

"I do. I saw it there this morning."

"Where did you meet?"

"Right there at that tree or close to it. Further in, I think, than the tree."

"While approaching each other, did anything happen?"

"We were pretty close together—we may have still been walking— but the second shot was fired," stated Denhardt explicitly.

"What was said by you or Mr. Baker as you met there after the second shot was fired?"

"Well, he said, 'Did you hear that shot?' I said, 'Yes, I did. Did you?' Speaking of the first shot. Then I said, 'Isn't it awful!' That was because I realized what happened, and it was the worst thing that ever happened in my whole life. I said, 'I'm afraid she has taken my gun and gone,' and in the meantime, I had looked in and found it had gone, and she had taken that gun."

Myers covered for his client, "You mean you walked back to your car?"

"Yes. He saw me and said so."

It was after they walked back to inspect Denhardt's car for the gun that the general also noticed that his keys and flashlight were both missing.

"When you didn't find your flashlight, what did you do or did Mr. Baker do or either of you say?"

"I asked Mr. Baker for a light. That is what I had started to his house for—to get help to help to go find Mrs. Taylor. I was afraid she had done what she had did—killed herself. I wanted a light, and I wanted help. I was there alone. That is what I asked him for, and he later did go and get a lantern."

Again, Myers attempted to help shore up his client by asking a prompting question. Denhardt had just said that he found that his flashlight and keys were missing after he and Baker had walked back to the car to confirm that the shot they had heard was from Denhardt's gun, which contradicted Denhardt previously saying that he knew he did not have a flashlight, so after the first shot, he went to go get a flashlight from Baker.

"You mean, when you went up after the first shot was fired, you were going to get a light?"

"I was going to get help," Denhardt said generically.

Denhardt's new time sequence deviated wildly from George and Nettie Baker's consistent testimony that the farmer did not come out until after Denhardt had disappeared back into the darkness looking for a phone, after the Shepherd's car had passed, and at least ten minutes after the first shot because, as Baker admitted, "I were scared." Then, the farmer slowly comes out, meets up with Denhardt by his car. On the walk over, he sees Denhardt still moving, partially blocked by the rear of the car when the second hollow shot goes off.

But Denhardt's new sworn version also contradicted Denhardt's *other* sworn testimony, the affidavit of January 16, 1937.

Here's how he described the event sequence then:

"[B]efore [Denhardt] reached Baker's home, Mrs. Taylor called for him to return, he then turned and started back, but when he reached the car, he found Mrs. Taylor had disappeared in the darkness; that at that time he called to her, but there was no answer to his call. That shortly thereafter he heard the first shot and after that was heard, he found that his revolver, which Mrs. Taylor knew was always in the glove compartment had also disappeared. Then, for the first time, affiant states that he felt the worst had happened. The second shot followed when affiant was in the presence of Mr. Baker; it was a muffled shot."

In sequence and substance, these two official, legally sworn versions of Denhardt's story (never mind the various unofficial versions suggested directly to the press or stated publicly) are irreconcilable in several key places. Certainly, whenever a prosecution witness varied at all in his or her testimony, Denhardt's legal team was unrelenting in its criticism, but for their own client, silence. But there is yet another version of Denhardt's story that his attorneys knew very well, a rambling, unpleasant narrative so full of sex and paranoia that if Myers and Berry had any integrity at all, it would have made the men seriously question the sanity of their client. It was all in "Folder 8."

CHAPTER FOURTEEN

According to the confidential letters in Berry's files, the Denhardt legal team deserves a lot of credit for keeping the real story of their client out of the press and out of the courts. For example, on February 15, 1937, Beckham Overstreet again was taking his case of non-payment from Denhardt for legal services rendered to Oldham Circuit Court. "No gentleman will stand to take the insults and the assaults that I have from you and continue as your counsel," Overstreet writes to Denhardt. He says that after several attempts at a settlement, he will give the general five days. When it comes to payment, though, Overstreet would have to get in line.

Just prior to that, Denhardt received an itemized statement from Berry listing "monies advanced and some expenses for which I feel I am entitled to reimbursement." Not only are the Denhardt lawyers not getting paid and not getting hard costs like phone bills covered, they also had been advancing him money! These men had made Denhardt a top priority in their law practices, but in return Denhardt is nickel-and-diming them financially.

On February 24, 1937, Overstreet filed his suit to recover wages in Oldham County. In his letter to Berry, with a copy of the suit, Overstreet backs off on the threat to totally spill the beans on Denhardt, but only for the time being. "You will observe that I have prepared this petition so as to conceal the threats against my life which General Denhardt has made thereby avoiding publicity and to avoid any injury or hurt to his case by reason of his personal violence toward me, because I am fearful if that fact came out it would substantially injure his case and I want you to know I am doing all that I can to withhold that from the public," Overstreet wrote.

That said, Overstreet does remind Berry that if he were put under oath, all bets would be off. Then he closes, "General Denhardt has been unfair to all of his attorneys and particularly myself, and this suit may be the cause of him being more fair and considerate of you and other counsel left in this case to defend him." It was a noble effort.

With a trial date coming after the flood waters receded, Denhardt's legal team may have had bigger concerns. Perhaps Myers and Berry would have been more concerned with their client's mental state in regard to his upcoming testimony if they had read "Folder 8," a thirty-three-page pre-trial witness statement narrated by Denhardt. Folder 8 was a strictly internal document; there is no mention of this content in the public record. Also, there are no dates or signatures on this text, only notes from what looks like two different styles of cursive scribbles in the margins and a third writer, perhaps a woman, who might have been the law firm's secretary. Were the margin notes from Berry, Myers, or both? This untitled document was in Berry's files, labeled only in pencil as Folder 8, so that's as good a name as any.

The purpose of this pre-trial statement from Denhardt appears to be to prep him for his turn on the stand and for the lawyers to better understand his version of the events that led up to, during, and after the death of Verna Garr Taylor. From there, as the marginal notes indicate, the lawyers were breaking up his story into simple Q & A segments and framing questions that he would be asked so that he could supply the appropriate content. Judging by Madelyn Baldwin's court transcript of Denhardt's testimony under oath in April, his attorneys worked strenuously with the general to get this convoluted story in line with their defense team goals.

In broad strokes, the Folder 8 narrative found in the Berry files is thick with cheap shots at Verna, her family, her daughters, Denhardt's enemies—or at least perceived enemies—as well as the "truth" about Verna, sex, and the revelation of the real mastermind behind the tragedy. The reader is wise to be skeptical of Denhardt's rants on every level, but because they are so untethered to the Garr family reality, Folder 8 ends up saying more about him and the conspiracy he feels is all around him.

Folder 8 starts with a diatribe against Doc. It's fair to say, in the entirety of this document, Denhardt is obsessed with putting down Doc, either the real one or the boogeyman version of Doc that Denhardt has created. Denhardt explains that shortly after moving to the area, Doc sought him out at his new farm and presented himself as a fellow Overseas veteran. "When he introduced himself to me, he almost immediately began by telling me the story of his services in the army, which seemed to consist largely of his affairs with girls and married women in France.

"He told me of having disputes and disagreements with officers and did not impress me as having been much of a soldier," Denhardt wrote. "Later he told me of his divorce suit. He said that one of the causes of his trouble with her was because of the fact that she had talked about and slandered his sister." To Denhardt, Doc's visit was a largely social call, veteran to veteran. At a future date, Doc returned to the farm because he had heard the general was looking for a place in town to rent, too, and the family had such a property. Denhardt looked into the house, but he was warned away from the place because it was infested with bedbugs.

Doc was the brother that spent the most time with Verna. He came to her house often, frequently to eat lunch and dinner and when he was lonely. Doc needed extra attention from Verna, and she was willing to give it to him. Doc got preferential treatment over Denhardt. When Denhardt was over visiting Verna once, Doc came by and stayed, while Denhardt had to leave. Denhardt wrote that Garr family friend Ballard Clarke told him Doc "was or had been crazy and had been confined in an institution." In Folder 8, Denhardt seems fixated on Doc's mental state.

Also in Folder 8, Denhardt goes into detail about how Verna was furious at the way he acted around other women, especially her sister, and that she did not want Denhardt spending time alone with Juanita or Mary Cole, the teenage daughter of his tenant family. Folder 8 relates the story of Verna telling Denhardt he was not allowed to bring Juanita to the train without her because it would encourage Juanita to think "more than she did already that she had 'vamped' me." In Folder 8, Verna is framed by Denhardt as both a woman who is cripplingly insecure about her appeal and simultaneously sexually aggressive.

In another story, Denhardt and Verna had not seen each other for a couple of days when they agreed to meet in Louisville at the Pendennis

Club. "When I returned and saw her in the ladies' waiting room in the Pendennis, her attitude seemed to have changed, and she was anything but cordial." In this anecdote, this is the day that Verna "confessed" to Denhardt about her ongoing romantic affair with Chester Woolfolk. "She told me that Ches brought her to town that day, and now I can account for the change of attitude by reason of the fact Ches brought her to town and of conditions which must have occurred in my absence." While he was away, they were being intimate, Denhardt claims.

In Denhardt's testimony in court, he said that exchange that took place after Verna stopped by KMI to settle her laundry account: "In that conversation, which extended down the road, she said she was deeply troubled, worried very greatly, because of the mistreatment accorded her the night before by Ches." But as described in Folder 8, after returning from the business office of KMI, Verna "told me of her love affair with Ches, which she stated had been going on ever since about two years after her husband's death. She said that she had thought she was in love with Ches up to the time I came along." That was the reason that Ches "roughly handled and mistreated" Verna after she showed the other ladies in the laundry her ring—because she and Ches had been lovers since he was twenty-three. Neither event happened, but in Folder 8, Denhardt appears to be writing a very different draft of what later would be his court testimony.

Verna's supposed confession of a three-year-long sexual affair with her laundry truck driver was not even the half of it. Because she would be giving up her laundry business upon marriage, in return for her sacrifice, Verna wanted to be deeded half of Denhardt's estate—and she wanted "a place" (farming land, a house?) for Ches on that property because "Ches would not cause trouble if a place on the farm were provided for him." She admitted to being a "ratter" for trying to "put this over on me," but she was in love, Denhardt said, speaking for Verna. Even though Miss Bertha was old and frail, Verna heartlessly wanted her out of the house, period, Denhardt claimed. Denhardt's "spinster sister" out, Verna's controlling boyfriend in. Later they compromised on making a separate apartment for Miss Bertha in the home, on Denhardt's request, while "[Verna] planned to let Ches live in one of the houses on the farm and help run it for her."

"She told me on the day or night of her death, that was entirely a cold-blooded proposition urged by Dr. Garr and one she hoped to use for the benefit of Ches." Doc, therefore, was the mastermind of the plot to cuckhold Denhardt. "She told me that her brother had planned having me meet her ostensibly to rent the house, and that it was on his insistence that Verna had started to go with me." In the Folder 8 narrative, Denhardt has Verna saying that Doc had forced this arrangement on Verna, but Verna still had no conflict of conscience about it. "She, of course, had let it go at that, and I had not the slightest thought that she, at that time, was leading a double life."

But Denhardt said he just had to ask her, "Why have you deceived me in this manner?"

And Verna said coyly, "That was very wrong of me, but I was simply trying to lead you on, therefore, I deceived you as I did."

There were many times that Denhardt says she strung him along on purpose before he knew she was being "intimate constantly" with Ches. "While on the way home one night (Verna was driving), I put my left arm on the seat behind her and gradually let it fall around her and pulled her gently toward me. She made no objection to me, but on the contrary said, 'I like that, it is the first time I have ever let any man touch me or caress me since Barc died. I am letting you do this because I like you and trust you and believe you really like me.'"

In fact, seemingly contradicting the chastity of their relationship, there may have been more than just the caress of a shoulder for Denhardt that night; he hints at one "happy ending" from Verna. According to Folder 8, "instead of driving down the street leading to her home, as I thought she would, upon her own volition, she proceeded down Highway 22 in the direction of Crestwood. We drove down this road some distance before turning back... I left her a happy man that night."

The image of Verna in Folder 8 is a pious, innocent church woman *and* a sex-mad-cougar-gold-digger who callously was leading an old man on in order to set up a lust nest with her boyfriend on his property. She shows no sign of remorse about how this is impacting Denhardt until the last day when suddenly she is so overcome with guilt for her "double life" that she must kill herself in order to make amends.

"She was very much depressed and told me that Ches said he was going to do something to fix it so that I would not marry her, that he was going to do something to break us up if she persisted in going ahead with me," Denhardt said. "Of course, this confession, next to her death, was the greatest shock of my life, I was simply dazed. I could hardly believe it was anything but a terrible dream, yet, it was true that the woman to whom I had confessed everything early in our affair so that there might be no 'rude awakenings' for her later when we might become really serious, and on whose account I had been better than ever in my life and had absolutely avoided every appearance of evil, [this woman] had been intimate constantly with a twenty-six-year-old boy." It's implied that most of their intimacy happened while she was alone with Ches in the laundry truck or on trips, according to Berry's Folder 8.

Of course, per Denhardt, "When [Verna] saw how she had absolutely crushed me, she became more thoroughly depressed than before, and said she couldn't possibly go to Mrs. Lee's party." In the Aetna Parking Lot, though, Denhardt forgives Verna for her "constant intimacy" with Ches in hopes that this would cheer her up and make her less depressed about hurting Denhardt's feelings. When they later stopped for dinner, Verna bought Denhardt the pint of whiskey to help him "get over the shock." She talked constantly of suicide as a way of atoning for her sins to Denhardt. "Next to God," she told him, "you are the best man that ever existed." She told him that she had "thumbed her Bible through and read it over and over again trying to find where she could get forgiveness." Denhardt then told her, "The Bible is filled with promises of forgiveness when a person asks and repents." But, per Denhardt, Verna insisted, "No, I can't find anything in it that would give me forgiveness."

Yet, at many points in the Folder 8 narrative, Denhardt stressed that *he* had instantly forgiven her. It was "the fact that I forgave her and excused her in regard to this that she said, 'I was next to God, the best man that ever lived.'" She was amazed at his godliness no matter what she threw at him, he wrote. But the more halos Denhardt tries on, the worse Verna feels about herself. Death is the only way she sees "out of the mess I have made of my life."

Still, even though she had brought up her suicide-atonement many, many times during the day and night of November 6, Denhardt refused to believe she would go through with it. Undeterred, Verna promised to leave a note specifying Denhardt's innocence, the first thing she would do before she killed herself after she got home that night.

Miss Bertha might have been less surprised. Just a few days before her death, Denhardt, Miss Bertha, Mr. Cole, and his daughter Mary Cole drove to La Grange and stopped by the laundry. "She came out as usual and sat by me in the car. We talked for some time. During the time we were there, Ches drove up in the laundry wagon. When he came, Verna scarcely looked at Bertha or me, but kept her eyes almost constantly on Ches. Whether she did this through fear of his doing something to me or because she loved him so, she could not keep her eyes off him. Or whether she was only interested in the amount of laundry he might have brought in, I do not know. As soon as I told Bertha of her death and the cause, Bertha, at once, remarked, saying, 'Did you notice her watching him… when we were at the laundry?' I think I understand now why she did."

The impact of her death was so great that when Denhardt finally made it back home that night, Miss Bertha tried to console him with Peacock's Bromides and some whiskey. It's funny to note that in the Folder 8 document, *whiskey* is crossed out and written above it in ink in what looks like a woman's cursive is "aromatic spirits of ammonia."

Did Denhardt's lawyers knowingly sculpt a highly sanitized version of the Folder 8 witness prep into the sworn testimony he would later give at his trial? By the time Denhardt had been massaged and molded back into the recognizable image of the heartbroken fiancé, he had replaced, "Mrs. Taylor had been intimate constantly with a twenty-six-year-old boy" with "She had a wonderful influence over me and tried to help me in every way. I thought and still think and will always think she was one of the best women I ever knew, and I loved her, because she was so good."

Some bizarre Folder 8 content did surface during the rest of Denhardt's testimony in court. Knowing that Denhardt told different stories in his sworn deposition of January 16, Folder 8, and under oath at his trial for willful murder, at what point would his lawyers suspect that their client was committing perjury? Legal scholars would caution that rules regarding the handling of witnesses have changed over the years, and that, according to the protocol of the time, there may have been nothing at all unethical about how Denhardt's lawyers were shaping his testimony.

It should also be noted that to Denhardt, truth was relative only to what he needed it to be to get what he wanted at the time. In other words, because only his reality mattered, regardless of what Denhardt was saying, he truly thought it was the truth. The only thing consistent about Denhardt's stories was that, no matter the tale being told, Denhardt was either the exemplary hero or the misunderstood victim.

CHAPTER FIFTEEN

Without knowing about the existence of an inner thigh bruise, Denhardt had told undertaker Smith Keightley at the scene of the crime, "We had tussled over the gun before I took it away from her and locked it up. You know I didn't kill her. I loved her. We were to be married in a few weeks. I couldn't kill her." Standing on the metal of SR 22, Denhardt offered this as proof that he did everything in his power to keep Verna from going through with her misguided self-destruction.

Under direct examination by attorney Myers, however, Denhardt denied that he had ever struggled with Verna at all. His heroic "tussle" over the gun could have explained the thigh bruise, but Denhardt insisted that he never said that, and that there had been no physical confrontation.

In fact, the end of Myer's direct testimony of Denhardt turned into a "the lightning round" of denials. Denhardt copped to owning a fountain pen pistol but said that it remained in a box in his attic the entire time he lived in Oldham County. His keys and flashlight were not found where everybody else testified, they were found nearer to the gate at Baker's farm. He denied repeating statements such as "My, my, ain't if awful!" on his own. He said that others kept prompting him to say it! Denhardt denied asking anybody what they thought the Garr Boys would do upon learning that their sister was dead. Instead, he testified that his only concern was for "Dr. Garr, and I, of course, expressed myself deeply for the family, and sorry for them, and mention was made of Dr. Garr because of his inflammable condition." These condolences were heard by no one.

On the witness stand, Denhardt admitted saying that he had said both of Verna's daughters opposed the marriage, but by that, he only meant

Frances. According to his own narrative in Folder 8, Frances was sullen and moody and frequently talking back to her mother, but she loved to go riding with the general and be taken out to dinner by the general and taken to football games with her girlfriends. Denhardt also said that Frances was using Denhardt to lean on her mother to be less strict, but names her in court as one of the forces behind Verna's suicidal mood.

Denhardt testified he wanted to go tell the family personally about the tragedy, but that Ricketts suggested, "I had better not on account of the nature of this Dr. Garr." Denhardt said both Keightley and Ricketts were wrong when they said Denhardt told them that he and Verna had broken up and that she had given him the ring back. Clearly and definitively, Denhardt claimed that only out of guilt over having attracted the affections of Chester Woolfolk did Verna attempt to give the ring back. His reason for not mentioning Ches to either Keightley or Ricketts was that he did not know them, and he thought it would be ungentlemanly to speak on such a personal matter.

Myers asked then, "Did you relate the story on the subject wholly to anybody that was in the family?"

"Mr. Ricketts brought Mr. Lee to the house. Mr. Lee married Mrs. Taylor's first cousin, who was as dear to her as a sister could be and whom she loved as much as she loved anybody. Her husband came the next morning to find out what had happened in the last hours, what led up to it." The jury was left to infer "the story on the subject" was the one he had just told in court, that Ches had misconstrued Verna's kindness to him into feelings that she might be in love with him. It was her guilt over Chester's vague threat about stopping the wedding and her daughters' disapproval that forced her into a suicidal depression, according to Denhardt's court testimony.

In the defense investigator's notes found in lawyer Berry's files, however, Denhardt was still drunk from the night before. Left alone with Mr. Lee, the defense knew that Denhardt attacked Mr. Lee and was assaulting him when the sheriffs jumped on Denhardt and restrained him. Myers must have known that Denhardt never "wholly" related anything to Mr. Lee except vulgarity, drunken ramblings about "publicity," and the swing of his firsts. After Miss Bertha entered the room and took the gun away that was under Denhardt's pillow, the general rolled over and started to cry because of how he was being "mistreated" and told everybody to get out.

Even in his own words in Folder 8, Denhardt tells it very differently from his own sworn testimony. Without ever mentioning how drunk he was, Denhardt said,

> When I awoke in the morning, I found myself standing in the middle of the floor with several men rough-handling me. Mr. Cole finally came in and I told them I would do what he said. He got the men to let me get back in bed. I have read that they shoved Bertha aside and pushed their way into the room where I was...
>
> D.F. Lee came into the room after Ricketts had arranged for a conference, all had left except Bertha. He said the family had sent him to see me wanting to know had happened during the last hours. He said they either felt or knew I was not to blame but wanted to know how it happened and what took place during the day and night. I frankly told him that Ches did not want her to marry me, and had been giving her trouble.

Myers then asks him, "Did you relate to [Mr. Lee] in substance what you have told the jury?"

And Denhardt said quietly, "Briefly, yes, sir. I couldn't finish the story because I turned over and wept bitterly." This is never mentioned in his Folder 8 version.

"General, do you know how the stains, part of which have been termed by experts here as blood, got on that coat?"

"I do. I cut my finger, right there, just a small cut, putting on or trying to put on a wire to a defroster on my car," said the man who claims to know so little about automobiles he let his fiancée walk in the cold night to get help for a dead engine. In Folder 8, Denhardt said, "I really don't know how it was done." Once more, his go-to witness was the deceased Verna. On the stand, he said, "I didn't know it was bleeding until Mrs. Taylor held out my handkerchief and held my hand." Denhardt says he spent the rest of the night with his handkerchief wrapped around the bleeding finger, something nobody else ever saw. And when in the timeline did Denhardt get into fixing the defroster? The only time he was under the hood was after Verna was missing.

In Folder 8, the ghost of Verna is also very conveniently vocal about another matter that was important to Denhardt, the return of Verna's diamond ring to Denhardt. Although Verna does not argue explicitly that *her* ring should given back to the general, Denhardt quotes her at length expounding on the propriety of returning *all* engagement rings to heartbroken suitors. In the Folder 8 witness prep, Denhardt said,

After I had given her the engagement ring, she informed me that when an engagement was broken or in the event of a a divorce or a death, an engagement ring should revert to the man giving it and she insisted that I write my former wife in regard to the diamonds and wedding presents given by my friends and certain other silver and articles of value that my wife had asked to keep during her life. After some insistence, I wrote a letter to Mrs. Denhardt intimating that I was about to marry and asking for the diamonds and other articles I had left with her.

Denhardt said, "Verna asked me to let her see the letter before I sent it, and I showed it to her, also Mrs. Denhardt's answer thereto when it came. Verna was still urging me to push this matter right up to the fatal day." So, in other words, it's not Denhardt that now was asking crassly for the ring to be returned to him—it was Verna saying it from the grave!

But that particular argument never got any farther than the Folder 8 document. Verna's supposed last act of Southern politeness was never raised in court, although the engagement ring would be the center of much conversation when Captain Kinsolving got his chance to cross-examine Denhardt later on.

CHAPTER SIXTEEN

If the first days of Denhardt's trial had started with broadside cannon fire from two legal juggernauts, the final days came down to hand-to-hand combat. In fact, in the last few hours of testimony, neither side seemed to have many weapons left at all, so they contented themselves with legal biting and eye-gouging to gain the last-minute upperhand. Kinsolving's cross-examination of Denhardt promised more than it delivered. If the packed crowd of the Henry County Courthouse expected a pistol duel or cinematic swordsmanship, what they got was Denhardt cleaning his fingernails while the prosecutor snapped at the general's ankles.

There might be forums where Kinsolving could have either forced or tricked the general into telling the truth, but a court of law gave Denhardt every advantage. One could push a Chevrolet Master Sedan through the logic gaps of Denhardt's narrative, but it did not matter: Kinsolving was still just a tourist in a world of Denhardt's creation. According to the rules of court, even when a witness is obviously lying, a lawyer can only do so much in contested territory.

For example, after the second shot, Denhardt obviously had no thought of finding the body himself. Common sense says he could have done it at any time if he had wanted to. The urgency of "we must go find the woman" was projected onto others and premised on notions of a rescue operation that strangers were to perform for him. If Verna were hurt or dying in a ditch somewhere, though, why was Denahrdt waiting for others to snap into action?

"When you didn't find her [with the car], did you get out of the car and attempt to search the ditch or the area outside of the road line?" Kinsolving pressed.

"We did, after we had come back to the car and were fixing the car. It was agreed on by all of us. They thought at the time we would use both cars, then we decided to walk and find her that way. I agreed with them and they with me that that was the proper procedure. I urged haste, but they thought they had better fix the battery first."

Kinsolving asked, "Did you get the lantern and make any endeavor to go up the road and search the ditch for her before the battery was put in?"

"No, sir," insisted Denhardt as if this made sense. "They all agreed that we would go together."

"Fifteen minutes later, when the car battery was installed, what happened?"

"We went up the road... Mr. Hundley on the right, and I was in the center, and Mr. Shaver on the left."

"Where did you walk?" Kinsolving sneered.

"In the road." Denhardt was walking in the one place where there was no chance Verna would be—they had just been down the middle of the road in a car—twice.

"In the middle of Highway 22?"

"Not in the middle exactly."

The defense posturing of a distraught fiancé searching desperately for his injured betrothed just doesn't jibe with a guy who had waited fifteen minutes merely to walk slowly down the middle of road they had already driven up and down twice. Of course, Denhardt's languid walking path was consistent with a man who knew this was a staged recovery mission, not an authentic rescue mission, but there is just no way to elicit that from a witness willing to perjure himself.

Kinsolving tried pointing out other farces, such as the way Verna is only suicidal to Denhardt, while the rest of the world described her as normal, jovial, and companionable. Denhardt simply called Kinsolving's bluff.

"Did you notice anything unusual about [Verna's] condition when she went into Stewart's Dry Good Company to transact the business there that she had?"

"Well, she of course may not have shown it to other people, but I know, of course, her depressed condition."

"Was her appearance, so far as you could notice, and her demeanor at Stewart's her normal and usual demeanor when she was in there?"

"When [Verna] got out in the public, it was more or less normal."

Incredulous, Kinsolving double-checked what he was hearing: "She only exhibited that depression to you?"

"She didn't have much to say but attended to her business quietly, and we were quiet together a good deal of the time because I knew her state of mind."

"What was her demeanor or deportment while engaged in that business with Mr. Gorman, in the Citizens Union Bank?"

"Outwardly, all right."

Outwardly pleasant and happy, inwardly a hot boiling caldron of crazy when she was around Denhardt. Denhardt absorbs what is meant to be a jab by simply agreeing with Kinsolving.

Kinsolving went on the attack about Denhardt's new compressed time sequence with much of the same result: "Isn't it a fact that Mr. Baker didn't come out of the house until about the time of the second shot?"

"No, sir," said Denhardt.

"Isn't it a fact that an interval of ten minutes had elapsed?"

"No, sir, that is not true. A very small interval had elapsed. I went immediately to the house after the shot was fired. The gun and the flashlight were gone. Baker had come from the house and saw me looking for the gun."

"After he came, that was after the second shot," Kinsovling restated.

"No, sir, it was after the first shot."

Even though this solemn attestation is in conflict with George and Nettie Baker's testimony and even contradicts Denhardt's own previously sworn affidavit, it's Kinsolving's handling of the witness that gets him reprimanded by Judge Marshall for badgering.

Myers' silence on this issue is revealing and damning at the same time. During Denhardt's *examining* trial, Myers had declared to Judge Morgan that the Bakers' story was "clear and straight" and "corroborated by *every* witness in this case." Myers lauded the Bakers' version of the timeline as the reason why Denhardt should be exonerated, but in the actual trial, he sat idly by while his client changed his testimony significantly. Myers' primary obligation is to support Denhardt, of course, but these are the contradictions that emphasize that, with lawyers, there is difference between getting a client off and getting at the truth. Any assertion that Berry, Myers, and Otte were truthseekers have to be taken with a grain of salt.

There were occasional moments when Denhardt would falter while Kinsolving leaned on him, but they were brief and harmless stumbles, such as when Kinsolving was trying to get Denhardt to admit what he had told many others, that he always carried some kind of pistol.

"I will ask you if it isn't a fact that you were carrying [the pen pistol] in your pocket, with part of it exposed, a few days—a week or ten days—before Mrs. Taylor's death?"

"That is not a fact at all, and it is not true," said Denhardt, "I never carried it for... at all." For the prosecution, mostly, Kinsolving's ability to nail down Denhardt was no match for Denhardt's ability to change his story on the fly.

"I will ask you if, at the time Mr. Ricketts came back into your residence, just before he left, and asked you for that coat, if you didn't tell him, in the presence of Clayton Renaker, 'Now, Ricketts, don't put anything on that coat. You see, there is no blood on it now, and don't let anybody put any on it,' if you didn't use those words, or in the substance, those words?"

"I never said, 'Don't you, Mr. Ricketts, put any blood on it.' I never thought he would. I was trying to make sure he was going to keep it in his possession and not turn it over to somebody that was not as responsible as he was."

"Didn't you tell him there wasn't any blood on there," Kinsolving reloaded, "and say, 'Now I don't want anybody to put any on there?'"

Unfazed, Denhardt said, "I said, 'I don't *think* there is any.'"

The mop-up was pretty routine after Kinsolving gave up the cross-examination of Denhardt. By the time final evidence presentation closed, there were minor victories both ways. The defense had called its own blood expert, Dr. Alexander S. Weiner from Brooklyn, New York, who testified that the spots on Denhardt's coat did indeed come from a small cut on the general's hand or a shaving cut, perhaps, that might have trickled without Denhardt noticing. Dr. Weiner testified it was "impossible" that the blood on the general's coat could have come from the victim because if "the blood stains on the coat had been caused by blood from the deceased's garments, they would have been smudges on the sleeves, not on the tail of the coat." Dr. Weiner was of the somewhat comical opinion that the blood on Denhardt's coat came from the general flicking blood at himself (which he demonstrated with a finger motion) but did not explain why somebody would do that. Dr. Weiner claimed that all of the blood found on Denhardt's coat could fit into one-eighth of a teaspoon.

In its response to Weiner, the Commonwealth put Coroner Ricketts back on the stand. With great self-assurance, Kinsolving said, "Coroner Ricketts, you were present and helped to apply the paraffin solution to General Denhardt's hands on the morning of November 9, the Monday after the death of Mrs. Taylor, correct?"

"I was present, and I watched them prepare General Denhardt's hands for the paraffin powder test."

"Did you observe any cuts to the general's hands?"

"His hands were perfectly sound," Ricketts replied matter of factly. "Not a scratch on them."

"And the general's face? Was he bleeding, or did you see any cuts?"

"No, sir, I had several encounters with General Denhardt both the night before, the next morning, and the Monday afterward, and at no point did I observe any cuts on his face or hands. No blood, whatsoever. When General Denhardt handed us his coat for testing, he told us that there was no blood on it and warned us not to put any on it to make him look guilty."

Deputy Sheriff Clayton Renaker also testified to having seen Denhardt after the shooting and did not observe any cuts on his hands or face.

The defense countered with Denhardt's lifelong friend, physician, and bondsman, the Commonwealth of Kentucky Health Commissioner, Dr. Arthur T. McCormack, who said that the general was a "profuse bleeder" by nature and that Dr. McCormack absolutely observed a "small laceration" on the general's right index finger days after the shooting. But would a profuse bleeder only discharge an amount that was only one-eighth of a teaspoon? The question was never asked.

Denhardt's farming tenants, the Cole family, came up one by one to say that the fountain pen pistol had been in the attic all along and that they never showed it to anybody. They all but called the Roberts boys liars. The paraffin wax tests were dismantled by competing experts, who said farm fertilizers and matches could have left nitrate traces on Denhardt's hands. Denhardt returned to the stand to testify that he lit a lot of matches and was exposed to fertilizers on the farm.

A ballistics expert for the defense examined the fountain pen pistol that Denhardt owned and declared that, along with the tear gas cartridges, it could fire a single .38 shell instead. He also explained how loud the .38 cartridge would sound, supposedly defeating a prosecution theory. All that proved, though, was that Denhardt had more than one pen pistol: one that could fire a .38 was in a box in the attic, and another, smaller caliber one had been downstairs with his gun collection.

The prosecution also attempted to rebut Denhardt's testimony with regard to Verna's supposed debilitating headache of November 6, by recalling her daughter, Mary Pryor. The prosecution intended to point out that Verna ate a normal breakfast the morning of her death, showing no signs of this physical strain on which Denhardt based so much. Mary Pryor had been sitting at the table during Verna's breakfast. She took the stand and was sworn in, but then the defense objected to her testimony on the grounds that she had been in the courtroom during Denhardt's time on the stand. Mary Pryor sat while the lawyers whispered their arguments back and forth to Judge Marshall until she left the box without ever being able to say out loud to the jury what had been on Verna's breakfast menu. However, in what was considered a compromise, what Verna ate that morning—bacon, eggs, toast with preserves, tea and oatmeal—was dictated statically into the court record.

One rebuttal witness who was noticeably absent—and, in fact, could not be found anywhere even by the most resourceful reporters—was Chester Woolfolk. Ches had been in Wirt Turner's office during the last part of the trial, in case he was needed to testify about whether he had a "social relationship" with Verna. The prosecution asked that he not give any interviews to the press. Chester went so far as to disappear. "In La Grange, newspaper men seeking the dark-haired youth whose suggested friendship with the La Grange widow has injected a new and puzzling note into the murder trial here, met a general atmosphere of hostility," wrote Dave Brown of the *Courier Journal*. "Reporters asking for directions on how to reach his home received many indefinite answers and, in some cases, no answers at all."

But in a special to the *Chicago Tribune*, reporter Philip Kinsley wrote that he had detected a shift in the community sentiment in favor of Denhardt's case on the basis of the prosecution's unwillingness to refute Denhardt's suggestions about Chester Woolfolk. Was Denhardt saying Ches had threatened that people would die if the engagement did not cease? Would Ches kill Verna within fifteen minutes of going home as Denhardt claimed? Did Ches really have some Svengali-like power over Verna that clouded her mind? Kinsley observed that not hearing from Chester "had the effect of leaving that story unchallenged and supplying the defense with a motive for suicide."

The prosecutors had had a long talk about putting Chester on the stand to refute Denhardt's insinuations that Verna was "[v]ery depressed, very nervous, very much distraught over this Ches affair, over which she had no control and for which she was in no way responsible," as Denhardt described it. The prosecution's reasoning was, the very premise that this laundry truck driver was Verna's sex-mad lover was something that nobody in the jury ever would take seriously. Anybody who knew Chester described him as so shy he was difficult to converse with. His cousin, Joseph Woodson Oglesby, wrote in a family memoir, "I was always fond of him, but he never said two dozen words to me in his lifetime."

Kinsolving confronted Chester about the base story of some sort of love triangle, according to the accounts in true crime magazines. "Mrs. Taylor was like a mother to me... Mrs Taylor would never have thought of me like that!" Ches insisted. The prosecution's conclusion was "Chester Woolfolk is considered a thorough young gentleman and highly respected by all who know him." But who knows? Maybe he was sweet on her. Verna was fond of the quiet, hard worker whom she indulged with her attention. Ches was everything Denhardt was not: young, handsome, humble, and liked by Verna's girls.

In the Folder 8 document, Denhardt insists that Verna must fire Chester as her righthand man at the laundry—something to which Verna agrees in Denhardt's narrative, of course—but it may have been a fight over keeping Chester at the laundry over the general's wishes that finally won Verna to the side of her family. She had been wooed by the general, but if this is what marriage was going to be like with Denhardt, it was time to give the general his marching orders.

Kinsolving may have been worried that if he put Chester on the witness stand to rebut Denhardt's claim, Myers would cut him to ribbons. Perhaps Kinsolving feared Chester's shyness might come off as if he were hiding something. Who knows what damage a flustered Chester might cause by accident? To put Chester on, Kinsovling felt, would only make it seem like there was some validity to Denhardt's bizarre claim. Besides, they still had more blood evidence to focus on before closing arguments. Kinsolving decided to sleep on it for the night and reconsider it in the morning.

Kinsolving was confident that forensic science would be enough to overwhelm the power of Denhardt's lies. John Marshall Berry was confident that he had found a way to show how Verna killed herself with Denhardt's service revolver and still not test positive for firing a weapon in the paraffin wax test.

The Garr Boys were assured of little, but they were still hopeful that the legal system would produce justice for Verna when the case went to the jury.

CHAPTER SEVENTEEN

S tarting with its decision *not* to put Chester Woolfolk on the stand to deny Denhardt's crazy accusations and save the rebuttal to Chester's "death threats" for closing arguments, the prosecution felt it had made all the right moves toward the goal line. Kinsolving had even chosen not to cross-examine a couple of the defense witnesses. Perhaps that's why the defense tried one more time for a directed verdict of not guilty from the bench before the jury was given the case. The motion was denied.

Closing arguments in *The Commonwealth of Kentucky v. Henry H. Denhardt* were scheduled to begin on April 29, 1937. Each side would be represented by closing arguments from three attorneys. It would be a day of passion and disputation, of shouting and crying, of accusations and orations. Those who had been there many times wanted to see the conclusion; those who had yet to make it once fought harder for a seat to say they had witnessed history. As the local papers reported, "red-faced farmers with their wives occupied points of vantage as counsel summed the case for the jury." The weather was good, with only a hint of rain in the forecast, and everybody wanted to be there for what was called "the speaking," and "a feast of oratory."

Once the testimony had been concluded, however, the court stenographer was done. There is no transcript of the closing arguments and final instructions from the judge. What survives are multiple, daily press descriptions and lengthy quotes from the participants, long-form news magazine and true detective magazine accounts, and part of John Marshall Berry's closing argument, written down by a third party. The note at the top of this partial transcript says in pencil, "This was Miss Ella's attempt to reproduce my argument. She only started and quit. In this she lost out many times!" From those sources, this much of "the speaking" can be reassembled.

Before putting in his chew, once more, Judge Marshall welcomed the crowd that was about twice the size of New Castle itself into his courtroom with his usual caveats. "I warn you against demonstration of any kind, for or against the defendant or the families involved. A trial is one of the most solemn occasions that a free man under a free government engages in—trying a man for his life and liberty.

"Conduct yourselves," he concluded as was his custom, "as you would in the church of your religion."

Myers opened for the defense.

> Gentlemen of the jury, the Commonwealth of Kentucky would have you believe that you are here to decide the guilt or innocence of Brig. Gen. Henry H. Denhardt, a man who has served his state and his country for forty years. But you want to know why we're really here? Messmer and politics! General Denhardt, the former lieutenant governor of Kentucky and a man who brought peace to counties overcome by labor wars, is the victim of the ambitions of Sgt. John Messmer of the Louisville Police Department Crime Lab and typical Frankfort politicians that saw a chance to get an old enemy. I accuse him of secrecy in the taking of paraffin tests by which the Commonwealth hoped to establish that Denhardt had fired a revolver that night and Mrs. Taylor had not.

Messmer's face flushed red with anger, and he glared at Myers as the latter continued.

"You've seen the so-called evidence against the general. You've heard about all the problems with it. Messmer was either very careless with his exhibits or deliberately tampered with them; that's how anxious Messmer is to make a name for himself. For his own personal gain, he is willing to send an innocent man to the electric chair."

At this, Messmer walked the few steps over to Judge Marshall and whispered something in his ear. To whatever was said, Judge Marshall shook his head "no" and jerked his thumb toward the door. With visible consternation, Messmer went back to his chair and stared at Myers.

> The prosecution's case rests on the absence of the stain of gunpowder on Mrs. Taylor's underclothing. But Messmer

is smart enough to use a gunpowder with light smoke discharge in making his ballistics tests instead of pistol powder No. 6, which makes a heavy discoloration and was used in the cartridges with which General Denhardt's gun was loaded. Yet a grayish stain that could have been the missing gunpowder mark, the very proof that Mrs. Taylor had held the gun to her own body, magically disappeared from the exhibit while in the hands of the ambitious Messmer, the man you see here today. If that stain had not just simply washed away, we would not be here today. Gentlemen of the jury, you know better than to believe in magic. There is always a magician's hand behind it.

Judge Marshall interrupted Myers to warn spectators to cease talking. "If you don't," he thundered, "I'll come down there myself, and you will leave this courthouse."

For the prosecution, J. Ballard Clarke was called on to respond. Tall, big-boned, with working man's hands, Clark looked more like one of the jurors than any of the other lawyers. Before defending Messmer, Clarke explained:

I am not just here because I have been paid to do so. I guarantee you that none of us are. We're all here because we saw an injustice being done. Verna Garr Taylor has been attacked twice. A murder was committed first in body and then attempted in reputation. We're here to defend Verna. We're too late to stop Denhardt from killing her on the side of the road because she wanted to end their engagement, but we're here in time to save him from doing violence to her good name. I have known the victim since she was a girl in pigtails, and I can assure you that nobody loved life, loved her family, loved her girls, more than Verna. I appeal to you, as one man to another, to send this murderer to the chair like he deserves.

But if Clarke started slow and folksy, the more he went through some of the defense's claims about the evidence, the more passionate he became about the loss of Verna. As he worked himself up, Clarke began moving and waving his arms in excitation as he spoke. "It's either murder or suicide—and we all know that Verna did not kill herself." As Clarke paced, his big body seemed to take up more of the courtroom space, and his arms came ever closer to almost touching the defendant. "Verna Garr was a sweet, lovely woman who fell victim to this unrepentant Lothario." One passionate plea after another, Clarke paced in front of the jury until the gallery laughed softly when Clarke appeared to reach a crescendo.

Judge Marshall threatened to clear the court if there was any more laughter. Clarke concluded, "It's either murder or suicide. If Denhardt killed her—and we know he did—it was in cold blood."

W. Clark Otte made the second argument for the defense, taking nearly two hours and forty-five minutes. Picking up where his colleague had left off, Otte slowly held up Verna's black dress and her pink undergarments to show to the jury. Shaking his head, Otte continued the attack on Messmer.

"So, just what are the qualifications to be considered an expert in criminal science? Whatever they are, clearly Messmer does not have them. What do we have here? A woman's slip with a hole in it? Skin from the side of a hog that bullets had been fired into again and again until the so-called scientist finally got the results he was looking for? My friends," Otte said with a chuckle, "a little knowledge is a dangerous thing."

But in Otte's estimation, Messmer was not the only liar heard by the jury. "Remember, it's Messmer *and* politics, that's why we're here. There are invisible hands at work, a cabal of dark forces that produced witnesses like Clarence Roberts, the young farm boy who lied to your face when he said that he had seen the general with a gas pistol just days before Mrs. Taylor's death. The boy ought to know better than to be lying in court, but the man who got him to come into court and tell that story should be hunted out. I hope and pray that the young boy will mend his ways and step aside from his path of sin."

That would be it for the night. The next day would be Wirt Turner and Kinsolving for the prosecution, with John Marshall Berry closing out the final argument for the defense. Denhardt was turned over to Henry County jailer, J.D. Simpson, who secured the general for the night in his damp, one hundred-year-old cell. Outside, a party atmosphere reminiscent of a county fair continued long past sundown. Townsfolk and visitors from all over Kentucky gathered wherever food and drink were still being served. It was reported the only New Castle establishment with a nickel phonograph was still serving customers while high school kids danced until an unheard of hour—almost midnight. Denhardt would be able to hear the swing music from his ground floor jail cell.

Tuesday, May 4, Denhardt awoke in the basement of the old, red-bricked Henry County Courthouse after finding whatever rest he could before what was expected to be the last day of closing arguments.

As the defense had ended the previous session with the closing argument of Clark Otte, the prosecution began with Wirt Turner. Once more, the pleasant May morning allowed for the windows to be open and a breeze to blow in. The lack of May showers and the increased interest in the final arguments before the jury was expected to begin deliberations that evening had brought back larger-than-average crowds on the lawn once more.

> Good morning, gentlemen, I am special assistant prosecutor Wirt Turner, and I have been retained by the victim's lovely daughters, Mary Pryor and Frances, with whom Mrs. Taylor was living quite happily until the day of her death. I'd like to start this morning by addressing the attacks that good, hard-working people have suffered at the hands of the defense, who, it seems, will say anything to distract you from the simple fact that their client killed Mary Pryor and Frances' mother because she no longer wanted to be engaged to him. The defense has claimed that Verna Garr Taylor, who survived the devastating loss of her true love, the girls' father Barclay Taylor, shot herself in a most impossible way because her daughters opposed her marriage to Denhardt. The defense has claimed that the only reason that Denhardt is on trial is because of 'Messmer and politics.' They have said with innuendo that Messmer tampered with and changed evidence in this case. If John Messmer changed one speck or spot of evidence and Captain Kinsolving, as the Commonwealth's Attorney, knew of it, he would prosecute just as hard and viciously as he is prosecuting General Denhardt. The defense has said that if it were not for Messmer and politics, there wouldn't be any

case. I tell you there would have been a case because I was retained by those two orphan girls before I even knew that John Messmer lived! And these two girls are not interested in politics.

A subtle but strong point. The defense wanted to focus on the Commonwealth's police procedures, as though the family would have done nothing if it had not been for "Messmer and politics." Instead, the timeline was that the Garr family immediately hired attorneys and pushed their own case forward, independent of the Commonwealth. If anything, Sergeant Messmer was part of the Garr family prosecuting team, instead of the Garrs being a part of a public prosecution.

Before closing his remarks, Turner attacked Denhardt's suicide theory.

"Verna Taylor had been left with two of the loveliest daughters in our community. She was in excellent health, pretty, popular, and the manager of a successful business. Verna Taylor had no reason to die and every reason to live.

"We are not asking for special treatment on political grounds. We only ask that you treat General Denhardt as you would anyone who made orphans of your children."

The defense objected. The judge sustained. The point was made.

The day's most dramatic moments came when defense attorney Berry made Denhardt cry about his circumstances again—a lot.

May it please Your Honor and the gentlemen of the jury, for a decade or ten years in this county, I participated in many a fight, both in and out of the courtroom, and I have fought when sentiment was for me, and I fought when the sentiment was against me, and I have never ceased to fight regardless of the condition, and I never saw it fail in my experience and in all these years, but that when the public became informed, the sentiment that was hostile and opposed vanished in the sunshine of the truth and of reliable information, and gentlemen of the jury, in this fight, hard and long as it has been five months and more, bucking every obstacle and every adversity, I have approached this trial and witnessed again the same sensible re-action that always comes and always responds to truth...

"Now, gentlemen, since those days to which I have eluded in the beginning, we have pursued by every litigation and correct method and process and investigation of the facts and the truth in this case, and I know as certainly as I know I stand here, that the man had no more to do with the death of that woman, lovable and sincere, adorable, charming, and good as she was, than I had to do with it... We know what she was, and we loved her. Just as much as you, her daughters, lament and grieve for her passing, we grieve and lament..."

Denhardt made no attempt to hide his tears. Berry paused compassionately. "I don't blame anyone who knew Mrs. Taylor for displaying emotion at this time."

The jurors waited impassively while Denhardt regained composure.

A few minutes later, Denhardt broke down again when Berry argued, "The defendant is facing the electric chair, but the prosecution has yet to prove a motive. All the prosecution has been able to prove is that General Denhardt took a live woman out and a dead woman back with the general's gun near her body." Emitting a faint wailing sound, Denhardt cupped his large hands around his face with this elbows on the defense table. "I just wanted to appeal to you to forget the prejudice which existed here in Henry County at the start of this trial. No longer do you hear the hissing murmur of a hostile populace that five months ago asked for blood."

Again, the jurors showed no reaction.

Did the defense really believe that they knew what Verna was, and that they loved her, and that "just as much as you, her daughters, lament and grieve for her passing, we grieve and lament"? How could the defense reconcile the image they projected of Verna, as well as the one they did not state but implied, with a woman who was "lovable and sincere, adorable, charming, and good"?

Berry did raise some eyebrows when he demonstrated a way that a right-handed woman with twenty-six inch long arms could shoot herself through the left side of her body with a footlong, two-and-a-half pound gun in an upward, left to right trajectory. Holding Denhardt's service revolver upside down, cradling it in her palm, Berry showed how Verna could have just barely managed to push the trigger with her right thumb. In this manner, Berry claimed, Mrs. Taylor would have cleverly avoided getting any nitrate to blow back on her hands either. What nobody in the courtroom noticed was how close Berry came to fumbling Denhardt's gun in that awkward, upside-down position. Years later, when confronted by the author's mother, Berry confessed that he almost blew it when he struggled to demonstrate how Verna might have held the gun. He almost dropped it. My mother told me later, "He knew that I knew that HE knew that Verna couldn't have killed herself with it that way."

In Berry's version of Verna' suicide, she took Denhardt's gun down the road, set down his keys and flashlights, went farther down the road in complete darkness, fired a test shot to make sure the gun worked, and then after she positioned herself on the edge of the road, used both hands to turn the gun upside down and then counterclockwise before she aimed at herself just below her left breast. The reason why the shots sounded different was because the second one was muzzled by her coat.

From there, Verna's still momentarily living body fell backward, flat on the ground. Berry did not explain how the service revolver that Verna merely cradled with her hands as she pushed the trigger with her thumb and that would have discharged downward, away from Verna and to the left, ended up in the ditch to her right, almost parallel with her head.

Just before the first shot, which presumably Verna fired normally, she would have been only a couple hundred feet *in line of sight* of Denhardt, who, by his own account, was somewhere near his car, standing on this very straight road. How did he miss a person that close walking with a flashlight and then firing a weapon? Between the bright muzzle flash (the sparktograph of the weapon was already a matter of court record), the sound of the gunshot, and the light of the flashlight, Verna would have been hard to miss on the dark empty road, but Denhardt testifed, "Only [after the second shot] did I think the worst, that she might have taken my gun."

And would not the firing of the first "test" shot have covered her right hand in nitrates?

Denhardt sat through Barry's demonstration with his typical steely grimness, but as the mid-afternoon clouds began to roil outside, the general did break down in tears one more time before the lawyer concluded his summation. A soft rain plink-planked on the courthouse roof as Denhardt was touched when Berry read a message from William E. Bater of Tuxedo, North Carolina, who served under the general in the trenches of France during the Great War. Remembering his appreciation for Denhardt's courage under fire, Mr. Bater expressed his faith in the general's acquittal. With his shoulders slumped, the general shuddered as Berry patted him dramatically on the back. It was Berry's intent to let that moment linger in the thick, humid air of the afternoon shower, but Kinsolving fractured that mood of conciliation very loudly when he abruptly started his summation.

"Even though the defendant has been the lieutenant governor, the head of the National Guard, and a war hero, he had no right to murder an innocent woman," he exclaimed.

"You must put aside your respect for his honorable accomplishments and focus solely on his actions as a man who acted dishonorably," Kinsolving insisted. "Just like any dishonorable man, those actions require that you find him guilty of the willful murder he committed. In my opinion, the evidence in this case justifies a verdict of guilty, and if you give him the death penalty, you will be giving him no more than what he deserves."

The eleven tobacco farmers and one garage mechanic had a menu of sentencing options to consider. As the rain intensified on the tin roof and gusty winds blew in from the open window, Judge Marshall instructed the jury that it could decide on willful murder and the death penalty, or after a fiery debate between counsel in the judges' chambers, the jury could compromise on manslaughter and unplug the electric chair completely because there was evidence of a struggle between Denhardt and Mrs. Taylor in the form of the thigh bruising and heel marks off the road. The range of imprisonment for manslaughter was two-to-twenty years. Other alternatives included self-defense, with some jail time or just a fine. To be clear, Judge Marshall said, "Or you could find the general innocent completely in the death of his fiancée. The case is now yours. You are instructed not to discuss it or form any opinions except in the jury room."

The case went to the jury on May 4 at 5:25 p.m. Five minutes after that, the bailiff notified the judge that the jury had retired for the day but asked that the exhibits of the case be transferred to the jury room during their recess. At 6:16 p.m., the jury went to dinner. The members of both legal teams packed up their papers as the large, orderly crowd filed out. Some people in the gallery lingered just in case the jury came back after a short deliberation. Nobody seemed in a hurry to deal with the steady rain outside.

In front of a thinning gallery, closely watched by Jailer Simpson, United Press newsman Martin Kane observed only Denhardt lingered in the drab courtroom. His clothes wet from perspiration, his suit rumpled, his eyes tired, his hands shaking, Denhardt wanted to sit a spell before being taken to his cell. Nobody bothered him. In the end, the crowd had left, and it was just Denhardt alone with his thoughts. When he was ready, Denhardt moved across the slanted courtroom, streaked with mud from the boots and heavy shoes of people coming and going, hoping for a last second verdict on the first night. Jailer Simpson later told the press that Denhardt ate a hearty dinner and cooperated willingly in being locked up while the jury considered his fate.

After coffee, the jury reconvened for its evening deliberations and worked until 11:15 p.m. when the newly elected foreman, Richard Adcock, notified the judge that deliberations would continue in the morning. The judge then instructed the bailiff to lock the jury in its modest but comfortable country hotel for the night, kept away from the press, families, and each other.

Through the outer, narrow, two-bar arrow slit window of the jail cell, Denhardt chatted with his attorneys, who were working on two new motions, and with Miss Bertha, to whom Denhardt succumbed one more time in self-pity. "The people around here don't like me," Denhardt told Miss Bertha, "They want to see me done for." Murder or suicide. Denhardt did not know it yet, but he—and the rest of the world—would have to wait until until Thursday, May 6 to find out how wrong or right he was—exactly six months to the day since Denhardt's explosive temper got the better of him that cold November night.

Privately, always the cheerleader, special prosecutor Wirt Turner told Doc, Roy, and Jack confidently, "Boys, we're going to hang him."

On the lawn, a small group, dripping wet from May showers, stood vigil for the general. The light went out in Denhardt's cell at 11 p.m., and then directly above him, the jury room went dark fifteen minutes later. For the first time in the history of the Henry County Courthouse, however, exterior lights stayed on outside the jail to keep an eye out for any would-be troublemakers.

Denhardt had a lot to think over in his cell. His defense had been eloquent in its praise of what a great woman Verna was, but try as he might, Denhardt would never be able to remember a single sentence where his own lawyers said that he was a great man.

Chapter Eighteen

On his second morning in the dungeon of the Henry County Courthouse, Denhardt awoke in his wrinkled suit and dingy shirt, unshaven and unwashed, to hear that a group of reporters wanted to visit for a quote. Denhardt tried to be sociable, but what he wanted was news for himself.

"Has the jury done anything?" he asked a visiting newsman, who handed him a copy of the May 5 morning edition. Denhardt poured over it. The muffled voices of the jury room above him were tantalizingly close last night, but Denhardt had not heard any indications that the jury was back at work that morning.

They weren't. Just after 9 a.m., the twelve jurors had filed "sheepishly" into Judge Marshall's courtroom. "Um, Your Honor," said the Foreman Adcock, "we just wanted to let you know that we have not yet reached a verdict."

"Then get back in there and get to work!" Judge Marshall bellowed through his ubiquitous cheek wad of chew. "Who told you to come in here?"

"Somebody said you wanted to see us, Judge."

"Well, I don't," the judge snapped. "Now get out of here."

Maybe the jury missed the relative comforts of the court. The small room where the big men had to meet was lit by two bare, glaring light bulbs that dangled over twelve uncomfortable wooden chairs. This was a room better suited for interrogation than deliberation. By 10 a.m., though, the old battered jury room table was cluttered with ashtrays, papers, and the requested exhibits. Amid breakfast refuse, cigarette butts, and chewing tobacco spit cups, a glass jar with the bullet hole-broken flesh cut from under Verna's left breast floated in a thick solution. Murder or suicide: Perhaps the electric chair, a prison cell, or freedom for Denhardt came down to how twelve tired men in shirt sleeves viewed what that part of Verna's body in a bottle was trying to tell them.

By 11:15 a.m., Judge Marshall was ready to meet with Denhardt's attorneys to hear two motions. The first motion was evidentiary. Defense lawyer Otte sought to exclude the paraffin wax exhibits on the basis that Mrs. Taylor's molds had not been made until after she had already been cleaned "with a strong antiseptic" and General Denhardt's molds were not made until sixty-five hours after her death. If Judge Marshall ruled in their favor, the jury would have to ignore all of the nitrate-related evidence that, in turn, eliminated any roadblocks to a "not guilty" verdict. To the jury's face, of course, the Denhardt team had spent considerable time explaining how faulty and inconsequential that evidence had been all along. Now, it seemed of paramount importance that the molds be excluded from the trial.

In the time it took Judge Marshall to hit his spittoon, the motion was overruled. Next.

The second motion got a little personal. Otte asked that the entire jury be dismissed on the grounds that the judge himself had been instructing the jury improperly. According to the law, Otte argued, the judge was obligated to remind the jury at *every turn* not to discuss the case or form any opinions outside the jury room. Instead, when the judge gave the order to sequester the jury last night, the judge failed to admonish the jury to refrain from conversation related to the deliberations, as he had neglected to do this morning, as well.

Leaning back in his chair, Judge Marshall defended himself laconically to Otte. "Counselor, once this case goes to the jury, it's out of my hands. I'm not going to babysit them every minute. They're grown men. When I told the jury the case was theirs, I said, 'You are instructed not to discuss it or form any opinions except in the jury room.' That meant ever. They can decide this case anytime they see fit. Motion denied."

At 12:10, the jury left for lunch and then returned to the jury room.

By the end of May 5, the judge called all the lawyers from the Commonwealth and the defense and the defendant back to the courtroom to notify them that the jury was still out, but it was adjourning for dinner, with the expectation that it would resume deliberations again that evening. The judge looked over at the pitiful, sweaty defendant continually rubbing his bald head. Because Kentucky law requires the automatic revocation of a bond while the jury deliberates, Denhardt was in the jail's care until the end of the trial. Seeing Denhardt's ashen complexion, the deep worry lines in his face, and his deferent walk, Judge Marshall suggested that tonight, if it were okay with Jailer Simpson, General Denhardt could sleep in the same hotel where the jury was being sequestered, just as long as the jailer or his son could stand watch on the general's room to make sure there was no contact.

"I can't," the older Jailer Simpson said. "I am a candidate for reelection and so is my son."

"I understand," said Denhardt humbly. "I'll be okay." Left with no alternative except another night on the jail cot, the shaking Denhardt was led by the jailers down the small corridor for another night of sleep in the same clothes he'd been wearing since the jury began deliberating.

A few reporters came by after dinner to Denhardt's arrow-slit window—also known as loophole—for a comment. Although the press had never failed to point out how lovely and amazing Verna was, some of the boys, like Martin Kane, had been fair enough with him, Denhardt thought.

So, on the night of May 5, Denhardt found a kid outside his window to fetch Kane and bring him to Denhardt's jail window. Kane became a witness then to the fear that the Garr Boys could "inspire in the eyes of the man they hated." As Kane told it for UP, "I went into the bare jailyard. Peering through a window in the granite wall (was) a big man with a gray blob of a face. The jail corridor's single unshaded electric light glared down on the back of his bald head, but I saw his bulging eyes first. They were frightened. He reached a hand part way through the window.

"'Have you a drink?" he asked.

As if Denhardt did not have enough problems, he was likely suffering from *delirium tremens*, the fabled "D.T.s," the characteristic trembling and sweating caused by alcohol withdrawal. The D.T.s usually take effect after three days, almost exactly how long it had been since Denhardt had had a drink. Kane was always looking for the best story, and he did not see a problem if that sometimes put him right in the middle of it.

Without taking sides, Kane took pity on the prisoner, and he found a place open that would sell him a pint of bourbon. He brought down the bottle and a glass tumbler with water in it to Denhardt's arrow-slit window. Kane held out a 50/50 water/bourbon mix, but when the general reached for it, he could not stop his hand from trembling, the same frightful shaking that Kane had seen earlier when the jailers had led Denhardt from the courtroom after the last court session. Once he steadied himself, Denhardt drank the whisky in two gulps and set the glass down nervously on the ledge of the window.

"I needed a drink," Denhardt said before a long pause. "The longer the jury stays out," Denhardt noted with a ring of authority, "the better it is for me. A quick verdict would have been 'guilty.' I used to be a lawyer."

After Kane left the general in his cell, he stood on the lawn and watched the jury deliberating in the window of the courthouse. That's when Kane noticed the silhouettes of Roy and Jack Garr ambling down the streets of New Castle. He recognized their shadows right away, these two stout men. In a story about the first day of the trial, Kane had described Roy and Jack as mild and soft-spoken with cheeks of "berry red... they look to be of good-natured fellows under normal circumstances." By contrast, Kane found Doc, "gaunt, his cheek bones are high, his expression constantly is somber. Denhardt feared Dr. Garr most. He told reporters that he believed the veterinarian was carrying a gun."

During the trial itself, Denhardt feared the Garr Boys less because he felt "they would not harm him so long as there was a chance that the jury might convict." Thoughts of the end of the trial ahead did not decrease Denhardt's concerns.

Roy and Jack sauntered up to the tree under which Kane had been watching the ruddy-complected farmers in the harsh light of the jury room.

"Have you heard anything?" Roy asked the reporter. Kane replied, "Only the usual rumors."

"My sister," Jack said, "never intended to marry that man. She never wore his engagement ring. She just took it because he made her, and she was afraid of him. He told her, 'Take the ring. You don't have to wear it, just take it.' Our sister told us he was a nuisance."

Kane wrote that when he went back to Denhardt's cell window, the prisoner was out of sight probably because "he had seen the Garr Boys from the window."

Foreman Adcock reported to the judge that the jury wanted to call it an early night, so they were locked in to the hotel at 8:45 p.m. After lights out, it was another long night of the soul for Denhardt on that jail cell cot. On the morning of May 6 (twelve hours before the crash of the airship Hindenburg in Lakehurst, New Jersey), the general woke up to a choir of angels. Specifically, a group of religious workers from the Volunteers of America sang outside his jail and exhorted him to "Have faith in the Lord!"

"I have always put my trust in God," Denhardt yelled back, with stale liquor on his breath from the night before. Standing in the early morning sun of the surprisingly chilly courtyard, the devoted Miss Bertha waved and wished her brother well that day, too.

Judging by how vacant the Henry County Courthouse was on the morning of May 6, the Denhardt jury caught everybody off guard when it showed up with its announcement. This was the moment that thousands of people had been waiting for, the big news-making event that they would have paid cash money for, and most missed it. Because the call to court came early and suddenly on May 6, only ten folks were in the gallery.

Denhardt had not heard an announcement that the verdict was in, either. If there had been, he reasoned, the courthouse would have been mobbed. Instead, with no opportunity for even a morning coffee, Denhardt was brought in by Jailer Simpson up the back stairs to Judge Marshall to a quiet court. The jury was standing already in a semi-circle behind the bench. Berry and Kinsolving were present. Miss Bertha was not there; neither was Doc, Roy, or Jack. Neither of Verna's girls had gotten the word, either. Something was off. The room was so empty that it sounded especially cavernous, almost ominous. Denhardt, his light Florida tan replaced with a prisoner's pallor and three days growth of beard, took his seat next to John Marshall Berry and waited. Nervously, Denhardt rubbed his hands over his bald head and worked hard on a piece of gum. Finally, the judge spoke through his quid of tobacco.

"I regret very much, gentlemen, that it appears to be necessary for us to try this case again."

The courtroom was silent. Only the more experienced lawyers sensed exactly what was happening. "Isn't that right, Mr. Foreman?" The judge sighed.

"Your Honor," Foreman Adcock said solemnly, "the jury stands at seven for acquittal of General Denhardt, five for conviction."

"Mr. Adcock, I hope there is a chance for you all to come to a decision. This has been expensive to both the state and the defendant, and it will have to be tried again. It will be even more expensive to both next time. If you think you can come to some kind of verdict, I will let you go back and consider through the day."

One of the other jurors responded, "Judge, we stand here today now as we did on the first night." Judge Marshall polled the jury standing behind him just the same, and it was still seven to five.

Denhardt looked cold and beaten. After a fortnight of the trial, his disheveled suit hung on him a little looser, but as thoughts of freedom dawned on him, a brightness began to return to his blue eyes.

> Judge Marshall then reaffirmed that no resentment would be held against the jurors, regardless of what their views were of this case: "This has been a long trial, and there was a great deal of evidence to be weighed and considered carefully. It has never been my practice to punish a jury into reaching a verdict. I thank you for your careful attention throughout the length of the trial. I direct you to not speak of how your fellow jurors voted because this case will have to be tried over again, very likely this September. You are finally discharged, with the court's appreciation."

With that, the jurors left.

Denhardt then turned to Berry and just shrugged as if he did not know what to make of it. Jailer Simpson put a hand on the general's shoulder and guided him back downstairs to his cell so that he could confer with his attorneys in private. Denhardt was still under arrest technically, but as soon as the bond was renewed by Dr. McCormack, he would be free to go.

Denhardt was sitting in his dingy cell, waiting for the paperwork to clear, when reporters who were just finding out about the hung jury clamored for quotes and pictures. With bulbs bursting, Denhardt smiled widely for the newspapermen, despite his salty appearance.

"General Denhardt, what did a hung jury in your favor mean to you?"

"It was a total vindication of what I had said from the beginning," Denhardt boasted with renewed vigor. "It was a great victory for me. It was wonderful. I'm going home now to Bowling Green."

"General Denhardt, would you pose a couple shots for us?"

"Hell, yes!" Denhardt roared jubilantly. "I'll pose in the cell or top of the jail or any place you want!"

"Do you think you'll do as well with a retrial, General?" asked a reporter.

"Boys," Denhardt said with that swagger back in his voice, "they have no case. I'll never be tried again."

Outside the Henry County Courthouse, an angry Commonwealth's Attorney Kinsolving refused any statement other than, "This man *will* be tried again."

And just like that, whatever humility had been welling up in the tearful pockets around Denhardt's brokenness suddenly drained and dried. Not a word about Verna. No apologies for what Mary Pryor and Frances had had to go through in the trial or for any of his attorneys' excesses when it came to the reputations of people like Sergeant Messmer. No regrets, no looking back, just a claim of a "great victory" because of a hung jury. A vote of seven to five after twenty hours of deliberation still meant that 41% of the men were committed to killing him, but that was beside the point. Any measure of the jury confirms the prosecution was not even close to a conviction.

Many people who have followed his case still insist he was railroaded, but even if one were to believe Denhardt's version of Verna's suicidal breakdown, the question has to be asked: Which of the many versions of Denhardt's story does one believe—and why?

Ever mindful of Garrs real or imagined, Denhardt quickly moved out of the courthouse entrance. As Kane described it for UP, the cars pulled up as Denhardt's "blue eyes darted into the crowd, across the street, and especially up at windows in houses across the street—vantage points from which a hidden assassin would have a clear view of him going down the steps."

The Chevrolet Master Sedan was waiting to take him back to his roots, back to Bowling Green, away from Garr territory. Miss Bertha was already in the car when it took off. A chaser car full of Denhard's lawyers trailed behind it. "It had gone only a few yards when it stopped," Kane wrote, and Miss Bertha "got out of it and into the following car. Denardt decided that it would be safer for her if she did not ride with him."

In New Castle's drugstore, holding soft drinks, Roy and Jack Garr stood at the soda fountain, depressed at having heard the jury's outcome. Reporter Jane Dixon's questions were met with monosyllabic responses. "Their lips were tight, their eyes were dark," but Dixon recorded that they only spoke softly to themselves in their sorrow.

"He did it," they repeated to each other. "Maybe we didn't prove it on him, but he killed sister."

CHAPTER NINETEEN

If Berry thought he had to buck every obstacle and every adversity to get Denhardt free, it would be easy compared to getting paid by Denhardt now that the trial was over. Denhardt had a very different view of what would be a fair compensation to those who had worked so tirelessly on his behalf. Days before his main trial was to begin, having heard that his attorneys were grumbling already, Denhardt wrote to Berry, "It is to be regretted that we did not agree on the amount that I was to pay you in the way of a fee at the time of your employment.... I very much appreciate all you have done in my case. You have been loyal and faithful and given me splendid service, and I wish I were able to pay the fee you suggested. . . I am absolutely unable to pay the sum you indicated."

In typical Denhardt fashion, his feigned confusion was part of a larger ploy to renegotiate Berry's fee. Denhardt had a figure in mind, one that covered all of his legal debts: "I inquired to find out what fees for similar services in important cases in my county had been paid by men of my supposed financial standing. The largest fee I heard of being paid was to a group of four lawyers—the amount paid all of them was $3000 or $3500 or something less than $1000 a piece. The case was great deal worse than mine."

What could be worse than being on trial for murder? Denhardt doesn't say, but he does challenge Berry on whether he really did all that much work:

> You were quite busy in the case November 12, 1936 to the writ of habeas corpus which I believe was on December 8, 1936. Then there was a lull in the activity until the grand jury met, I think, on January 18, 1937. I myself prepared

the affidavit which was used at that time. After that, for a week, you were busy in securing affidavits for a change of venue. Then the flood came that kept you busy for some three weeks. Since then you have done a great deal toward the preparation of the case... but I do not believe that you have had to have really neglect or give up on any of your practice on account of my case.

Denhardt then goes on to offer Berry $2000, maybe a hundred more, take it or leave it. On May 12, Berry wrote to Myers to notify him that the check Myers gave Berry from Denhardt's account at the American National Bank of Bowling Green bounced. Berry also notified Myers that, although the general had refused to sell his Oldham County farm for $110 per acre to the Commonwealth for a new prison facility, there was an offer on the table for $50 an acre from another interested buyer. This would bring Denhardt roughly $42,000 and clear him of all of his debts.

After the end of the trial, Denhardt appeared to dodge Berry and the other attorneys on the issue of their fees on his way out of town. "Last I was hopeful of an opportunity to talk to you about my fee, but did not have one," Berry wrote on May 14. "Inasmuch as it has been five and a half months since my employment, I feel that the time has arrived when I may, with due propriety, ask that this matter be settled. If we cannot have an opportunity before, I should like to dispose of this with you when I am next in Louisville."

Apparently that meeting did not take place because Denhardt responded immediately in a letter of the same date:

Dear John, I have been very much under the weather ever since reaching home... Besides a lot of medicine, the doctor insists on complete rest and quiet. Walking only a few blocks fatigues me greatly. I feel very much as I did after four months on the Western Front, only I am not getting myself together quite as rapidly... I note what you have to say in regard to the sale of the farm. Land values are advancing rapidly and I do not feel that I should sacrifice this farm even it is in Oldham County. I do not have to sell from a financial standpoint and I hate to be driven to it for any other reason.

Trying to soften up Berry while he gets his accounts in order, Denhardt got folksy by saying, "Rodes and I were discussing the fee angle of the matter last night and I appreciate more than I can tell the fact that we country lawyers do not have the same attitude toward our clients as do men from the city." The letter ended with a P.S. apology for a returned check of $100.

On May 21, Berry received a letter with a new check for $102.50—a hundred to replace the previous check and $2.50 for the bank charge for insufficient funds—a check that itself would later be returned to Berry because there was a problem with it. Berry's letter of May 21 addressed a couple of issues from Denhardt's letters. Apparently, in a postscript on another recent letter of Denhardt's not in the file, Denhardt ranted about how dissatisfied he was with the seven-five jury decision and the possibility of another trial. Based on Berry's response, Denhardt had questioned both the quality and the loyalty of his legal representation and saw that as part of the reason why he was not acquitted completely and had to endure a retrial.

In Denhardt's letter of May 22, it was clear that Clark Otte had become the new Chester Woolfolk in his life, somebody on whom all things could be blamed. "As I suggested in my letter of yesterday, in the postscript thereto, I am astounded at some of the things that I have heard that our mutual friend Otte did in connection with my case." For several paragraphs, Denhardt then proceeds to trash Otte for his lack of work, for Otte's efforts in trying to organize a united front of lawyers with regard to their fees, and balked at paying him for his services or even reimbursing him for his expenditures to the private investigator of the "secret angle."

Reading between the lines, whether Otte ever was as defiant as Denhardt suggests, Otte's instinct might have been correct. Denhardt had been stringing along three attorneys for months, paying piddling expenses here or there, sometimes bouncing checks, and avoiding a clear agreement about how much they were going to get paid in the end. Otte may have sensed that the moment the trial was over, Denhardt would cry poverty and try to manipulate his legal team into accepting deep discounts. Perhaps Otte's timing was off on the eve of the trial, but his insight was dead on.

In Denhardt's letter of May 22, however, Denhardt agreed to pay Berry $3,000, at least in principal.

"While I consider this to be a very large fee, it will be paid or secured," Denhardt promised. The problem with that concession is that $3000 was not Berry's fee. Berry was expecting their agreed upon rate of $5000, but "if you would pay me the $3500 I would accept it. That was too large and you suggested $3000, and I said, 'All right, give me your check for $3000 right now and I will accept it,'" Berry wrote.

There is no response from Denhardt, so Berry fires off another letter reminding him that he is very much past due. On May 29, Berry sent a letter that he described as "warranted a reply" immediately but still no word. In another correspondence a couple days later, Berry complains about being stonewalled again, adding,

The reason for my feeling uncertain and dissatisfied over your failure to hear from you is, that a few days ago one of my good friends in Henry County, an elderly gentlemen, who attended your trial regularly, reported very hurtful remarks you made in Louisville recently when you were at the Bourbon Stockyards, selling some hogs. In view of all that has taken place, and all the effort that was made, remarks such as you are credited with, cause me to want to know what you mean, what your attitude is, and what your intentions are. Surely I am entitled to see you in person.

Denhardt takes a while to respond because, he says, his stenographer was on vacation. (If Denhardt had been using a professional typist on his previous letters, he was owed a refund. All of his letters are filled with typos and handwritten corrections.) In a letter dated June 14, Denhardt pledged, "I have asked my good friend, Hon. E.J. Felts of Russellville, Kentucky, to work out the details of the settlement for me... He is fair and will do what is right in the matter. On account of my nervous condition, my doctor advised that I refrain from actively participating in any conferences unless absolutely necessary."

Explaining the insults that Berry's elderly gentleman friend reported to him, Denhardt adds passive aggressively:

Please be assured that at no time have I made anything but favorable comments with regard to you and Mr. Myers handling my case. A man by the name of Tinley, or something like, that recently stopped me in the Bourbon Stockyards, said he remembered me and had been present at the trial... Tinley, in the presence of (other) men, said that he was surprised that all of the five men who were for conviction came from your part of the county. He did this of his own volition, and without any thought from me because I did not know where they came from.

As instructed, Berry wrote and scheduled a visit to Bowling Green so that Denhardt did not have to tax himself by traveling and so he did not have to go anywhere near La Grange. Berry was quite content to allow this Felts fellow to do the negotiating, and he was grateful that, pursuant to Denhardt's letter, the bill would be resolved finally and that he and Denhardt could settle their personal issues face to face. No big surprise, however, Denhardt was nowhere to be seen the day Berry arrived, and Judge Felts was unprepared to arrange payment of Berry's bill. Felts did suggest, apparently, that another meeting was in order—perhaps next time in Bardstown!

"Dear General, I was very much disappointed in not seeing you yesterday, but I saw Mr. Felts and he said that as soon as he could get in touch with you he would arrange for an appointment at Bardstown or some other place. I do not want to drive to Bowling Green again because it is a long hard drive and really takes a day and a half to make the round trip."

But where was Denhardt when he had agreed to see his friend and lead counsel in Bowling Green? According to a letter to Berry from early July, the man who was under doctor's orders to settle all his financial worries, the near-invalid too exhausted to travel and too nervous to leave the safety of his home town, had driven his car by himself to his farm in Oldham County, just a few miles from Doc's house, the man Denhardt supposedly feared the most.

Chapter Twenty

It took a couple weeks after the hung jury for things to get back to normal in New Castle. In *The Henry County Local*, jurors said they were "highly elated to be excused by Judge C. C. Marshall. Strict observance and being cooped up for over two weeks was no fun, to say the least, they report."

Yet, the *Local* captured a certain, self-deprecating pride in being the center of the news universe for a period of time when it editorialized, "Not within the history of Henry County was there ever occasion for 'New Castle' to be the initial words in the opening paragraphs on most of the front pages throughout the nation for two solid weeks. Fortunately for the Coronation of a new king in England it came after the closing of the Denhardt trial. Had both happened at once, it is hard to imagine what would have gotten prominence," boasted the *Local*. "To say the least, 'the old brick courthouse' with the 'barnlike courtroom' stood the test with the 'tobaccer chewin' jedge' keeping the situation at hand all the way. The 'natives' had a delightful time out of the 'roman holiday' and all is well in the valleys once more." It was a well-earned "humblebrag."

"We're glad to get settled down again," one New Castle restaurant manager told Isabel Stephen on assignment for *American Detective*. "We're not accustomed to all the excitement of the queer—of the, uh— of the folks from the big cities." Despite doubters, people in New Castle were confident of how a Henry County jury had handled the case. "Now, if it had only been in Harlan County!" joked one bus driver to Stephen.

If nothing else, the hung jury in the Denhardt murder trial proved that Berry, Myers, and Otte attorneys were flat-out wrong in their claims that it would be impossible for the general to get an impartial jury in Henry County or that Denhardt would be marching into certain death if the trial were to go through in New Castle. Despite the defense team's attempts for a change of venue and their hysterical "Chicken Little" affidavits, the jury was split slightly in Denhardt's favor, and there were zero attempts to wrestle him out of jail to pass the case up to a Higher Authority with a bullet.

"I suspect that someone on the jury was paid to hang it... only the most stupid jury, or one corrupted with a payoff, would hang," one criminology professor told me after reviewing the case. "The story reeks of jury tampering by a man used to getting his way, no matter what."

Could jury-rigging have been the "secret angle" that could never be associated with the lawyers or that "dangerous element" never explained in the December 18, 1936 Berry letter? Very probably not, but Denhardt traveled in cynical circles, and his low regard for the rule of law, especially when it came to him, is a matter of record. It could explain Denhardt's nonchalance through most of the legal process and his jaunty first day in court for his trial. Maybe it was not a hard promise to fix the verdict for a price, maybe it was just a whisper that got back to him that he had some fans inside the jury who had his back.

The nascent crime science evidence was flawed and sometimes clumsily presented, so the non-verdict could have been a case of a small-minded jury that saw newfangled, "big city" forensics as, to borrow a word from a New Castle restaurant manager, "queer." Maybe a phallocentric jury was prejudiced by sexist concepts that women were such emotionally unstable creatures that they would be susceptible to spontaneous suicide, or even some combination of these ideas. Denhardt's disorientation during the jury's final deliberation might have been influenced more by his alcohol withdrawal than a fear he might actually lose.

Whether the defense did something to hedge its bets, or the result was 100% organic, the outcome emphasizes that, in hindsight, the revenge-minded Garr-led mob" coming to kill Denhardt story was exaggerated from the beginning in order to manufacture a false urgency for a delay and/or a change of venue. Vigilante justice for Verna's death was one of Denhardt's primary concerns the night her body was found. The coroner's inquest was moved, more security was brought in, the general was sent to a safer jail in Louisville—all these measures came out of a fear that the Garr Boys would take the law into their own hands. Other than rumors, there is no account of Doc, Roy, and Jack planning any harm to Denhardt or Miss Bertha, and no shots were ever fired at Denhardt's house and none of the Garr brothers ever bothered Denhardt in the Henry County Jail—not so much as an angry note.

Looking at the entirety of the record, in fact, the opposite was true. As reporter Martin Kane related, if there was no hope of a jury conviction, Denhardt reasoned, that's when the Garr Boys would be at their most dangerous. Roy was a man of his word when he said before the trial, "We all feel pretty bad, of course, but it's got to be straightened out. If everyone who gets on to that witness chair will only tell the truth, it'll get straightened out somehow." Denhardt may not have been just paranoid in his belief that Doc was always armed in court, but nobody ever saw a gun, and Doc walked away from a hundred chances to shoot Denhardt at point blank range.

Newspaper reports that the Garr Boys were scurrying around looking for revenge was likely built on a smidge of anti-Southern Yankee prejudice/fascination with Southern culture. *Gone with the Wind* had been the bestselling book of 1936; author Margaret Mitchell won the Pulitzer Prize in May 1937. The bloody Hatfield-McCoy feud on the Kentucky border with West Virginia was not even fifty years old and it continued to inspire classist and regionalist tropes in Hollywood about Kentuckians. The many references to Denhardt fearing reprisals from the Garrs, true or not, fed the narrative in the North that Southerners were always feuding with somebody because it was their low-born nature.

The most plausible explanation behind Doc, Roy, and Jack's lack of effort to avenge their sister's murder, however, was that each brother had a career, a family, and responsibilities. The Garr Boys were not barefooted yokels in overalls and straw hats drinking moonshine in the back of a truck. They were educated, small businessmen between thirty-five and fifty-years-old who paid their taxes and believed in allowing the legal process to play itself out. They did stare at Denhardt a lot, and Jack said to the press after the jury was hung, "All I gotta say is he'd better stay out of Oldham County," but Doc and Roy remained silent, and nothing came of any of it.

Just as Denhardt told reporters he would do, he did beat it out of Oldham County and moved back to Bowling Green. Denhardt felt "home," but in the words of *True Detective Mysteries,* in light of his ugly divorce and ungentlemanly past behaviors that had made him unpopular with many friends and neighbors, "members of the old, proud families in that section did not share his happiness. They were resentful of his freedom, of the cocky air and egotistical self-assurance." The Garr Boys did not follow him to Warren County, however, and they never pestered him. Denhardt was still a public figure and a businessman; hunting him down in Bowling Green would have been easy. Despite Denhardt's skittishness, the Garrs were content to wait for Denhardt's retrial to be scheduled, the next step in the legal system. In Denhardt's reasoning, with the hope of a jury conviction still lingering, the Garr Boys would be patient.

There was, however, in the distance, the faint, tinny squeak of Lady Justice's scale rebalancing. When Verna's obituary was on the front page of all the local papers the day after her death, a little "startled looking" man who remembered seeing Denhardt in the lobby of the Seelbach Hotel the same night that another beautiful, self-sufficient widow supposedly killed herself violently, started talking. Was it just coincidence that Patricia Wilson had died just after Denhardt had begun courting Verna? Did Mrs. Wilson reject Denhardt, too? Others also pinpointed that the man arguing with Patricia Wilson in the early morning hours sure looked a lot like Denhardt.

Edward C. Langan, the public administrator for Jefferson County, accused Denhardt of being responsible for the 1936 elevator shaft death of "party girl" Patricia Wilson. The $75,000 "damage suit" filed in Jefferson County was based on testimony that established Denhardt had a relationship with Wilson and eyewitness reports that identified Denhardt as being in the Seelbach Hotel the night Mrs. Wilson's broken body was found. In Langan's court action, Jefferson County officially contended that Denhardt "beat and assaulted" Mrs. Wilson prior to pushing to her death.

Counseled by Berry and Myers again, Denhardt countersued Langan in Warren County for $150,000 and claimed that Langan was part of an orchestrated effort to imprison and destroy Denhardt "financially, politically, and socially." Named as co-defendants was James T. Robinson, a Louisville attorney, The Sun Indemnity Company, and others "at this time not definitely known."

In his counteraction, Denhardt contended that "political foes" inspired the murder charge against him in Henry County, and "When the defendants became aware that their conspiracy in the first overt act was failing," the suit laid out, "they moved into Jefferson County and maliciously, unlawfully, and wickedly" libeled him in order to deprive him of his military rank. This was, to Denhardt, further evidence of the "invisible government" that had been thwarting his greater political aspirations for years. Denhardt sought damages for the injury to his reputation as an attorney and as brigadier general of the U.S. National Guard in Kentucky.

According to the *Park City Daily News*, the Denhardt family's rival newspaper in Bowling Green, "the plaintiff states that... her case was accepted as suicide until the defendants began to seek ways and means to cause the courts to issue a warrant" for Denhardt.

Perhaps Langan's lawsuit was politically motivated, although that seems unlikely because, by this point, Denhardt was already un-electable. Putting Denhardt on trial for Mrs. Wilson's death did not even hurt any of Denhardt's political allies because there is no evidence that he had any of those left, either. Hung jury or no, associating with Denhardt was political poison. It just may be that holding Denhardt responsible for Mrs. Wilson's death was based on principle. Since it was a civil case, different trial rules of evidence and testimony apply, which might have increased the chance of success. Then again, it might have been a populist headline grab by Jefferson County Administrator Langan, who saw how the voters were so furious that Denhardt had gotten off that he decided it would help his career if he were seen as Verna's avenger.

Hearings for both lawsuits were scheduled for fall of 1937, but Denhardt would not live long enough to be either a defendant or a plaintiff in Langan's crusade. If Denhardt had kept a lower profile, perhaps he would have lived longer. These were lessons that Denhardt should have learned from the last time he was freed from jail on a writ of *habeas corpus.* As Berry observed then, if Denhardt was eating and drinking somewhere, he ought not to make "a dam fool" of himself.

Berry was prophetic when he wrote to Myers, "Denhardt's persis-tence along the line of his present behavior will defeat every otherwise successful effort his attorneys can possibly make." For reasons known only to him, Denhardt rarely missed a chance to brag to the press that there was no way he would ever be convicted in Kentucky.

CHAPTER TWENTY-ONE

After a professional review, Denhardt was reinstated as commander of the Kentucky National Guard in July of 1937. Had he kept a low profile, that might have been the last anybody heard from him. Instead, he used his reinstatement as an opportunity to flaunt his status as a free "unconvictable" man. A widely publicized photo of General Denhardt leading the annual military exercises at Fort Knox was accompanied by comments reflecting a happy, self-satisfied attitude and a taunting certainty that he would never be tried for Verna's murder again.

"Brig. Gen. Henry H. Denhardt paused today as he directed the Seventy-fifth Brigade of the Thirty-eighth Division in mock maneuvers to predict that his second trial on a charge of murdering his fiancée, Verna Garr Taylor, would not be held as scheduled this fall," wrote the *New York Times* on August 10, 1937. "'They don't have enough evidence,' the general said mopping his brow, 'I didn't do it,' he added."

Publicly, Denhardt maintained he did not even know that he had been relieved of command of the Kentucky National Guard. "The suspension," Major Joseph M. Kelly, the executive officer of the Kentucky National Guard told the *Louisville Courier Journal*, "was from May 27 to July 24." This means Denhardt's duties as the head of the Kentucky National Guard were suspended *after* his hung jury, not before his trial. There would have had to be grounds for a suspension, but none were stated. Conduct unbecoming to an officer? A perception of cowardice? How could a general lead men into battle if he were too scared to go up a dark road by himself to look for his presumably dead fiancée? At the Pentagon, "no official cognizance whatever" was given to his trial because it was not a military court. So why was he suspended from duty in Kentucky?

Because, the family believes, *they knew.* In the Kentucky National Guard, his reputation was as a brutal man given to violent outbursts against those less powerful, and those who worked closest to him considered Denhardt to be "power drunk" and "cruel and inhuman." Because he helped to organize it, Denhardt was "grandfathered" into the Kentucky National Guard. The testimony against Denhardt must have been too much. This was the Guard's best chance to get rid of him. But if that were the case, why did his suspension last only until July 24?

In a letter that summer from Myers to Berry discussing, among other things, that Denhardt "has not paid me anything on his fee," Myers mentioned off-handedly that "All the money that the General has paid me was just small amounts for expenses when I was going back to Frankfort to get him re-instated." In short, Denhardt used his lawyer to twist the Guard's arm into lifting the suspension.

Myers and Berry also shared their frustrations concerning Denhardt's unwillingness to recognize and plan for his retrial on September 21 in New Castle. To Berry, there was no doubt a retrial was going to take place, the only variable was if the case would be heard again in Henry County with another Henry County jury, whether it would be heard in Henry County with a jury brought in from another county, or whether there would be a complete change of venue. Myers appeared to be the last of Denhardt's attorneys who was still talking to Denhardt because Berry writes, "If you will pardon some frank suggestions, which will not set well with General Denhardt when you tell him of them, I should like to observe that we had better make up our minds that this case is going to be tried in September, and prepare for that ordeal; General Denhardt should refrain from his cocky interviews even if he is to participate prominently in the mock warfare at Fort Knox."

"I suggest that we tell General and if he does not follow instructions, it is his own fault," wrote Myers in return to Berry. "Put your views in a letter, and I am quite sure that I would coincide with them, and I will read the letter to him, and let him accept the responsibility."

On September 4, Berry wrote out his views to Myers, which he also copied and sent to Denhardt. As Berry explained, he had no expectation that Denhardt would read it, but he asked that Myers read it to Denhardt, whether the general liked it or not.

> I feel under my obligation to him, regardless of what General Denhardt's opinion may be about the strength of the Commonwealth's case and its in insufficiency at the tri-

al, he should be made to realize that meager facts and circumstances, plus the type of sentiment there is, combine to make a serious threat. Some unpleasantness has occurred between him and some of his counsel since the trial. It is to be regretted and is unfortunate, but I think it is all traceable to some lack on the part of both of an essential and mutual understanding and attitude.

This reads like a fancy way of saying that Denhardt and his lawyers should have had their service contracts down in writing from the very beginning, so they were both to blame. Berry then goes on to mandate that regardless of the past conflicts, Denhardt needs to arrive at a settlement with Clark Otte, "upon reasonable terms," because his expertise could not be replaced. Berry's stern warning to Denhardt is that if does not find a way to bring Otte back on the team, "it is his party and not mine." In their communication, Berry and Myers agree that it would be better for all concerned that, if only one lawyer were to be paid, it should be Otte so that he would return to the team.

With the retrial just seventeen days away, Berry asked for a group meeting and advised that they should argue for a change of venue before it was too late. Counting the number of times that Berry references Denhardt's reluctance to recognize how fast the retrial is coming and how much work is ahead, the takeaway Berry wanted Myers to impress upon the general the most was for him to "stop acting like there never could be a conviction." Perhaps the general felt reenergized because he was literally surrounded by an army, but for whatever the reason, the photos alone seemed intended to goad the Garr Boys, if not the whole state, into hating him even more.

"Natives of Kentucky, for the most part, studied the smiling, confident pose of the General with distaste and read with rising indignation the quotation from Denhardt, the boast that he would not be brought to another trial," wrote *True Detective Mysteries*.

But if his very public return to good graces in the Guard put Denhardt back in the gunsights of the Garr Boys, they did not pull the trigger. As mad as Doc, Roy, and Jack had been about seeing the general's official standing restored while the Garr family still mourned, nothing compared to hearing about the new version of Denhardt's story about what happened on November, 6, 1936, which, according to *True Detec-*

tive Mysteries, Denhardt had started telling after beers and bourbon in taverns all over Bluegrass Country. For the upcoming trial, the word was that Denhardt finally was going to testify to the complete, *unedited* story of Verna Garr Taylor, the unvarnished truth that he was sure would win him total acquittal. Denhardt was dusting off the narrative of Folder 8, with some spicy new additions that were reported like this.

—ᗰ—

"Oh, you have no idea how bad it is," Verna cried. "You are the most wonderful person in existence outside of God himself—and to think that I have done this to you... ."

"Done what, my dearest?" Denhardt tenderly prompted in his new story.

With appropriate solemnity, Verna explained that her daughters and her brothers were interfering with their marriage plans and being in the middle was tearing her apart psychologically. She did not know what to do. She professed her love to Denhardt but added that her family expected so much from her that she feared it would eventually come between them. But there was more.

"How can I tell you? If you and I alone had only this to face." Verna stopped herself as she sobbed, according to this story. "I have brought pain to you—you the most wonderful man God ever put breath into. What will I do? What will I do? I've gone through the Bible over and over again for something that covers what I have done to you, dear, dear Henry."

Reading between the lines, it sounded as though Verna were implying that she had been with another man, even though her relationship with Denhardt had remained appropriately chaste.

"Who is the man's name?" Denhardt intuitively braved.

Verna revealed, "Chester Woolfolk," her twenty six-year-old laundry truck driver. Denhardt could only sigh heavily. Perhaps he even had suspected something. The poor woman would never have stood a chance against Chester's charms, but the true story, as Denhardt relayed it, was even worse than he feared.

"It all started two years after my husband died," Verna confessed. "You know how it sometimes is when a woman has been without a mate and is terribly lonely. Well, this boy came along on a business trip with me one day. We were in my car. On the way back we had some motor trouble. He got out and remedied the trouble. We were in a lonely spot. When he got back into the car, he put his arms around me. I was helpless—Oh, Henry, I didn't want this to happen."

Although crushed, Denhardt knew his love for Verna could conquer all. As hard as it was for him to bear, and as much as he needed a good stiff drink, he encouraged Verna to go on.

"Well, he had me in his power. He threatened to expose me, although it was really no fault of mine, in a way, if I didn't continue to receive his attentions. So, I continued."

Denhardt struggled with the next, obvious question. "This, then, was going on when you met me?"

"Yes, darling, it was. I tried to break it off then, but he wouldn't listen. He said, 'You'll do as I say, or I'll tell the general.'"

"And so you continued?" Denhardt asked defeatedly.

Verna hung her head in shame but admitted softly, "Yes, I continued."

Knowing now that all the while he had been faithful to her, Verna was constantly intimate with another man was all Denhardt could handle. He felt like such a fool for worrying whether he could be a little more forward with his fiancée, and here she was being blackmailed into sex with a man half her age.

"Oh, Henry, I just want to end it all right now! I can't live with myself!"

"We'll have none of that!" bid Denhardt. "To err is but human, my dear one. I'm frank to admit that this is the greatest shock of my life, but fortunately I am a man of broad understanding, and I can see just how this intolerable situation came about."

"But you don't understand, Henry. Chester won't let us live in peace."

"Now, Verna," Denhardt admonished, "I want you to get this idea of death out of your head. Honest confession is good for the soul and I want you to know that you are forgiven in my eyes. God knows I was no angel before I met you. So, I want you to forget completely about this entire unpleasant occurrence. Of course, there will be no reason for your not breaking this thing off immediately. As I understand it, the only reason you continued after you met me was that this truck driver—damn his dirty soul!—threatened to expose this whole thing to me."

"Yes, that's the way it was," Verna said, seemingly relieved. The tears stopped as Denhardt continued to comfort her, but then, after a while, the crying came back in uncontrollable waves, along with her thoughts about the gun in Denhardt's glove box. No matter how many times Verna said she wanted to die, though, Denhardt was there to say, "Shh-shh, I have forgiven you." But Denhardt's dispensation seemed only to make it worse for Verna by highlighting how she had fallen so short. With wary concern, Verna explained that everywhere she went, she carried a death sentence that also put others in harm's way, and she just couldn't live with that on top of her sin.

"Chester Woolfolk told me that if I ever ended our relationship or persisted in marrying you, he would kill me, anyway. If you take me home, I'll be dead in fifteen minutes. I love my children, my mother, and most importantly you, but I am tired of living. I'll make sure to leave a note explaining everything." Based on his years as a county judge, a soldier and a commander in the battlefield, Denhardt thought he recognized the signs of somebody having a nervous breakdown. Verna's crying fits, the talk of suicide, the rambling logic—he'd seen it all before.

Fearing for her life from her jealous lover, clinging to hope that she could be married soon to the man-god that she worshipped, and still recovering from her maddening headache, Verna kept driving into the night. Instead of turning left onto the main road that would have taken them north into La Grange, she steered eastward, of her own volition, against the general's wishes that she choose refuge in hearth and home. There they found a nice, quiet spot in the parking lot of the little country schoolhouse and sat together while the whole world melted away. Verna seemed to gain control of her erratic emotions when the rest of the night's events unfolded as Denhardt had previously reported, except that it was because of Chester's threats of killing Verna the moment she returned, coupled with her guilt for the affair, that led her to die alone so that nobody else could be hurt in the certain crossfire to come.

—⟨∭⟩—

This synthesis of the Folder 8 narrative and his first trial testimony was likely the script Denhardt was polishing around town. Unlike

Folder 8's emphasis on Verna's supposed near-hypersexuality, this version gave Verna the blackmail excuse to take the curse off her impiety. In fact, she becomes a martyr. Perhaps Denhardt thought the family would appreciate this concession. Denhardt's previous testimonies under oath were not perjuries, in his mind, because Denhardt explained that he was trying to protect Verna's reputation by falsely testifying to her benefit. "As a Southern gentleman," Denhardt's drinking buddies later told reporters, "I took a chance on the noose rather than tell the whole truth. That is to say, gentlemen, I couldn't bring myself to expose just why Verna shot herself."

There was another similarity between the Folder 8 narrative and this new dishonoring version of Verna's life. Sometimes in the telling, perhaps depending on the quality of the liquor or the quality of his audience, Denhardt even would find a way to mention that he and Verna had already consummated their relationship, as well. While Folder 8 implied that one recent night before her death, Denhardt had left Verna "a happy man" after a drive home detour, the new "just between you and me" bar story that he appeared to be honing for trial would make a similar inference about a hotel room in Louisville the last day they were together. This invention seemed intended to counter any claims of jealous rage for the sex she was having with Chester. Why should Denhardt kill the cow when he was getting the milk for free, too?

As the court date was set for September 21 in Henry County, the media was preparing tentatively to swarm New Castle once more. The hotel was booked up, but many reporters were waiting to hear whether the venue would be relocated before they made firmer plans. My mother remembers that the trial was the main reason why her family never moved from Kentucky after the big flood earlier in the year even though her family ended up waiting out the receding water in warm California with family. "The summer of 1937, Mom and Dad were soon homesick for Kentucky. Mom had Verna and her death so much on her mind, and there was the new trial coming up, so home we came."

The whole extended Garr family was distraught. If it were not bad enough that Denhardt kept bragging he would never be convicted, now he was going to get one more chance to abuse their sister publicly with salacious lies.

Doc had had enough. He had listened to his brothers and their pleas to be patient and let the system work it out, but if Denhardt were correct and there really was no way he would be convicted, then Denhardt had to be stopped before he had another opportunity to humiliate sister.

But before Doc, Roy, and Jack would do something that could end up with *them* going to the electric chair instead of this "pompous political petrel" (as one newspaper gadfly referred to Denhardt), they had to be sure of what their prospects were. There was only one person who they trusted to tell them the truth: tough-talking, ear-to-the-ground reporter Jane Dixon from *The Louisville Times*. She may not have been aware of it, but she was about to do what no judge in Kentucky would ever do: pass a death sentence on General Henry H. Denhardt.

CHAPTER TWENTY-TWO

J ane Dixon, an accomplished journalist and recent hire of the *The Louisville Times*, "Kentucky's Biggest and Best Evening Newspaper," had covered the Denhardt trial from the beginning. Married to Major W.H. "Cappy" Wells of the U.S. Army, Jane found employment in newspapers wherever her husband was stationed. In 1922, she covered the scandalous Hall-Mills trials, the New Jersey double homicide of a married Episcopal priest and his lover from the church choir. In 1935, while still in New Jersey, Dixon was a correspondent for the "Trial of the Century," the Bruno Richard Hauptmann trial, the convicted killer of the Lindbergh Baby. After her husband was transferred to Louisville in 1937 to oversee the Citizens' Military Training Camp, a now-defunct national defense program that allowed men to satisfy their obligation to serve in the military without being called up for active duty, Dixon signed on with *The Louisville Times*. The first Denhardt trial was one of her initial assignments.

Her Yankee, East Coast bluntness was too abrasive for many New Castle residents, and her journalistic celebrity often made her the butt of the joke in *The Henry County Local* newspaper columns, but she had earned the respect of Doc, Roy, and Jack. Even if they still refused to be interviewed, Dixon admired "their apparent stoicism in the face of an appalling tragedy and their quiet demeanor."

Less than a week before Denhardt's second trial was about to begin, Dixon was stopped by Doc on the sidewalk in front of the editorial offices of the paper in Louisville. As Dixon observed later in *The Louisville Times*, Doc seemed like a man in need of an objective opinion about the outcome of Denhardt's retrial.

"I'm afraid the old buzzard'll get off," Doc said to Dixon as people hurried by, paying no nevermind. "Of course, you know he killed my sister. We all know he did it. She wanted to get away from him. He's the kind of guy that always got everything he wanted, one way or another. He wouldn't let her go. She never killed herself. He did it, but the way things go in courts, it's a hard thing to prove. Do you think the second trial is going to be any different?"

Dixon tried to break it to him gently. "Unless some new and convincing evidence is introduced, Doc, it's not likely that Denhardt will be convicted. You know the law calls for proof beyond the possibility of doubt."

Doc just shook his head. "We can't understand why some of the evidence we had was not brought out in the trial. Kinsolving knew these things. We don't know why he didn't let the jury know them."

Dixon, who had been through a few high profile trials in her life, suggested, "Perhaps it was inadmissible. You know how it is in court. Lots of things that seem important to us are ruled out as trial evidence."

"That's the trouble," lamented Doc. "Looks sometimes like they don't want the truth." Then, as Dixon remembered it, Doc sort of drifted away in thought, as though he were talking to himself.

"If the old scoundrel would only admit that he killed Verna, we'd feel better toward him. We wouldn't persecute him if he'd admit he did it and was very sorry for what he'd done." That was a powerful compromise for Dixon to take in.

"It's the way he brazens it through and tries to put the blame on Verna that makes us feel the way we do. Why, he had the nerve to go out to Fort Knox this summer as the head of an army unit, just like he's always done. Him, leading men, after he's killed a poor defenseless woman in cold blood. A man who had any kind of shame in him wouldn't push himself out in the public eye with what he had hanging over his head. But he doesn't care. He doesn't care what happens to anybody but himself. Are you coming to the trial?" Doc asked.

"I don't know. Probably not," Dixon said.

"I guess it won't be much of a trial," Doc said sadly. "Maybe it will be postponed. Maybe they'll try and drag it along until it dies of its own accord. That's what they're after." After a pause and a sigh, Doc concluded with, "Well, he killed my sister. That's sure."

Dixon would later write, "His demeanor was that of one who wonders at the injustice of the inevitable but accepts it in sorrow. There was none of the nervous excitement, the fiery revolt, of the avenger about him." Dixon took that exchange on the sidewalk to mean that the "three Garr brothers... felt that somehow, somewhere Kentucky justice had gone awry in failing to convict the accused killer of the lovely widow. They had a conviction that it would fail them again at the second trial... [T]his indubitably was the reason that impelled them to take the law in their own hands and mete justice in the gun way."

But "meting justice in the gun way" would not be so much about the legal system failing them—it was about the Garr brothers not failing their sister. As sentimental as it might seem, the Garr Boys were raised with the ancient chivalric notion that womanhood needed extra protection. The word was out, Roy said: "Denhardt was going to try to slur my sister's character." If the past was prologue, Denhardt's lawyers ultimately would not stop their client from changing his testimony again to suit his current needs. He would have free rein under oath, just as he had before. Dread over Denhardt making Verna out to be a conniving, sexual libertine "constantly intimate" with several men at once might have seemed like a paranoid fantasy were it not for Folder 8 in Berry's office. Add to that how well known it was that Denhardt would get "voluble over his bourbon and spill not only the bourbon but also that yarn impugning the honor of the prettiest woman in northern Kentucky," as they put it in a 1937 issue of *Actual Detective Stories of Women in Crime* magazine. This is what pushed the Garr Boys to fall back to the Southern dictum, "Death before Dishonor."

The Filson Historical Society in Louisville explains that the Kentucky philosophy of "'Death before Dishonor' ruled the lives of Southern gentlemen for generations before the Civil War. As a result, personal disputes were often settled at gun point." The belief in a "Code of Honor" killing was that a real man would rather risk the loss of his own life than to risk the loss of his good name. None of the Garr Boys wanted to die, and it was proven that none of them wanted blood on their own hands if the courts—or even the accused—had been willing to make amends. But what Doc could not know when he said, "We wouldn't persecute him if he'd admit he did it and was very sorry for what he'd done," is that an admission of fault would be impossible for a narcissist/sociopath like Denhardt. The only dishonor Denhardt was concerned about was his, and to him, lying was not dishonorable, it was self-preservation.

"Death before Dishonor" was a solemn obligation then, one that Doc, Roy, and Jack neither shied from nor reveled in. The Garr Boys all had families and lives of their own, children they might not hold again, but the greatest inheritance they could leave their children was a respected family name, one that had been passed down for generations since Squire Boone led the first Garrs and Blankenbakers through Appalachia to the wilderness that became Kentucky. Because there had not been a "Code of Honor" killing in the state for so long, however, Doc, Roy, and Jack had no way of knowing how people would react to grown men standing up for a sister who had been so good to them. They could be the ones getting lynched or end up in the electric chair.

Either way, if the Garr Boys were to stop Denhardt from defiling their sister's memory by taking matters in their own hands, they knew they'd only get one shot, so to speak, at catching up to Denhardt with his guard down.

Chapter Twenty-Three

"The Death of General Henry" or "The Garr Ballad"
George Herndon

O, the harvest moon was shinin' on the streets of Shelbyville
When Gen. Henry Denhardt met his fate
For the Garr Boys was awaitin', they was armed to shoot to kill
And death and General Henry had a date

For pretty Verna Garr was alayin' in her grave
In La Grange just sixteen miles away
And folks from miles around claimed the General shot her down
Because she wouldn't let him have his way

If Verna's death had been obscured intentionally by Denhardt to shroud his guilt and avoid a trial, Denhardt's death was exactly the opposite. Whereas Verna was murdered just after 10 p.m. in the darkness of a lonely stretch of country highway, Denhardt was killed just after 10 p.m. on a brightly lit street in full view of people in front of a hotel—and his killers handed their guns over to police, confessed, willingly went to jail, and welcomed a trial. Just as certain as it was Denhardt that murdered Verna on November 6, 1936, Doc, Roy, and Jack executed Denhardt on September 20, 1937, just one day before his new trial was going to start in New Castle. As Doc had suggested to journalist Jane Dixon, unlike Denhardt, the Garrs were going to own up to what they did but then risk the legal consequences. Denhardt killed Verna, but created as much confusion around the victim as possible for the jury. The Garr Boys killed Denhardt, but their plan seemed to be to bring the victim into sharp focus for the jury.

For they knowed he killed their sister out on State Road 22
Though he'd been tried by twelve men tried and true
But they knowed they wouldn't rest til they'd seen justice done
So they done what Judge Marshall wouldn't do

Nobody knows for certain who notified the Garrs that Denhardt and Myers would be checking into the Armstrong Hotel on Main Street and 6th Street in downtown Shelbyville, but it was probably Ryan Blakemore, the owner of Blakemore Grocery, which adjoined the Armstrong. The hotel was to be the site of a pre-trial conference between Denhardt and all his lawyers. Due to concerns about Denhardt's safety, Myers thought it best for the general to travel the night before the trial to get closer to New Castle and not to lodge in Henry County. Denhardt and Myers checked in around 7 p.m. and were given a double front room on the third floor.

Roy started his morning in a brief meeting with Captain Kinsolving in New Castle and then had spent much of the day in Louisville with his wife so that she could see a physician at the Heyburn Building. Once back in La Grange, Roy asked his brothers to come with him to Shelbyville to consult with Kinsolving about new evidence they hoped would be introduced. Plus, he said, "Denhardt was going to try to slur my sister's character," and they wanted to see what Kinsolving could do to stop Denhardt from saying whatever he wanted about Verna in front of the whole world—and then to use that testimony to secure a not guilty verdict.

A change of venue from Henry County to someplace like Shelbyville had been on Berry's wish list all summer long, as well as a delay of the September 21 court date until later in the fall when Berry would be less bothered by his chronic hay fever. More importantly, Berry and Myers had been hoping for the return of Clark Otte to the defense table. Berry had written to Denhardt to "make peach" with Otte for months, and based on a September 11 letter from Denhardt, it still did not seem likely. In Denhardt's last correspondence to Berry, in the usual way he did things, Denhardt had triangulated others to trash an enemy for him in exaggerated terms. Referring to Otte, Denhardt wrote "Mr. O'Neal expressed extreme surprise at his conduct. He then submitted an excessive expense account which Otte had made up... [H]owever, I made him an offer of settlement which Mr. O'Neal said under the circumstances was eminently fair."

Denhardt had understood that he was the only one who could get Otte back on the team to take on the forensic evidence that Kinsolving was sticking with, but Denhardt still blamed Otte for his problems: "Otte has done nothing but cause trouble since the time he thought he was firmly fixed as one of my counsel. Had he spent one-fourth of the time representing me instead of talking fees and encouraging others to charge me fees, I certainly would have been acquitted. I regard his services as most harmful and not at all helpful." Imagine the gall of Otte wanting to be paid for his work and encouraging his co-counsels to get paid, too.

Kinsolving was home getting ready on the eve of the trial when the Garr Boys stopped by. The brothers and Kinsovling discussed the possibility of new testimony that had not been included in the first trial, such as a laundry worker who witnessed Denhardt threatening Verna if she would not marry him and a farm worker who was told by Denhardt that the blood on his coat had come from an attempt to dehorn some cattle that weekend. More importantly, Kinsolving had been told of an incident where "Denhardt threatened to kill a Negro with a fountain pen gun." A peace officer by the name of I.L. Totten had been called to the scene and was willing to testify.

The Garr brothers asked Kinsolving what he thought the chances were of winning this time. Kinsolving was still optimistic, but the Garrs remembered too well the promise of past iron-clad witnesses who fell apart like wet paper on the stand. The next morning was to be the start of Denhardt's second trial with the Hon. Charles C. Marshall, "the tobaccer chewin' jedge," but there still was some doubt as to whether or not that trial would take place. The Garrs never asked whether Denhardt was in Shelbyville, and Kinsolving never mentioned it if he knew. After several hours, the men thanked the household for the hospitality and promised to see Kinsolving in the morning in New Castle for the start of the new trial. Everybody seemed to be in good humor. Roy even sat awhile and joked with Kinsolving's young son before leaving.

Nothing they heard from Kinsolving changed their plans, however. Back in the car, they knew what had to be done to stop Denhardt from lying about Verna again. There were three brothers but just two guns. It was agreed in advance that they would all stand together for the honor of their sister, but because he had a new baby daughter, under no circumstances was Jack going to fire at or assault Denhardt. He was the little brother, and he had to do what Doc and Roy said. Jack could stand but not fight. Roy and Doc would do all the shooting that needed to be done, if the opportunity presented itself.

Berry had been led to believe that Kinsolving had been amenable to a delay until the allergy season passed and was prepared to submit an affidavit concerning his health signed by his doctor. Just in case the judge hit the spittoon and said, "Overruled," a secret pre-trial get-together between all of Denhardt's lawyers in Shelbyville only made sense. Topics to be addressed included a discussion of new approaches by Kinsolving, potential new prosecution witnesses, and Kinsolving's motions to eliminate some of Baker's testimony about Denhardt not being responsible because he was nearby when Baker heard the "pop" shot. Over a light supper served in the hotel room, Berry, Myers, Denhardt, and the prodigal Otte had finished their agenda around 9 p.m. Reaffirming plans to meet in the morning in New Castle, Denhardt and Myers bid goodnight to Berry and Otte on the sidewalk in the fresh night air. Berry left for Henry County, and Otte started the drive back to Louisville. Still early, Denhardt and Myers decided to amble up Main Street a couple blocks to the Court Restaurant for a bottle of beer and a late night bite.

"Well, Rodes, I feel better in mind and body than I did at this time before the last trial," Denhardt said, tipping a glass. "I have a hunch we'll come out of it this time all right."

Just about then, the three Garr Boys parked their car on the corner a couple blocks further west, on the east side of 6th Street, about twenty-five feet from the Armstrong Hotel, and they waited.

> Little did the general fear as he sipped a glass of beer
> With lawyer Otte up from Louisville
> That before one hour had fled, he'd be laying cold and dead
> With Verna's secret locked within him still

Myers would say later, "General Denhardt feared it was coming. After the first trial, he talked about wearing a bullet-proof vest. Then he decided he was letting his imagination run away with him and that he would not wear armor. Still, he had been ever watchful against attack.

"I saw the Garr brothers step out from behind a car as we started across the street. I knew instinctively what they intended. I shouted to the general, 'General, it's the Garr Boys! Run for it!'" Denhardt reacted to Myers' warning immediately, running hunched over in a military-style zig-zag toward the hotel.

There were plenty of witnesses who saw Denhardt and Myers crossing diagonally through the intersection toward the Armstrong when Doc, Roy, and Jack appeared and Myers shouted, but none of the bystanders were directly in the line of fire. Others, too, on the street echoed in astonishment, "There are the Garr Boys!" From there, it all happened very fast. It was a minor miracle nobody other than Denhardt was injured.

Roy fired twice in the general direction of Denhardt then vectored up the sidewalk to cut off Denhardt's path to the hotel entrance, Doc angled behind Denhardt forcing him toward Roy, and Jack followed up the middle of 6th Street with his hands in his pockets, standing unarmed between the general and any possible avenue of escape. Denhardt, however, was only focused on the hoped-for safety of the doorway of the Armstrong Hotel. But by running toward the hotel, Denhardt also was running roughly in the direction of Roy.

At first, Myers took off running westward up Main Street but bravely stopped, turned around, and came back, unarmed, to help Denhardt. There were seven shots fired at the general: two by Doc, five by Roy. Roy missed four times with his 1929 Smith & Wesson Hammerless .38 Special CTG. In this five round revolver, Roy had four steel-jacketed cartridges and one lead bullet. Doc hit Denhardt twice in the back with his own .45 caliber Colt revolver—an M1917 model virtually identical to the gun that Denhardt shot Verna with—as he was running toward the hotel. Denhardt stumbled forward and fell on the hotel's front steps, just shy of reaching the door. Both of Doc's .45 slugs exited Denhardt without hitting any major organs. Those wounds might have been survivable. Neither of Doc's .45 bullets were ever found. Denhardt was crawling on his belly, bleeding, desperately trying to get away from Doc, when Roy walked up from the left side.

"You won't need to go to trial, you son of a bitch," said Roy, aiming. "You killed our sister." Myers had run back up Main Street close enough to see Roy fire once, down toward Denhardt's head, from just one step away and then saw his client's body go limp mere inches from the Armstrong door.

Denhardt did not attempt any last statement before that last shot. At that final moment, though, one can only wonder if Denhardt recognized that the Garr Boys were closing the circle of death that he himself started? More likely, Denhardt's last thoughts were a list of all the people who had failed him and how unfair it was that he should have to die like this.

A car passed slowly up Main Street. After the last shot was fired, all eyes turned around toward Doc. According to the eyewitnesses, something had come over him. Suddenly, "there was none of the nervous excitement, the fiery revolt, of the avenger about him," as Jane Dixon described Doc on the sidewalk in front of her paper. After Roy dispatched Denhardt, Doc wheeled around to confront the returning Myers in the street with a kind of resolved sorrow. Nobody can say for sure what Doc was thinking, but Doc had the demeanor of a warrior.

As if he were back on the battlefields of Europe, proving that he was a real soldier and not a coward, Doc calmly was walking right at Myers with his gun leveled straight, staring down the site of his revolver at the lawyer as if he were about to shoot a Hun and erase forever the legacy of his shell shock.

"I haven't done anything to you, Doc," said Myers.

Without a tremble, without so much as a twitch, Doc put his finger on the trigger and half-smiled as he proclaimed, "You're the son of a bitch that defended the son of a bitch who killed my sister!"

With his arms raised in surrender, all Myers could do was plead calmly for his life. "Doc, for God's sakes, don't do that."

Then, just as the Great War veteran seemed intent to fire at the enemy in the manner that he had been trained, brother Roy gently pushed Doc's gun arm slowly to the right, thereby moving Myers' face out of the line of fire, saying, "We're not going to shoot the lawyer, Doc." His brother complied.

After that moment of grace, though, Roy motioned toward the hotel with his gun and told Myers, "Go in and keep your mouth shut." By that, Roy implied, he may not be able to stop Doc the next time, so don't taunt him. Myers did not have to be told twice. He moved quickly toward the hotel, stepped over the general's body in the doorway, looked down to make sure he was dead, and went in.

CHAPTER TWENTY-THREE

As the general left the doorway of the old Armstrong Hotel
He stumbled and he fell upon his face
Roy Garr came up behind him, smoking pistol in his hand
And with one shot passed on to God the case

"Oh, don't shoot me, I'm a lawyer," said attorney Rodes K. Myers
As he raised his hands and pleaded for his life
His frantic words were heeded by Dr. E.S. Garr
Who saved him for his children and his wife

Doc, Roy and Jack went toward Blakemore Grocery, as they had agreed in advance in case people decided to fire back, but all was silent. They found themselves just standing in the store's entranceway with a stunned crowd milling about talking about what they had seen. The three brothers looked at each other and shrugged. "Well, let's go to jail or find the law," Roy suggested.

Before they could move far, the law found them. Patrolman Jeptha Tracey and Claude Hammond were running up the street from different directions. Tracey approached the men cautiously with his hand toward his weapon.

"That won't be necessary," Roy said, and he immediately confessed: "I am Roy Garr, and I shot this man," pointing to the body of Denhardt in the doorway.

As Roy and Doc handed their guns to the policemen, handles out, Doc joined in, "I am Dr. Garr. I did some shooting, too." Pointing to his little brother, Doc added, "He had nothing to do with it."

"I give myself up, anyway," Jack volunteered even though nobody was asking.

"Before any shots were fired," Roy said to the patrolmen, "I saw Denhardt go for his gun, and I went for mine. We thought he was reaching for his gun. It was self-defense." They all agreed. Tracey searched Denhardt's body for a gun but found none.

"I'll have to take y'all to lock-up," said Tracey as he led them away.

Having heard the shots during a quick errand up the street, the Armstrong Hotel's proprietor, Harry Flood, dropped what he was doing, hurried, and was the first to reach the body. Flood had his son, the night clerk, call for Dr. A.C. Weakley, but there was no real thought that Denhardt had survived. Flood also had his son call Coroner F. L. Lapsley.

Without any further conversation or resistance, Tracey marched the Garr Boys the short walk to the Shelbyville County Jail, a small, square, castle-like stone structure next door to the jailer's house, where they were placed in the custody of Sheriff Forest S. Barnes, Jr. Commonwealth's Attorney Kinsolving of Shelby County ordered that no one be allowed to talk to the Garr brothers. Obviously, because of their longstanding personal and working relationship, Kinsolving eventually would have to recuse himself from this case.

Dr. Weakley examined the body and declared that death appeared to be instantaneous. Coroner Lapsley then ordered that Denhardt's corpse be transferred to the R.L. Shannon Funeral Home. Dr. McCormack, Denhardt's other attorneys, and a few prominent Shelbyville citizens were notified and came to the funeral home to be there when Denhardt's body was ready to be released, prepped for burial, and returned to Bowling Green.

Outside on the street, the townspeople came out to 6th and Main to watch Denhardt's body be removed. Investigators took statements from about a dozen witnesses, including 13-year-old Shelbyville Junior High School student Bruce Tracey, the son of Patrolman Tracey, who was walking out of the nearby pool hall as Myers yelled out and the shooting began. There was no dispute on the sequence of events, but not all the witnesses heard the same things being said. No witness reported seeing the general brandish a weapon, but a couple of people thought they saw Denhardt reach for the right pocket of his coat as he ran, almost as if by force of habit.

Newspeople and photographers arrived, and after the body was taken away, some local citizens posed as though they were Denhardt laying face down in the doorway. Similar to his trials, Denhardt's death scene soon developed a carnival atmosphere and the Kentucky State Police were sent in to maintain order. At the request of attorney Myers, the State Police also would to take over the investigation from the sheriff's office.

After being booked, the Garr Boys followed Shelby County Jailer George L. Minch, Sr. to the stony stairs that descended into the dank basement of the Shelbyville County Jail. Doc, Roy, and Jack took a left before the two doors of solitary confinement cells and crouched as they passed through the barred hallway that ended with two small holding cells. There were three cots for sleeping. Roy and Jack stayed in one cell, and Doc had the other, but they were not locked behind cell doors for the night, only behind the barred gate at the beginning of the hallway. This gave the brothers a little extra room to move around. They gave Jailer Minch no trouble. It was a long, quiet somber night.

> Now ladies don't you worry if you've got a brother good
> That you might have to meet poor Verna's fate
> Not if you've got lovin' ones to protect your womanhood
> And the law is what it is in this here state

Throughout the night, Coroner Lapsley worked on Denhardt's autopsy. In Denhardt's pockets were $17.97 in cash, and a letter from his ex-wife. The only item that could be called a weapon that Denhardt carried that day was a small, pearl-handled pocketknife, which Myers took with him. In the final report, it was determined that three bullets had entered Denhardt's body: one .45 slug in the middle back, one .45 in the shoulder, and one .38 bullet that entered behind Denhardt's left ear and remained lodged behind the general's forehead. In order to gauge how close Roy's revolver was to Denhardt, Lapsley would have required analysis of the "ballooning" and the burned powder patterns of the wound courtesy of the Louisville Police Department Crime Lab.

Tuesday morning came early for the Garr Boys. Well-wishers, the curious, and the press started to come by the ground floor window bars opposite the basement cells, offering the brothers encouragement and praise for their act of honor.

Myers did not get much sleep, either. At about 4 a.m., a transatlantic call was put through to his Armstrong Hotel room from a reporter with the *London Star* in England. The British press had been covering the Denhardt trial all along, so Myers shared the latest facts of the shooting as he knew them, stressing that the general neither yelled anything at the Garr Boys nor made any threatening motion. Jailer Minch got a similar call, but he had little to report to the London paper, either. The "code killers" had been perfect Southern gentlemen, so Jailer Minch presented the boys with a hearty breakfast of bacon, eggs, toast, and coffee.

By Tuesday morning, the story was front page news across the U.S., although much of the reportage was misinformed. *The New York Times*, for example, got much wrong in a short piece headlined, "Gen.

Denhardt Shot to Death by the Kin of his Dead Fiancee." Like many newspapers, *The Times* reported that Denhardt had been hit by seven bullets, the killing had happened after Denhardt left the hotel at 10 p.m., and that the Garr brothers ran up to the stationary general from the shadows and shot him as he attempted to reenter the hotel. Papers further west had more time to rearrange their front pages, so the Denhardt killing got more play and better reporting in newspapers such as the *Arizona Republic*. "General Denhardt Slain" was the front page headline on Tuesday morning, September 21, with the sub-head, "Fiancee's Death is Avenged."

Breaux Ballard, a Louisville automobile dealership owner, secretly drove J. Ballard Clarke, Mary Pryor, and Frances to see the Garr Boys behind bars by permission of Captain Kinsolving. The meeting was largely silent, with more hugs and hand squeezes being exchanged than words. There were expressions of pride, devotion, and gratitude from the girls to their uncles, but few tears. Clarke announced that he had been retained by the family to lead the defense team and that several prominent lawyers would assist their defense. To keep their spirits up, Ryan Blakemore brought them special meals throughout their stay.

Patrolman Tracey told the waiting press that, according to what the Garr Boys had told him, they planned to plead self-defense, and Clarke did not dispute that. A coroner's inquest was held and determined that the cause of death was the three bullets and that it was no suicide or misadventure. An examining trial would have to establish the charges.

As hundreds of sightseers gathered to take photos at the Armstrong Hotel vestibule, Kinsolving had a court date in New Castle. Appearing in front of Judge Marshall again, Kinsolving came to the Henry County Courthouse to close out the case of the *Commonwealth of Kentucky vs. Henry H. Denhardt*.

"It was a terrible tragedy," declared Judge Marshall.

"I wish to call the court's attention to the death last night of the defendant and request that the prosecution be dismissed," Kinsolving said.

"Granted," Judge Marshall replied as he signed the formal order.

In Frankfort, Attorney General for the Commonwealth of Kentucky Hubert S. Meredith was frustrated because Commonwealth's Attorney Kinsolving had not yet recused himself from the role as lead prosecutor. General Meredith was dropping plenty of hints to the press that it was time for the Commonwealth to take over the case because there was "too much pro-Garr sentiment among the local authorities."

Meredith nudged Kinsolving publicly by saying, "I will render any assistance to the Commonwealth's Attorney that he asks for. The last legislature defeated a bill designed to put the attorney general in charge of such cases, so clearly, I have no right to take charge."

Meredith just needed to be patient. Later Tuesday morning, Kinsolving drove to Frankfort to request that Attorney General Meredith take over the case officially. In doing so, Kinsolving stepped aside for his second in command, Coleman Wright, who swore out the murder warrants for the Garr Boys. Arraignment was deferred until Friday so that Myers had sufficient time to lead an automobile cortege with Denhardt's body to Bowling Green. Elaborate funeral arrangements were underway. Before leaving town, Myers said, "I intend to go on the witness stand and state that Roy Garr saved my life. I'm going to credit him with that much, anyway." Asked how he felt after surviving a shoot-out and a gun in his face, Myers said, "It's like I'm living on velvet."

Tired of the enthusiastic distractions of passersby, Jack hung a blanket up over the jail cell window.

"What about posing for a photo, y'all?" asked a pressman.

"At least not until we have time to shave," Jack joked through the blanket, although he may have been the only one in a relaxed mood. Before Jack blocked the view, one reporter noted Doc sat by himself, "uncommunicative." Roy was his usual calm, detached self, but he might also have been in pain. Dr. W.H. Nash of Shelbyville was brought in to treat a nagging foot injury that Roy had suffered a couple months ago in Canada when his horse fell during a hunting dog field trial.

Sheriff Barnes served the murder warrants to the Garr brothers behind bars. His impression was that they had had a "bad night," but that Doc seemed somehow less affected, Barnes said. When Barnes told Doc that they each had been given warrants for murder, Doc's only response was, "Who are you?"

"For what little talking was being done, Dr. Garr was the spokesman," Barnes said. Told that they were going to be held until the examining trial on Friday, in reference to how long Denhardt's legal proceedings dragged on, Jack joked sarcastically, "We want a quicker trial" as Barnes walked away.

A main concern by investigators was how the Garrs knew that Denhardt and his lawyers had agreed to meet in Shelbyville the night before the new trial in New Castle. "I think I know how the Garr brothers found out we were here, but I cannot afford to say yet. There was a leak somewhere," Myers commented to the press.

At least part of Tuesday was spent by Clarke securing the services of respected former U.S. Congressman and State Senator Ralph Gilbert for the defense. Coleman Wright had also reached out to Senator Gilbert to convince him to be a special prosecutor, and he had received an entreaty from Attorney General Meredith, too. Clarke saw such a value in having him on the defense team, however, that some funds were raised by wealthy friends of the brothers to pressure the politically influential Gilbert to join their side of the case. By Tuesday evening, Sen. Gilbert had said "yes" to the Garrs. This was significant because Denhardt himself had once asked for Gilbert to be his attorney for his first trial, but Gilbert had declined to help him.

When Jane Dixon came by the jailhouse window opposite their cells, the Garr Boys took down their blanket for a while for her and chatted like neighbors through a picket fence.

"We're feeling all right," they all agreed. "We're more comfortable now than we have been for a long time." Dixon observed to her readers, "They looked all right, too. Despite the stone bars, the tenseness that characterized them during the April trials in New Castle which eventuated in a hung jury... is gone. They appear relaxed, quiet, cheerful but obedient to orders."

With the blanket down, Doc seemed content to just smoke and marvel at the crowds of supporters and reporters crowded on the streets near the jail. With just a wave or a smile, he would respond to shouts of "How you doing, Doc?" Jack would sometimes yell back to a call from somebody in the throngs that he recognized. "I don't see how you could have done anything different, boys," encouraged a distant relative. Roy, "the big brother" of the group, as Dixon called him despite his status in the middle, made an effort to greet her at the window to say, "I am doing well and feel as good as could be expected."

Dixon concluded, "The three Garr Brothers are about the last in a crowd of miscellaneous citizenry one would pick out as potential gunmen."

Wednesday morning, for the first time since being detained Monday night, the Garrs were allowed to leave the jail in order to meet with their attorneys, but Gilbert wasn't there. The conference was held in the Shelby County Courthouse office of a former judge, The Hon. George L. Willis, Jr., now part of the defense counsel, along with Clarke and John K. Todd, veteran practicing attorney for forty years and former county clerk of sixteen years. Six witnesses would be called for the defense, and the *The Shelby Sentinel* reported that all three of the Garr Boys left Willis' office in high spirits, Jack even whistling as he walked down the hallway back to jail.

County Attorney Wright promised that everything would be in order and that Sheriff Barnes was in the process of issuing subpoenas for the prosecution and looking for any information about who was in the car that drove by during the shooting. Attorney General Meredith announced that he would personally handle the prosecution of the Garr Boys and would be in Shelbyville by Friday for the examining trial presided over by County Judge Harry F. Walters. Clarke asked Judge Walters to issue a bond for his clients on Wednesday, but it was denied. Judge Walters said he had no alternative "under the constitution." Wealthy friends and strangers had already contacted the Garrs' attorneys and committed to providing for a bond up to $1,000,000.

By Thursday, the judge had still not decided whether to have the examining trial in the little courtroom usually used for hearings or the larger court. A contingent from Oldham County was expected as most businesses in La Grange had already posted signs that they would be closed on Friday for the trial. Wright had confirmed that the Commonwealth was willing to establish a bond, but it would not likely be as high as $1,000,000, an unheard of amount for a local trial.

In preparation for Denhardt's funeral on Thursday, Myers issued a statement he had prepared, condemning the actions of the Garr Boys and maintaining the innocence of his client. His message read in part, "[T]he sorry part of the whole ordeal is that his death leaves him still unjustly accused, not only by the law, but by hundreds of people who never learned the truth.

"I can tell you now that he is dead, as I stand here over his body, that General Denhardt did not kill Mrs. Taylor and that he loved her with as true a love as man ever had." It's hard to know whose legacy Myers was protecting more: Denhardt's or his own.

Sometime before his death, Denhardt said, "I feel that I haven't a friend left." It is doubtful that anybody could have argued with that much any more than they could have disagreed with Denhardt's other prophecy that he issued during the military games at Fort Knox in the summer: "I will not be brought to trial again." He was right on both counts.

Because Denhardt was not brought to trial again, there would be no new scandalous testimony about the woman he supposedly loved "as true a love as man ever had." Instead, it was Denhardt's honor that would be in question at the next trial. And in death, just as in life, there were no crowds waiting at the Bowling Green city limits to receive the body as it arrived from Shelbyville.

> Oh, sad the fate of General Henry, as everybody knows
> With his military record clean
> For he's layin' neath the sod, and his soul's gone up to God
> And he's buried in old Bowling Green*

*George Herdon wrote these lyrics as a spoof of Denhardt's death for a skit at the exclusive Pendennis Club. "The Garr Ballad" was sung to the tune of the bluegrass standard, "Jesse James." Denhardt attorney Clark Otte was also a member of the Pendennis Club, which is probably why he got a mention in the song even though the beer he shared with Denhardt was in his room hours before the shooting.

CHAPTER TWENTY-FOUR

Before the public viewing for Denhardt in Bowling Green's Armory from 10 a.m. until 2 p.m., a private service was held at 1034 Laurel Avenue, a modest two-story bungalow that had been the home of Denhardt and Miss Bertha since his self-imposed exile from Oldham County. In the home funeral service, the Presbyterian minister, the Rev. Dr. George W. Cheek, said flatly, "We are not here to speculate where the soul of this man may be today. That is a secret between him and God." At a funeral, usually a hometown pastor will give the deceased the benefit of the doubt. As many bridges as Denhardt had burned in his turbulent life, however, a cheeky comment like that may be the best that anybody could hope for from an honest minister.

Public reaction in Bowling Green to Denhardt's shooting was "one of interest but not surprise," wrote *The Louisville Times.* "Knots of citizens gathered on the streets talking about the shooting but not in a bitter vein." There was a respectably consistent line through the Armory to view Denhardt's open casket before his his burial at the family plot in Bowling Green's Fairview Cemetery under the direction of Lieutenant Averett of Louisville, the Army chaplain of the 149th Infantry, which Denhardt had commanded as a colonel. Despite his recent suspension and then reinstatement as adjutant general and the two legal cases for murdering two different women pending against Denhardt at his death, the general was accorded full military honors. "Three volleys by a firing squad of eight local National Guardsmen under command of Lieutenant Edwin Topmiller concluded the services at the grave," reported the *Park City Daily News.*

Five of the largest newspapers in the U.S. sent correspondents, as did two of the biggest news agencies. Photographers and reporters included a pair each from *The Chicago Herald-Examiner* and *The Chi-*

cago Times, and Charlie Nerple (!) from the *Cincinnati Post*. The Associated Press and the United Press made sure that photographs were in newspapers all over the country the next morning.

Rodes K. Myers was listed as head pallbearer, but many political and military dignitaries came by to pay their respects, even those who refused to stand by Denhardt during his trials. Judges, former governors, and many state legislators who served with Denhardt were in attendance, including W.J. Fields and Ruby Laffoon, the man who had pardoned Denhardt after the elections in Bloody Harlan. Despite doing the main part of the work to keep him free, Berry was among two dozen people named only as an "honorary pallbearer." Otte, the lawyer who perhaps almost single-handedly dismantled the prosecution's forensic case in the first trial, was not even invited to be an honorary pallbearer. As the main witness to the events to Denhardt's shooting, Myers was expected back in Shelbyville on Friday to attend the examining trial. At stake would be whether the Garr brothers would be held for trial, and if they were, whether they would be eligible for bond, pending their day in court.

Myers would not be going alone. As a result of four death threats, Myers had a security detail of two State Police officers to accompany him until further notice. Myers had received four threatening letters, one stating "We need more Garr brothers!" The FBI was brought in.

In a written statement, Myers wanted to make it clear that he was ending his association with this case. "Due to the numerous inquiries that have been made of me relative to whether or not I would assist in the prosecution in the case of the Commonwealth of Kentucky vs. the Garr Brothers... [m]y services as an attorney in this affair ended with the death of General Denhardt." Myers would testify if so called.

As it turns out, the Denhardt family would not hire any extra help for the prosecution. Miss Bertha let the public know,

> We have no intention of participating in another roman holiday such as disgraced the previous trial.... If the officers whose duty it is to enforce the law are derelict in the discharge of their sworn duties in the case of obviously cold-blooded murder, there will rest on the state and dignity of the Commonwealth a stain which will not degrade them in the eyes of the nation.

Even six-feet under, Denhardt was not paying for his legal help.

Miss Bertha, enamored with her brother to the end, was overestimating the national popularity of Denhardt. Judging by the volume of letters, telegrams, and overseas cables that were coming in support of the Garr Boys, the national reputation of Kentucky appeared to rest on whether Doc, Roy, and Jack would be celebrated by the court for doing the right thing. The post office was described as feeling "harassed" and unable to keep up with the fan mail for the three. "You have upheld the highest traditions of the Commonwealth and of manhood," one woman wrote. "A large portion of the population of Kentucky was loud in its praise of the Garr brothers," the press noted because "[t]hey had sacrificed themselves to the extent of facing execution for murder in order that the good name of their beloved dead sister would be protected." Many people were contacting the brothers to offer financial support.

All the boys had to worry about was themselves. On Thursday night, September 23, 1937, Ballard Clarke told the press, "They did not know General Denhardt was in Shelbyville. They did not come over here with any idea of that kind in their minds. They are ready and rarin' to go." He promised the country that Doc, Roy, and Jack would all take the stand and tell a "story reasonable, plausible, and true, which will refute the Commonwealth's idea of this case." In fact, they would tell *a lot* of stories.

CHAPTER TWENTY-FIVE

Over twelve hundred people crammed into the largest room in the Shelby County Courthouse for the start of the examining trial on September 24, 1937, just four days after Denhardt was killed in front of the Armstrong Hotel. The courtroom itself was full two hours before the proceedings were set to begin. Judge Walters would preside and Attorney General Meredith and Commonwealth's Attorney Wright would prosecute. Attorneys Clarke, Gilbert, Willis, and Todd comprised the defense. As promised, a car caravan had moved slowly down from Oldham County, and family and friends were well represented in court.

From the jailhouse to the courthouse, the Garrs heard nothing but applause, hoots, and "Attaboys," with special attention paid to the defendants by the women in attendance. Judge Walters admonished the gallery that he would not tolerate any disruption in his courtroom and he would clear every seat if necessary. *The Shelbyville Sentinel* reported, "the three brothers, freshly shaved, powdered and slicked up" settled in between their prominent attorneys.

In his opening remarks, Meredith said,

> The Garr Boys are not the only ones on trial here. Every officer of this community and our judicial system is on trial. Our jury system is on trial. If General Denhardt cheated the law, he bamboozled the jury. I don't know whether they should or should not have found him guilty. If the law is cheated here, it will have to be because of the jurors and not because any officer failed to do his duty. This is the first time I ever heard anyone claim self-defense when they shot the victim in the back as he was running like the devil to

get away from him. Here is a case of willful murder: killing a man to avenge the death of their sister. I had the most genuine sympathy for the Garr brothers up to the time they took the law in they own hands.

Myers was the first to testify for the Commonwealth. After some suds at the Court restaurant, "we left shortly after 10 o'clock. We walked toward the hotel. When we reached the corner, we angled across the street. As we neared the middle of the street, I saw three men standing outside a car parked on a side street. They were Dr. Garr, Roy Garr, and Jack Garr. I said, 'General, there are the Garr Boys!'"

Myers talked about Denhardt's attempt to make it to the hotel, about the flurry of shots, a pause, and then a single shot, which he indicated was a *coupe de grace* fired by Roy just a foot away from the fallen Denhardt's head. Myers testified about being confronted by Doc, and Roy's intervention. "Roy told me to go on in and keep my mouth shut," Myers said.

"What did you do?" Meredith asked.

"I went on in," Myers said to a laughing murmur that broke the tension in the courtroom.

The defense did not question Myers.

Thirteen-year-old Bruce Tracey and his patrolman father, Jep, as well as Harry Flood and former Sheriff John Dawson Buckner, who also saw the shots fired, all testified in concert with Myers' recollections. Drs. Lapsley and Weakley rounded out the case for the prosecution.

Unlike Denhardt's examining trial, Doc, Roy, and Jack happily took the witness stand. Their testimony was offered calmly and sincerely. Their expectation was that they would be tried for murder, but their hope was to be out on bond in the meantime. To achieve that, the judge would have to be convinced that they were not a threat to society and that there was evidence of extenuating circumstances in the death of Denhardt. Roy was the first to take take the stand.

After a preliminary discussion of how he got to know the general, Roy testified that he had not seen Denhardt between the day of the hung jury from his first trial and the "chance" meeting in Shelbyville. Roy said that they had had few personal encounters during the trial, such as during one lunch break when Roy and his nieces Mary Pryor and Frances had been seated at a restaurant in Eminence, Kentucky. After "Denhardt walked in, and when he saw me, he backed out of the restaurant with his hand on his hip. He didn't take his eyes off of us," Roy testified.

On the day in question, Roy said that it was just a coincidence that he, his brothers, and Denhardt had all been in Shelbyville at the same time. "I wanted to talk to Mr. Kinsolving about some evidence. Denhardt was going to slur my sister's character." He also had heard that Myers and Berry were trying to get a change of venue to Shelby County, so they had wanted to line up a local attorney in advance, such as State Senator Gilbert, but they had stopped by Blakemore's Grocery to get advice from a relative of their late brother-in-law. All three entered the grocery about 8:30 p.m. and talked with several persons in the store until Mr. Blakemore came by.

"We left the store, I imagine, about ten or a little after," Roy said. When all three left in Doc's car, they took a right a 6th Street and took a u-turn to come back to the intersection at 6th and Main. "When we got back up to the corner, it occurred to me that I never did find out what time Mr. Blakemore would be at New Castle for the trial on Tuesday. I said, 'I'd better stop and make certain.' Doc said, 'Aw, you've always got someone else to see. We'll never get back home.'

"We parked the car near the corner. Jack was in the back and didn't get out. I got out, and I imagine Doc got out about the same time I did." That's when Roy heard someone shout their family name nervously— "There's the Garrs!"—or something, and Roy saw Denhardt running in his direction.

"I saw Denhardt go for his right hip, and by God, I went for my gun. I knew he'd kill me just like he would a rat if he had the opportunity," Roy said. "When he threw his hand toward his pocket, I really started shooting. I was scared, and I started shooting, and I didn't stop shooting until I emptied my gun," he added. Roy freely admitted that when the shooting started, his mind flashed to the reports that, at his second trial, Denhardt planned on testifying he had been intimate with Verna in a hotel.

"I went wild. I had a vision of my dead sister, and I went toward them, and I went shooting. I know he killed my sister, and I knew he would kill me." After it was all over, Roy said, "I looked at my two brothers and said, 'Let's go to jail or find the law.' Then the officer came up, and I told him, 'I shot this man. Here's my gun.'"

But Roy denied Myers' claim of a point blank shot to the back of Denhardt's head. On the contrary, Roy claimed that at one point he got wind of a local plot to capture Denhardt and force a confession or kill him, whichever came first, but he interposed some sanity into that plan, and it went no further. In effect, Roy was saying that he had saved Denhardt's life once.

After an hour of testifying and answering questions, Jack followed Roy. He substantiated Roy's testimony about the chance meeting, adding that he only started to pay attention when he heard "Garr!" being shouted. "I looked up and saw Denhardt and Myers. Just then somebody shot. I don't know whether it was Roy or Doc." Jack also claimed to have seen Denhardt reach for his right pocket as he ran toward Roy and that he never saw Roy deliver a *coupe de grace* to the fallen Denhardt. He was only on the stand twenty minutes.

Due to his nervous condition perhaps, Clarke and Gilbert saved Doc for last, in case he could not handle the stress of testifying, but he did well. In a brief autobiography, Doc openly admitted to being hospitalized after a nervous breakdown following the war. Questioned by Clarke, Doc chimed with his brothers that they had been to Shelbyville many times to talk with Kinsolving, not to confront Denhardt. "We never had any suspicion he or his attorneys were in Shelbyville." Doc explained how, as Denhardt ran toward the hotel, he "squirmed kind of like this, and his right hand went back in the direction of his right pocket like this," he said, demonstrating. Denhardt always had bragged about being armed at all times.

"I didn't see who fired the first shots. I pulled my revolver and shot," Doc testified. "I'd been warned General Denhardt was a dangerous man. People have told me, 'Doc, look out for him.' I had heard of him drawing a pistol on people. I shot twice. I don't know if I hit him. I didn't see Myers at first and then I went out there and covered him. I had no intention of shooting Myers unless he was to shoot my brother or me. When the officer came up, I told him Jack had nothing to do with it."

Meredith had many more questions about this coincidence of them running into Denhardt carrying fully loaded pistols, but Doc stood firm that he "had been warned by people ever since the tragedy of my sister being killed. Yes, I was alarmed, that's why I had been carrying the gun."

"You had no desire to harm General Denhardt, of course!" Meredith sneered sarcastically.

Doc paused before speaking slowly, "I didn't especially love him," which got some snickers from the gallery. Doc, too, had been on the stand about an hour.

Kinsolving was called to verify that the purpose of the conversation on Monday evening was to discuss new evidence, "particularly that of Mrs. Webster." Mrs. Webster was one of the laundry ladies who had heard Denhardt threaten Verna but did not think her testimony would be needed in the first trial and had not wanted to get involved. Upon questioning from Meredith, Kinsolving admitted that he gotten a call from Sergeant Messmer telling him that there was to be a conference between Denhardt and his attorneys in Shelbyville, but the Garr brothers knew nothing of this, as far as Kinsolving was concerned.

If it were true that it was a Denhardt defense strategy to keep delaying the general's murder trial with the hope that the pubic would lose interest and emotions would wane, it could be said that the Garrs' defense team felt it would benefit more from a trial being held quickly while emotions ran hot. Regardless of how soon a trial could be scheduled, none of the brothers wanted to spend the time in jail waiting for it, so it all came down to whether Judge Walters was going to allow a bond.

In his summation, Meredith had gone over the testimony one more time and declared that when put together, the evidence clearly showed this was a cold-blooded, premeditated execution of a man still presumed to be innocent, and demanded that the Garrs be held without bond.

In his closing remarks, however, Gilbert said that all the Commonwealth's witnesses demonstrated that it was not murder, that it was "a very unfortunate circumstance that they chanced to meet" in Shelbyville Monday night. Gilbert criticized Meredith for his misleading statement that Denhardt was attempting to run away from the Garr Boys when he was shot: "Mr. Meredith is unacquainted with Shelbyville, or he would know that Denhardt was running toward them. He couldn't have run away from them and run to the hotel to save his life."

Gilbert even called into question the rock-solid testimony of Myers, which had led the prosecution's case. "Mr. Myers told it in a way it could not possibly have happened. I do not accuse him of perjury, but in his excitement, he confused the situation. There was not a series of shots, a pause, and then that one shot."

Gilbert then moved in for the kill himself. "We feel that we have overcome the presumption that these men should be held without bond. Thank you, Your Honor."

Before he ruled, Judge Walters asked for total silence in the court and once again promised that he would clear the room if necessary. He wanted order and he would not tolerate a demonstration, he scolded. The Garrs stood humbly for the ruling. Judge Walters reminded Meredith this was merely a court of inquiry, the subtext of which was that he was about to break bad news to the attorney general gently. He said that the defense had repeatedly asked for bond all week, but he had refused. Walters then paused before ruling with Clarke and Gilbert, "The proof is not evident nor the presumption great enough to hold these men without bond."

Despite the judge's warning—or because of it—the crowd of more than twelve hundred spectators broke out into immediate, rafter-shaking applause, which then became sustained shouts of support for the Garr Boys. Women screamed; men hollered. Mary Pryor and Frances threw their arms around their uncles and kissed them as hundreds of friends and family from all over rushed to the defense table from all sides. *The Courier-Journal* described it as "a demonstration that for fervor and spontaneousness probably never has been topped in a Kentucky courtroom."

Finally quieting the court one more time, the visibly annoyed Judge Walters said to the prosecution, "If I were to deny bond, I feel that they would be released within a week by the circuit judge on a *habeas corpus* hearing." Bond was set at $20,000 each for Doc and Roy and $10,000 for Jack. Dr. A.G. Ellison of New Castle, Shelbyville tobacco merchant James Bright, and the Garrs' wealthy neighbor, William Belknap, joined forces to furnish the amount that guaranteed the Garr Boys' freedom. "I'm awful happy to go home," Roy said. "This is the way I hoped it would be." Doc gave no sign of nervousness or instability, just joy. "I feel like a million dollars. I feel better now than I have in the last few months. I'm going home to see Mother."

Back on their farms but not out of the woods: Doc, Roy, and Jack would all be tried together, their defenses shared, in the Shelby County Courthouse with Circuit Judge C.C. Marshall presiding. Shelby County had been one of the preferred places for a change of venue for Denhardt's trial, considered more objective and less hostile to the general, but after the examining trial, Meredith immediately pushed for a change of venue. He would not get it. Everybody would have to take their chances in Shelby County sometime in October. Everybody but Doc.

The loss of a sister who loved Doc so dearly, the trials, the jail time, the publicity, all finally caught up with the shell-shocked veteran, and he had to be hospitalized again in a private sanitarium in Pewee Valley. Doc's breakdown was complete. It was reported that among the things Doc would shout in confinement was, "I shot him, too! Roy is trying to hog all the credit!"

The hate mail and the harassing phone calls continued for Myers until the trial, so his State Police protection continued too when needed. The FBI did track down some of the cranks sending those letters, but there were no prosecutions. It was all misguided anger vented at an innocent person.

With the evidence and testimony of the coroner's inquest and the examining trial, the Shelby County grand jury met on October 4 to consider the charges. "Should an indictment be returned, it was indicated that the trial would begin soon, possibly next week," the *New York Times* reported. Meredith appeared bored by the defense's plea of self-defense. "That old dodge about somebody reaching for his hip has been overworked in Kentucky," he said.

But the "man on the street" was firmly behind the Garr brothers closing the gap between a well-known bully willing to lie and this promising but still unreliable crime science unable to prove murder in the courts. "I think the Garrs should be left off with a five dollar fine and a severe reprimand—and never mind the reprimand," one court watcher was quoted as saying before the Garr trial.

At an October 7, 1937, pre-trial hearing in front of Judge Marshall, Doc was a no-show for his arraignment. Defense counsel presented an affidavit from Dr. H. B. Blaydes stating that Doc was in a "bad mental state... a person of unsound mind under the influence of opiates." In Dr. Blaydes' medical opinion, it was "unsafe and dangerous for him, and for the public, for him to be brought into court at this time." Defense then requested that Doc's trial be continued until the next term of the circuit court in Shelby County, but Judge Marshall overruled that motion because the defendant himself was not in the court to make the plea. It's possible that the opiates Doc was taking were not for his mental health but for a painful, untamed ulcer that was spreading.

Meredith was unrelenting on the issue of bond. Insisting that the overwhelming evidence from the examining trial showed "a premeditated and concert act" by all three brothers, Meredith pushed for Judge Marshall to take a harder line on allowing the Garrs to be free until the trial date. But as *The New York Times* covered it with the AP, "Over the strenuous objections of the Commonwealth, Roy and Jack Garr were released under $20,000 each today to await trial on October 18 on charges of murdering Brig. Gen. Henry H. Denhardt.

"At the same time, the court orders the $20,000 bond of their brother, Dr. E.S. Garr, forfeited when he failed to appear in court this morning for arraignment." Ouch. The hearing was typical of Judge Marshall, a little for the prosecution, a little for the defense, and the firm hand of the court reaffirmed. The defense said they would file a motion to set aside the forfeiture, but at least Roy and Jack were still free, and the trial date was just weeks away.

In a short, stand-alone piece in the *Chicago Tribune* on October 16, an unnamed writer cited the attorneys representing Roy and Jack as saying they hoped to stuff the jury with Ku Klux Klansmen. Since real Klansmen in the "secret society" would never identify another Klansman in public, the unattributed story seemed odd and perhaps another product of Northern, anti-Southern bias. While any large Southern, white, Protestant family might have some history of KKK membership, there was no family record, written or oral, of the Klan in the Garrs. On the contrary, many Garrs, such as my grandmother, were social progressives, especially with regard to racial issues.

Further confounding that solitary mention of the KKK in the Trib, when the trial started on October 18, the court found it almost impossible to get a jury at all. Starting with the standard jury pool of twenty-four, so many veniremen claimed that they had previously formed opinions about the case that one hundred more Shelby County citizens were called in the next day just to get a jury of twelve. If there really was a plan to fill the jury with Klan members who might resonate with the "Code of Honor" killing of a man like Denhardt (who was an open racist), the lawyers would not have broadcast that, and the jury would have filled up quickly with men willing to lie and not disqualify themselves. It would almost take longer to seat the jury of twelve tobacco farmers who claimed not to have formed an opinion than to try the actual case.

When the arguments did commence on October 20, once again the Shelbyville County Courthouse was bulging like the chew in Judge Marshall's cheek. Everybody was there from Oldham County again: Mary Pryor and Francis, every possible Garr-Blankenbaker-Tyler-Taylor relation, and a very special guest who arrived every day in a chauffeur-driven limousine, the Hollywood director, D. W. Griffith.

Griffith, or "Cousin David" as he was known to family, was La Grange's most famous native son. He directed more than five hundred movies in his career, but he's best known for *Birth of a Nation*, the epic, blockbuster movie about the South that forever changed how Hollywood movies were shot and how the role of the director was viewed. By the early 1930s, however, despite some other minor successes, he could no longer get work in Hollywood. Griffith came to Shelbyville to cheer on the Garrs and possibly connect on their story.

The Hollywood director's presence only added to the cinematic nature of the Garr trial. Contrary to the freak show circus energy outside the Henry County Courthouse for Denhardt's trial in April, all the people in attendance for the Garr Boys were openly rooting for the Garr Boys as if they were eating popcorn and watching their heroes in a matinee cliffhanger movie. Many times, Judge Marshall had to tamp down the pro-Garr enthusiasm of the room. Whenever something went well for the defense, it seemed that men, but again, especially women, had to sit on their hands to stop from applauding, squealing, or laughing. The charges were read, and Roy and Jack pled "self-defense." A motion was made by the defense to dismiss the charges against Jack Garr for lack of evidence. Judge Marshall tabled the motion for the time being. A new trial date of February 4, 1938, was set for Doc, the forfeiture issue having been resolved.

The path of both the prosecution and the defense was predictable in the trial of Roy and Jack, at first. Meredith remained incredulous that anybody would claim self-defense while shooting somebody three times in the back. Myers methodically testified to every detail that would build the prosecution's case for the premeditated execution of Denhardt by the Garr brothers. The Commonwealth effectively proved that Denhardt was unarmed and attempting to flee from, and not attack, the Garr Boys. As promised, however, Myers begrudgingly admitted that Roy saved his life from Doc, who seemed detached uncharacteristically during the shooting. The fact that Doc would eventually break down and could not be in court shone an even more favorable light on the leadership and bravery of Roy Garr. Sparing an innocent life, even if it meant intervening with your own kin, made Roy look even more heroic.

The defense offered reasonable doubt by explaining how Roy and Jack had accidentally run into Denhardt and Myers. Reporter Ruth Reynolds of the *Syracuse Post-Standard* preserved this exchange in her coverage:

"What did the sight of him do to you?" asked Gilbert.

"He scared me. I saw him go for his pocket. I went for my gun. He kept coming toward me. I emptied my gun at him."

"Why?" posed Gilbert.

"I knew he was a killer, and that if I didn't get him, he'd get me. I knew my life wasn't safe."

"Did anything occur to you to you while you were shooting?" Gilbert intoned suggestively.

"Yes, I had a vision of my dead sister."

Mrs. Verdie Bennett, Verna's housekeeper who was never called for the first trial, testified that she had overheard Denhardt tell Verna that he would shoot her three brothers—"especially that big bum, Roy, like a rat"—if they interfered with his proposed marriage to Verna. "All three of your brothers are yellow," Mrs. Bennett claimed Denhardt said. Mrs. Gus Brawner testified she witnessed Denhardt saying, "If it hadn't been for the Garr Boys, Mrs. Taylor and I would have been happily married by now."

But self-defense was not the only defense. Running on a parallel line, Gilbert also proffered what could only be called a "Denhardt deserved to die" defense. Denhardt's fellow officers from the Kentucky National Guard trashed their comrade. Judge Marshall did his best to curtail this testimony, but it just amounted to a series of bells that couldn't be un-rung.

Fellow Brig. Gen. Ellerbe Carter called Denhardt "the most domineering, violent, unscrupulous, brutal man I have ever known in my life."

"Disregard that answer," Judge Marshall instructed the jury.

Major Joseph Kelly testified, "Denhardt once threatened *my* life!" When Judge Marshall informed the major that his comment was "out of order," Major Kelly was the one who re-calibrated his words to say that Denhardt was "cruel and inhuman—a veritable Jekyll and Hyde."

And yet there was also a third, somewhat surprising, justification for Roy's actions: He was "temporarily emotionally insane" at the time of the shooting. In the words of Philip Kinsley of the *Chicago Tribune*, "The doctrine of irresponsibility, a 'mental explosion' that inhibited normal judgement, was invoked as the last plea this afternoon in the trial of Roy and Jack Garr." The medical testimony to Roy's "emotional insanity" was supplied by three different doctors, each of whom were brought in to answer a fifteen-minute-long hypothetical question that had been fashioned by Gilbert during a conference with Judge Marshall. The "question" was really a long summation of the major facts of the case from the defense point-of-view, starting with Denhardt's indictment for Verna's murder, his April trial, the warnings they received that Denhardt wanted to kill the Garr Boys, and ending with the recent drunken ramblings about Verna's sexual history. Listed as a "fact" for the jury to consider was Roy's vision of Verna's face when he saw Denhardt on the street. Accepting that all of these details were true, Gilbert asked each doctor separately, could Roy's actions have come as a result of "temporary emotional insanity"?

Drs. Milton Board, Leon P. Solomon, and John R. Peters, all "experts in mental diseases" in Louisville, concurred that Roy had been emotionally insane when he pulled the trigger because of a "mental explosion occasioned by seeing the general" in person. Given the scenario that Gilbert presented, the doctors more or less concluded that a man would be incapable of lucid reasoning at that exact moment. How long did the temporary emotional insanity moment last? The doctors all agreed that Roy felt much better right after he shot Denhardt.

Having established self-defense, the final day of the trial was spent putting a capstone on the "Denhardt deserved to die" defense and the "temporary emotional insanity" argument. Kentucky State Police Lieutenant J.C. Wyatt expressed his opinion that after several encounters with Denhardt, the former lieutenant governor and adjutant general had a "violent nature," an opinion shared by Louis Hall, a Louisville police detective also called to the stand.

Finally, local Shelbyville physicians Dr. E. B. Smith and Dr. W. H. Nash—the latter man being the same who had treated Roy's foot—endorsed the "emotionally insane" theory after hearing Roy was vexed by widespread reports that Denhardt's counsel was going to introduce testimony "casting reflection upon the virtue and chastity" of his late baby sister. The emotional build-up seeing Dehardt in the flesh was too great. Knowing what a bad man he was, knowing that he threatened to shoot Roy "like a rat," caused the mental explosion that led Roy to shoot for his life instead of run.

When the defense rested, the Commonwealth announced it would not offer any rebuttal to the defense theories or witnesses. Judge Marshall returned to the issue of the defense motion to dismiss the murder charge against Jack Garr because no evidence or testimony was entered indicating guilt or culpability. Without any fanfare, Judge Marshall sustained the motion. Jack was immediately a free man through a "directed verdict." An excited but muted hooray was immediately thwarted by a stern look from the bench.

In his summation, a dispirited Meredith went through the Commonwealth's case one more time and then mocked the defense by saying that in all his years prosecuting cases, "This is the first time I have seen the defense start out with a self-defense motive and end up with an insanity plea."

Closing for the defense, Gilbert asserted that Roy did act in self-defense from a known aggressor, that when he chased Denhardt it was because he had gone temporarily emotional insane, and as the defense had proven, that "Roy Garr had a right to put down a 'mad dog.' And we all know that is exactly what General Denhardt was, a 'mad dog.'"

Judge Marshall had minimal instructions for the jury. They could either find Roy guilty of murder or guilty of voluntary manslaughter or they could acquit him. The jury was gone for only one hour and fifteen minutes. As Denhardt himself told reporter Martin Kane the night he begged for a drink, "A quick verdict would have been 'guilty.' I used to be a lawyer." A seventy-minute minute deliberation did mean that everybody was in agreement, one way or another.

Local magistrate Judge Walters had warned against any demonstration before he ruled on bond for the Garrs, and he was ignored completely, but this was Circuit Court Judge Marshall, and he knew how to impose his authority. Whereas Judge Walters presided over a mere hearing, this was a full murder trial for a man's life, and Judge Marshall was intolerant of any inappropriate courtroom displays of emotion. "Treat this like a house of worship," Judge Marshall said, staring down the courtroom as he began his usual speech. When everybody had settled down to his liking, he asked the foreman, "The jury has reached a verdict?"

"We have, Your Honor."

"What say ye?" Judge Marshall asked, and the packed courtroom stopped breathing.

"We find Roy Garr *not guilty*!"

In that instant, before the foreman could finish the "t" on "not," Judge Marshall's authority vanished like spit on a griddle. Hundreds of people inside the courtroom screamed and burst into sustained applause and yelled out the windows to all of Shelbyville. On the street, others whooped it up, honked their horns, and hundreds of townsfolk came out of their shops and cars and celebrated with cheering, singing, and dancing near the courthouse. One historian noted that many of the men gave a "rebel yell," the Confederate battle cry, which startled several Yankee reporters. Perhaps in their attempt to treat the courtroom like it was their house of worship, everybody in attendance simultaneously decided to act like Pentecostals.

Judge Marshall, unaccustomed to having his courtroom instructions disregarded, frustratedly pounded his gavel for order for several minutes, standing and rapping louder and louder until the courtroom calmed down. Angry but so close to the end of the trial, Judge Marshall restrained himself long enough to wrap up the case once and for all. The jury was polled, the twelve were thanked by the judge, and court was dismissed. At the sound of the last gavel, the crowds picked up right where they left off and converged on the Garrs with such unbounded spirits that deputy sheriffs were forced to clear a path through the jubilance to get Roy and Jack outside to more praise and celebration.

Even stoic Roy let loose. Responding to a newsman's question about what was next for the family, Roy said smiling, almost laughing, "I am going back to La Grange and forget it all. My wife is sick, and I want to get back to her."

Jack was relieved and concerned about the sickness of their mother, too. "I believe the verdict will make her feel a great deal better."

After the verdict, an AP reporter writing for the *New York Times* asked Coleman Wright whether, as the prosecutor for Shelby County, he would move that the murder case against Doc be dismissed. His grumpy response was, "What would *you* do? If we couldn't convict Roy, we certainly couldn't convict Dr. Garr." The charges were eventually dropped.

Outside the courtroom, to the great amusement of the crowd, one anonymous juror explained the seventy-minute deliberation by saying that all twelve tobacco farmers actually found Roy not guilty on the very first ballot, but it didn't seem right to turn round and come back into the courtroom so fast. So, he said with a broad smile, "we stayed out to make it look as though we were thinking it over carefully."

Roy and Jack got a personal handshake from director D.W. Griffith, who asked the men whether they might be interested in letting him make a movie about their story, but they politely declined. They were not interested in more attention. Griffith was disappointed at having that honor turned down, but he understood. He said good-bye, got back in his limousine, and left. He never made another movie.

If a "not guilty" verdict was not justice enough for Roy, it might have brought the Garr Boys some satisfaction knowing that the man who administered the fatal shot actually got the courtroom treatment that Denhardt thought he deserved. Roy was found not guilty unanimously on the first ballot, and when the verdict was read, the entire town—if not Kentucky—celebrated. This was the kind of love and respect that Denhardt had craved so much. Ironically perhaps, if anybody should have used a "temporary emotional insanity" defense, it should have been Denhardt. Given his prominence, if Denhardt had admitted that he could not handle it when Verna broke up with him, that he sort of went blank before exploding with rage, with the right expert testimony, Denhardt himself might have been found not guilty just like Roy.

But by any measure, unlike almost everybody else in the Bluegrass State, Attorney General Meredith did not care for what he had seen in Shelbyville. When he addressed the media before leaving for his home in Greenville, KY, Meredith stammered out that what just happened in that courtroom was "a farce."

He had it sort of right. The Garr trial was not a farce, it was more of a satire.

Chapter Twenty-Six

In their trial for the murder of Gen. Henry H. Denhardt, the Garr Boys and their defense team did make a mockery of the American legal system. Not only did they perjure themselves by creating a pretense that their bloody run-in with Denhardt was accidental, that Roy went "temporarily emotionally insane," and that they really did feel that shooting him was an act of self-defense, but Verna's housekeeper, employees, and others also might have perjured themselves in order to secure a "not guilty" verdict for Doc, Roy, and Jack. It's hard to tell who had been legitimately prevented from testifying before, who was sincerely confused about whether their damning witness would have made a difference in the first trial, and who was just "helping" the cause. The evidence shows that the brothers had been orchestrating the circumstances that brought them within a pistol shot of Denhardt, intentionally waiting in Blakemore's Grocery, stalling until Denhardt returned from his beer, thereby creating the volatile conditions that resulted in the general's death. Murder and perjury are morally wrong and illegal, but was this philosophically indefensible?

Because if Myers, Berry, and the Denhardt family decried the state of justice after the Garr Boys trial, judging by the general's own legal files, they only have themselves to blame. To be exonerated, the Garrs merely ran the Denhardt legal team playbook. The Garrs' claim that Denhardt was killed in self-defense was just as ludicrous as Denhardt's claim that Verna killed herself. The Garrs' defense was that they were victims of circumstances; Denhardt's defense was that he was a victim of "Messmer and politics!" In his testimony, Roy Garr even saved Denhardt's life once— just like how Denhardt wanted to be seen not as Verna's destroyer but as her savior, too. Both defense teams exploited the difference between what was known to be true and what could be proven to be true in a court of law.

Myers, Berry, and Meredith were correct that the Garr defense team's monkeyshines were unbefitting a Kentucky court, but that may be more reflective of a clubby credo that maintains only lawyers should be allowed to game the system. When attorneys do it, it's good law-yerin'. When anybody else does it, it's unethical, by God. All the Garr defense team did was "out-Denhardt" Denhardt's defense team. The jury nullification verdict was a big "How-do-you-do!" to all the fancy legal book larnin' that allowed smart men to lose all common sense in defense of Denhardt.

Roy was right when he said once, "If everyone who gets on to that witness chair will only tell the truth, it'll get straightened out some-how." It may be the biggest lesson from this whole mess. If Denhardt had told the truth, it would have gotten straightened out somehow. Everything bad that happened started with Denhardt's unwillingness to be honest, first with himself, and then with anybody else. All le-gal systems are predicated on witnesses telling the truth. Denhardt's propensity for story molding—and his attorneys' deft sophistry that covered for it—broke down the legal system long before Roy Garr and his co-conspirators got on the stand. In a just society, it is wrong to take the law into one's own hands, but by lying and manipulating the legal system to cover for his murderous act, Denhardt put himself above a just society and onto his own plane. The Garr family was frustrated mightily when they were fighting to make Denhardt play by civilized society's rules; their great release came in joining Denhardt on the un-just plane he had created for himself.

In this way, "self-defense" and "temporary emotional insanity" were, in effect, satires of "Messmer and politics!" and "spontaneous suicide." This is why the Garrs' trial reads more like a sitcom than a courtroom drama. If satire is the use of humor to show that someone or something powerful is foolish, weak, or bad—a discourse with a moral purpose—then it would be fair to say that the Garr trial, with all of its arcane, specious expert testimony and over-the-top legal argu-ments, was a satire of the Denhardt trial. Of the many funny moments, my favorite was the testimony from the doctors that confirmed Roy's temporary emotional insanity was cured right after he shot Denhardt. No kidding.

Each Garr brother knew that to do right by their sister, they had to do wrong by the system. It was a trade-off they were willing to make, but there was no pride in it. Even within the family, the Garr brothers and their direct descendants would prefer that nobody bring up either Verna's or Denhardt's death. Researching this book, I reached out to two of my cousins that are more directly related to Verna than I am but neither would reach back. Maybe it's like Doc said to Jane Dixon, "A man who had any kind of shame in him wouldn't push himself out in the public eye with what he had hanging over his head." The Garrs eschewed their celebrity status because, according to the rules of Southern chivalry, it was not right to flaunt the victory in the Denhardt family's face, and more importantly, death had wiped Denhardt's slate clean. He had paid the ultimate price for his dishonor, but at least in the eyes of the Garr Boys, like any fallen enemy soldier, Denhardt was finally a free man.

When my mother first mentioned that she was researching this story back in the 1980s, Verna's sister, Mary Lillian, wrote my mother and called her a "family traitor." But it was not only about keeping the lid on the ancestral potboiler. Mary Lillian told my mom that if ANYONE should write about it, it should be her daughter, Mary Neal, who had finished college and written briefly for a local newspaper (mostly wedding announcements, my mother thought). "That was a dig to me because we ran out of money for college after I had begun," my mom told me. Later in life, my mother graduated from Northwestern University. "None of us liked Mary Lillian," my mother said, "She liked to 'put on airs,' as they say. She was jealous of Juanita for some reason—maybe her intelligence and common sense—so I'm sure she must have been jealous of Verna also, for her beauty."

Since a few historians have written already about these events in smaller articles, I hope I can be forgiven eventually by any of Verna's descendants for telling her story now.

One of those historians, William E. Ellis, honed in on something I think others have missed. "Long before the deaths of Patricia Wilson or Verna Garr Taylor, General Henry H. Denhardt appeared to be on a collision course with violent death." Looking at his history of being shot at, Denhardt did seem destined to be killed by somebody. If it had not been the Garr Boys, maybe it would have been a political quarrel after a bottle of bourbon, or a flirtation with another man's wife, or because Denhardt refused to pay a man for services rendered.

The other strong possibility was that if Denhardt had gotten away with killing Verna, it would have been just a matter of time until there was a third suspicious death in his presence. It's easy to imagine a third merry widow whom he also "loved too much to kill" enjoying a couple months of a honeymoon on the farm before drowning in an improbable bathtub accident or some such. Not to put too fine a point on it, but by killing Denhardt, the Garr Boys could easily have saved another woman's life.

But the sad thing is, in his own mind, if he had killed again, Denhardt would still have felt blameless after being around bizarre death #3, too. Ann Rule defined killers like Denhardt when she told me, "Looking back on what they did, they don't think they did anything wrong. In their minds, they are in the middle of the world, and the rest of us are circling around them like merry-go-round horses."

It's a reflex that narcissist/sociopaths cannot control. Denhardt's life of vituperation can be linked directly to a diagnosis that did not exist in the 1930s, so nobody knew to be on the lookout for it, how to handle it, or how to work with it legally. Back then, for want of a psychological understanding, Denhardt was referred to as a "mad dog," that is, seemingly fine at first but ultimately untrustworthy and potentially lethal. What else would explain a man who would dishonor a woman to save his own skin? Since there is no such proper legal defense on the books as "Death before Dishonor," Gilbert offered it in subtext, but the jury knew what he meant.

Like Moby Dick and Ahab, Denhardt took Doc with him to the deep end. Doc never fully recovered from his breakdown after shooting the general. He bounced back and forth from a doctor's care and the farm, but it was a downward spiral. He did make the news one more time, however. On December 8, 1938, Doc issued a public statement saying that Denhardt did not kill Verna alone. Denhardt was involved, Doc said, but he knew at least two other men played a part in her death that night. Doc said he made his secret report to Attorney General Meredith, but he took no action. A month later, Doc died in considerable pain from peritonitis and sepsis, probably brought on by a stomach ulcer. That alone could drive a man crazy.

Roy Garr lived out his natural life training champion dogs and living in seclusion. By chance, I talked to somebody who knew him once. "Let me tell you a story about your kin," a public relations executive from Kentucky once told me during a business meeting in New York City.

> My dad was a serious hunter, and every few years he would decide it was time to get a hunting dog trained right, and that would mean he would splurge and get a Garr dog. And that was always an exciting trip for us kids. When the dog was ready, my dad would pile us into the station wagon for the drive to Oldham County to see ol' Roy Garr. We knew to be on our best behavior. Roy never said much to us. We were always taught the Garr brothers were masters of the craft of dog training. Of course, we knew about the shooting, too.

Jack Garr continued to flourish outside of Cincinnati. That new baby girl who Jack's wife, Marguerite, was having that prevented him from being armed that night in Shelbyville went on to become Miss Ohio in 1955. It would have made her Aunt Verna so proud to see her niece, Margie Garr, competing in the Miss America Pageant, playing a zither and singing "Old Black Joe." There was a little bit of Verna Garr's magic personality in Margie Garr's winning smile.

When her husband Major Holmes died, Juanita returned to La Grange to take care of her mother. Mary Lillian moved to Birmingham, Alabama, where it's said she played up her own background as a "Bluegrass blueblood" in an attempt to fit in to a larger "society" crowd.

According to the book *Dinner with D.W. Griffith and Other Memories* by Joseph Woodson Oglesby, who was a cousin to both the famous director and Chester Woolfolk, Ches suffered after the trial. "Nobody in a sober frame of mind swallowed the defense attorney's flight of fancy," but after being publicly accused of being a tormentor of such a kind woman, Ches got out of town by joining the U.S. Air Force. After his service, he opened La Grange's first official dry cleaners and laundry (Verna always had to sub-contract her dry cleaning to Louisville) and used the profits from that business to buy real estate around Oldham County. Having already come from a wealthy family, when he died, Chester was one of the richest men in the area, but he died alone, unmarried, with no kids. "Chester was always peculiar," Oglesby's mother said. "[B]ut after Verna was murdered, he hardly spoke a word to anybody; crossed to the other side of the street if he saw a relative or a friend approaching." Another victim of Denhardt.

According to attorney Berry's letter file, sometime before Denhardt's death, Berry and Denhardt seemed to have come to an agreement about Berry's fee. The final amount was to be $1,977.50 (give or take $200 that Denhardt says he sent in the form of checks that Berry said he had no record of). There is no "thank you" letter in the file designating the close of the account. There is a notation at the bottom of the letter saying that a copy was going to Mr. Felts, so it seems likely that the negotiation still involved Denhardt's appointed arbitrator. In that same letter, Berry mentions that Hundley still was expecting a check from Denhardt for something unspecified and Hundley was getting "rather insistent," Berry hinted.

The next letter in the file came after Denhardt's death. Dr. McCormack was handling all of the general's personal estate matters, so Berry wrote to him in regard to money also owed to a Mr. Wright, but it's not clear who that is. "I am really quite humiliated in not being able to send checks to all of them," the doctor writes. "[T]he whole thing is in a tangle and I haven't been able to find any more blood in the turnip."

Unless a check arrived between the first week of September and September 20, Denhardt also died without paying Myers a penny. Maybe Myers got to keep the pearl-handled pocket knife.

The hotel itself burned to the ground in 1944, but the owners never rebuilt. A historical marker is placed just feet from where Denhardt died.

After Denhardt's death, the big battle in Berry's letter file was not for overdue legal bills, it was over who got to keep Denhardt's .45 revolver. Starting in January of 1938, an executive at the First National Bank of La Grange sent a letter to Berry asking if he could have it. A few months later, Berry makes a pitch to Dr. McCormack for the gun either on behalf of this guy at the bank or another friend.

On May 11, 1938, Berry received a letter from Jesse Denhardt, asking for his assistance in removing "the pistols and the overcoat" belonging to his brother out of a so-called "trophy case" in the Henry County Courthouse and sending it back to the family at once. In a return letter, Berry assured the general's brother that he was being misled by somebody, that the items were still being stored as evidence in a box somewhere, not in a trophy case, but as soon as they were released by the judge, Berry would make sure they made it Bowling Green. The Denhardts wrote back in gratitude, reaffirming they wanted the pistols and the coat.

The very last item in Berry's file pertained to the large diamond ring that Verna had tried to give back to Denhardt on the day they broke up, but that he insisted she keep, only for him to obsess about it after he killed her. In response to a comment by the family, Berry had written to Jesse Denhardt to explain that the ring had been released to the Garr family after they filed a formal motion in front of Judge Marshall.

"I think it's quite improper for the Court to have sustained the motion and order the ring returned to the Garrs, but the propriety of that action may be tested only by an appeal," advised Berry. An appeal was never filed in civil court over the ring, although a continuation of the "feud" would have suited many in the press just fine. Other than "The Garr Ballad" performed by bluegrass bands or the odd newspaper article here or there, the dispute faded over time. Each family had one dead. The Denhardts got to keep the gun and the Garrs kept Verna's ring. It seems almost too perfunctory to mention that the tragedy of November 6, 1936, would have ended quite differently if only General Denhardt had taken the ring back from Verna when she offered it, and Verna actually had taken Denhardt's gun and run away with it as he claimed. As for the tragedy of September 20, 1937, that, too, would have ended differently if, as my grandfather phrased it, Denhardt hadn't been such a "foul ball."

ABOUT THE AUTHOR

Although Ian Punnett was the first of his Kentucky mother's family born north of the Mason-Dixon line, he still was raised on a steady diet of grits, fried chicken, and Tennessee Ernie Ford's "Songs of the Civil War South." The pattern was set. No matter where Ian was living, his thoughts were never far from the South.

Photo courtesy of Fred W. Ullrich

As a professional broadcaster, Ian experienced success equally in Minneapolis-St. Paul and Chicago as well as Nashville and Atlanta. On top of his weekday radio and TV work, Ian may be best known as the weekend host of the nationally syndicated *Coast to Coast AM*, heard on more than 500 stations across the country.

In 2013, Ian left commercial media to pursue his PhD at the Walter Cronkite School of Journalism and Mass Communication, part of Arizona State University. He is the author of several books, including *How to Pray When You're Pissed at God* from Random House, which was featured on CBS Morning News, Esquire.com, and CNN.com, and two children's books written to raise money for canine charities, *Dizzy the Mutt with the Propeller Butt* and *Jackula the Vampire Dog*.

Index

Brown, L.R. 95
Brown, Mary Pryor (Mrs. Allen)
135, 136, 138, 140, 151, 196,
236, 249, 282, 291, 295, 298; *see*
also Mary Pryor Taylor
Bryant, James 133
Buckmaster, F.C. 146
Buckner, Sheriff John Dawson 291

C

Carpenter, George 67, 136
Carpenter, Preston 67, 136
Carter, Brig. Gen. Ellerbe 24, 299
Carter, Les 13
Cartwright, Duncan 64
Carver, Silliam O., Jr. 192
Chandler, Albert B. ("Happy") 25
Cheek, Rev. Dr. George W. 287
Chicago Daily News 131
Chicago Herald-Examiner 287
Chicago Times 287
Chicago Tribune 116, 144, 229, 297,
300
Chilton, Carl 133
Cincinnati Post 288
Clark, General George Rogers 23
Clark, J. Ballard 107, 132, 184, 194
Clark, William 23
Clarke, J. Ballard 42, 43, 135, 136,
137, 139, 149, 206, 215, 234,
235, 282, 284, 285, 289, 290,
293, 295
Cofer, Linden 133
Cole, Carl 147
Cole, Mary 85, 215, 218
Cole, Mr. 218, 222
Coleman, Mrs. 30
Columbus, Deputy Jailer E.J. 116
Community Laundry 30, 34, 49,
50, 56, 57
Connell, Mildred 34, 136
Connors, Jailer Martin J. 116
Courier-Journal 132, 229, 295
Curella, Brian 7
Curella, Heather 7

D

Denhardt, Bertha 27, 84, 86, 88,
95, 101, 123, 151, 216, 218, 219,
221, 222, 241, 247, 249, 287,
288, 289
Denhardt, Henry 10, 11, 12, 13,
14, 19, 21, 24, 25, 26, 27, 28, 29,
31, 32, 33, 34, 35, 36, 37, 38, 39,
40, 41, 42, 43, 44, 45, 46, 47, 48,
49, 50, 51, 52, 53, 54, 56, 57, 58,
59, 60, 61, 62, 63, 64, 65, 66, 67,
68, 69, 70, 71, 72, 73, 74, 75, 76,
77, 78, 81, 82, 83, 84, 85, 87, 88,
89, 90, 91, 94, 95, 96, 97, 98, 99,
100, 101, 103, 104, 105, 107,
108, 109, 110, 113, 114, 115,
117, 118, 119, 120, 121, 122,
123, 124, 125, 126, 128, 129,
130, 131, 132, 133, 134, 135,
136, 137, 138, 140, 141, 144,
146, 147, 148, 150, 151, 152,
153, 154, 155, 157, 159, 160,
165, 166, 167, 168, 186, 192,
197, 198, 200, 205, 209, 210,
213, 214, 215, 216, 217, 218,
219, 220, 221, 222, 223, 224,
225, 226, 227, 228, 229, 230,
232, 234, 235, 236, 237, 238,
239, 240, 241, 242, 243, 244,
245, 246, 247, 248, 249, 251,
252, 253, 254, 255, 256, 257,
258, 259, 260, 261, 263, 264,
265, 266, 267, 268, 269, 270,
271, 272, 273, 274, 275, 276,
277, 278, 279, 280, 281, 282,
284, 285, 286, 287, 288, 289,
290, 291, 292, 293, 294, 297,
298, 299, 300, 301, 304, 305,
306, 307, 309, 310
Denhardt, Jesse 95, 309, 310
Dent, Willie 26
Dietrich, Marlene 99
Dixon, Jane 130, 268, 269, 270, 273,
278, 284, 306
Donaldson, E.R. 146

Dr. Bill 6

Holtfretter, Kristy 6
Hoover, J. Edgar 146
Hundley, J.B. 57, 58, 59, 69, 70, 71,
72, 73, 74, 76, 108, 109, 110,
112, 114, 132, 136, 160, 225, 309

J

Jefferson County Jail 116
Johnson, Larry 17

K

Kane, Martin 241, 245, 246, 249,
258, 301
Keightley, Smith 74, 75, 76, 77, 78,
83, 88, 89, 106, 108, 110, 140,
146, 220, 221
Kelly, Major Joseph M. 261, 300
Kentucky Hotel 42
Kentucky Military Institute 22, 29,
124, 155
Kinsley, Philip 229, 300
Kinsolving, Captain H.B. 95, 96,
97, 98, 107, 110, 115, 131, 133,
134, 136, 140, 146, 147, 148,
223, 224, 225, 226, 227, 228,
230, 231, 232, 235, 236, 240,
247, 249, 270, 274, 275, 276,
280, 282, 283, 292, 293, 294
Kirchdorpher, R.H. 47
Knight, Claud 95

L

Lady in Blue, The 17
Laffoon, Ruby 25, 288
La Grange, Kentucky 20, 30, 34,
36, 49, 50, 51, 52, 57, 58, 85, 93,
94, 109, 116, 139, 152, 167, 180,
218, 274, 285
La Grange Methodist Church 88
Langan, Edward C. 259, 260
Lapsley, Coroner F. L. 279, 280,
281, 291
Lee, D.F. 84, 85, 87, 221, 222
Lee, Mrs. Bessie 33, 39, 136, 156,
157, 159

Lewis, Meriwether 22
LIFE magazine 116
London Star 281
Louisville Courier-Journal 21, 106,
118, 162, 261
Louisville, Kentucky 17, 33, 34, 35,
42, 188, 191, 254, 257, 267, 274,
276
Louisville Police Department Crime
Lab 111, 233, 281
Louisville Times 79, 95, 129, 130,
148, 268, 269, 287
Lucas, Mrs. Robert 33

M

Madison, Ambrose 23
Madison, James 23
Marshall, Judge Charles C. 117,
130, 131, 132, 133, 134, 135,
137, 140, 141, 142, 144, 148,
209, 229, 233, 234, 235, 240,
243, 244, 245, 247, 248, 256,
275, 282, 296, 297, 298, 300,
301, 302, 310
Martin, Pryor 133
Mayer, Elsie Frank 26
McCarty-Ricketts Funeral Home
83, 87, 103
McCormack, Dr. Arthur T. 84, 88,
95, 99, 117, 228, 248, 280, 309
McGuire, Candice Hadley 7
McGuire, Tim 7
Meredith, Hubert S. 282, 283, 284,
285, 290, 293, 294, 295, 296,
297, 298, 301, 303, 305, 307
Messmer, Sgt. John 82, 86, 87, 91,
101, 103, 105, 107, 143, 146,
176, 233, 235, 236, 237, 249, 294
Meyer, Jana 7
Middletown, Sheriff 25
Miller, Dr. A.J. 143, 145
Milliken, G.D. 108, 119, 121
Minch, George L., Sr. 280, 281
Mitchell, Margaret 258
Moise, Hayden, Jr. 192

W

Walsh, Dr. John T. 103, 105, 106, 108, 145
Walters, Judge Harry F. 285, 290, 294, 295, 301
Weakley, Dr. A.C. 279, 280, 291
Webster, Mrs. 294
Weiner, Dr. Alexander S. 227, 228
Wells, Major W.H. "Cappy" 269
Willis, George L., Jr. 285, 290
Wilson, Patricia 17, 18, 19, 162, 163, 259, 306

Woolfolk, Chester 31, 32, 37, 41, 44, 125, 126, 154, 155, 156, 157, 158, 187, 216, 217, 218, 219, 221, 229, 230, 232, 253, 264, 266, 308
Wright, Coleman 283, 284, 285, 290, 302, 309
Wyatt, Lieutenant J.C. 300

Y

Young, James 95